"This is holy ground"

A history of the Gettysburg battlefield

By Barbara L. Platt

Published by
The Gettysburg Foundation
Baltimore Pike
Gettysburg, PA 17325

Second Printing - 2003
Revised - 2003

Third Printing - 2006
Revised - 2006

Fourth Printing - 2009
Revised - 2009

Printed by Huggins Printing
2900 Sycamore Street
Harrisburg, PA

ISBN 0-9712661-0-7
Copyright Barbara L. Platt 2001

To

John Latschar

whose dedication and courage have brought to fruition
those visions men held in 1863

IV Chapter

Maps

As a frequent reader of Civil War books I continually deplore the lack of informative maps. Too often the reader is forced to utilize modern road maps and other sources to locate towns, roads, etc. important to understanding the text but whose location it is impossible to determine. Needless to say it is equally true of many of the buildings mentioned as being of importance. The five maps included in this book are intended to preclude the necessity of readers having to use their imaginations to find sites mentioned in the text, a number of which are located in areas of the town and battlefield with which most visitors are usually unfamiliar. They serve as well to illustrate the growth of the battlefield from the original 12 acres purchased by David Wills for the National Cemetery to the more than 5800 acres included within the current boundary of Gettysburg National Military Park.

CONTENTS

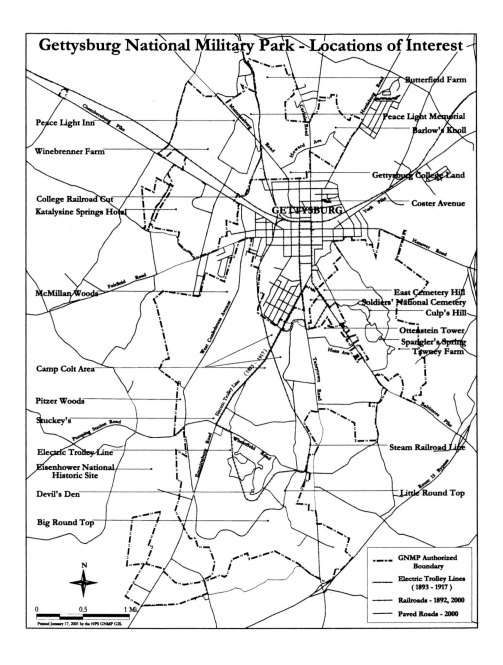

VI Chapter

Gettysburg National Military Park - Locations of Interest

Butterfield Farm

Peace Light Inn

Peace Light Memorial

Barlow's Knoll

Winebrenner Farm

Gettysburg College Land

College Railroad Cut

Coster Avenue

Katalysine Springs Hotel

GETTYSBURG

McMillan Woods

East Cemetery Hill

Soldiers' National Cemetery

Culp's Hill

Ottenstein Tower

Spangler's Spring

Towney Farm

Camp Colt Area

Pitzer Woods

Stuckey's

Electric Trolley Line

Steam Railroad Line

Eisenhower National Historic Site

Devil's Den

Little Round Top

Big Round Top

N

— ▪ — ▪	GNMP Authorized Boundary
——	Electric Trolley Lines (1893 - 1917)
——	Railroads - 1892, 2000
——	Paved Roads - 2000

0   0.5   1 Mi.

Printed January 17, 2001 by the NPS GNMP GIS.

ACKNOWLEDGEMENTS

This little book is not intended to be a complete history of Gettysburg National Military Park, that would be an undertaking of Herculean proportions. Rather it was written to dispel the notion that this national park was created out of whole cloth. It was not. It has evolved over more than 140 years and the process is not yet complete.

The development of the park through time has required the efforts of many people. The same may be said of this book, and to those "silent partners" I can only offer my heartfelt thanks. Park archivist Greg Goodall spared no effort in helping me find the missing pieces of essential material. Katie Lawhon, public relations officer at the park was a fountain of knowledge where newspaper resources were involved. Curt Musselman historian and GIS Specialist has few equals at creating maps. Debbie Darden, Chief of Resource Management and park planner, offered expert information on the park's recent history, wise insight into the development of the text, expertise on use of the computer – my nemesis during the whole project, and continual much needed encouragement. Without Richard Segars, the park's historic architect, and a whiz at computer graphics, the format and photographs used would never have been possible and the book quite literally would never have been published. Park Superintendent John Latschar provided not only moral support but served as a shining example of commitment to a cause that often renewed the writer's flagging spirits. Gerald Bennett, chairman of the park Advisory Commission and a fine historian and author, not only initiated the idea for this book but, with great kindness and expertise read the text as it developed, offering thoughtful council for, and keen insight into, my work. My sister Marjorie spent long hours typing an often altered manuscript. And from a person, himself not an historian, the quiet, steady encouragement of my literary efforts by Dr. Carl Pierson, my very special friend of 60 years, quite literally kept me at the task when words refused to come. Eventually the words did come and this is the result. Hopefully those who read them will gain new insight into what this most famous of all U.S. military parks has demanded of those who initiated its creation in 1863 and those who have served here through the often tumultuous years which have followed.

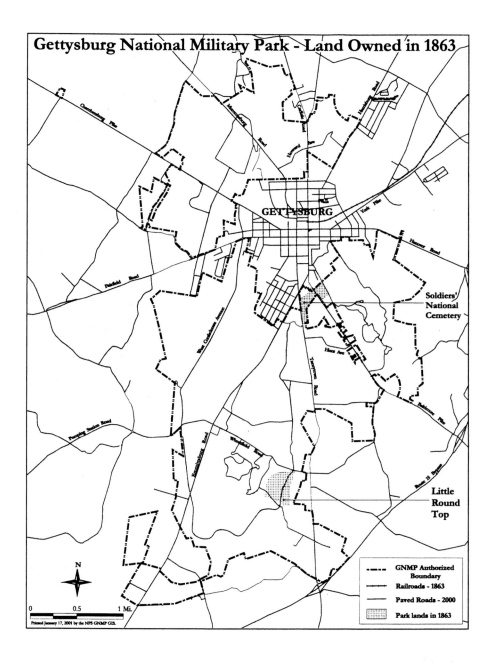

Gettysburg National Military Park - Land Owned in 1863

GETTYSBURG

Soldiers'
National
Cemetery

Little
Round
Top

N

0	0.5	1 Mi.

Printed January 17, 2001 by the NPS GNMP GIS.

- ▪▪—▪▪ GNMP Authorized
  Boundary
- ─┼─ Railroads - 1863
- ─── Paved Roads - 2000
- ▦ Park lands in 1863

PREFACE

Gettysburg, in 1863, was just a quiet country village of about 2400 souls in south-central Pennsylvania, serving as the county seat and enjoying a reasonable level of business activity. To the west and northwest of town the soil was good, farms were large, fences few and farmers prosperous. To the south and southeast of the village it was a different story. The land was poor and numerous fences marked the fields of the small struggling farms that dotted the area. Two prominences, Big Round Top and its lower companion, Little Round Top, dominated the landscape to the southeast while nearby the granite outcropping of Devil's Den faced Little Round Top from the west across what was soon to become known as the Valley of Death.

The town itself had grown up at the confluence of two major highways, the York/Chambersburg Pikes, now U.S. 30 east and west, and the Baltimore Pike, now Pa. 97. These intersected at the town square, or as it was called in earlier parlance, "The Diamond" and is in reality a circle. Six smaller roads connected with the two turnpikes in a spoke-like fashion. Reading in a clockwise direction, from the north came the Biglerville Road (Pa.34) and the Old Harrisburg Road (Bus.15), which joined to form Carlisle Street four blocks north of the square. The York Pike joined the Hanover Road (Pa. 116 east) two blocks east of the square, while to the south of town the Taneytown Road (Pa. 134) and the Emmitsburg Road (Bus.15) came together to form what is now Steinwehr Avenue. This road then joined with the Baltimore Pike to form Baltimore Street as it entered the borough. From the west the Fairfield Road (Pa. 116 west) and the Chambersburg Pike entered Gettysburg just a block apart. Finally the Mummasburg Road, which passed in front of what is now the Peace Light monument, entered the town at the northwest corner of the current Gettysburg College campus. It was this extensive network of roads that provided the lifeblood of the town and, in 1863, easy access for the two great armies descending on an apprehensive citizenry. Even now this road system remains virtually unchanged.

The appearance of the Gettysburg battlefield today, although a far cry from what it was when war passed over it in 1863, is far more like that early scene than it has been for at least 100 years and current National Park Service plans call for even more restoration within the next decade.

From 1863 through the 1880's most changes on what is now national park land took place through changes in the farms of the area. Some were sold, some divided among children within a family, some buildings were torn down or moved, others were built or enlarged. For example the Codori barn on the Emmitsburg Road was rebuilt after the war into the structure familiar today, considerably larger than the log barn which stood there in 1863 and interfered with the Confederate advance on July 3 known by most Americans as Pickett's charge. Soon too, a 2½ story addition was built onto the east side of the Leister house along the Taneytown Road which had served as Union General George Meade's headquarters during the battle.

When the fighting ended and the armies had departed, only a few men of vision gave thought to preserving the land over which one of the most significant battles of the Civil War had been fought. Their concept of honoring, in this way, the men whom the entire Union called heroes, was unheard of and few outside the borough had any interest in preserving every feature of the great battlefield as it had been during the battle. Families had a living to make and a war from which they were struggling to recover. "Development" and "tourism" were not a part of their vocabulary. They believed that the land would remain forever in farming and thus would be preserved as much as necessary. They did not, and indeed could not, foresee the enormous changes which the future would bring..

But time has altered that earlier scene both in the town and on the fields that surrounded it in 1863. Of the more than 16,000 acres, including the village, over which the two armies clashed, just under 6000 acres have been preserved forever as Gettysburg National Military Park. Much of the rest of the land has long since undergone the changes that continuing development inevitably brings. The national park now protects what remains of the battlefield as a lasting tribute to the men on both sides who fought, suffered, and died in one of the greatest battles of that terrible war. Therefore it is fitting that most of the monuments on the battlefield were placed there by the veterans themselves who sought to remember the heroism of both the living and the dead in the service of a cause they believed to be more important than life itself. For those who had worn blue, and as much for those clad in gray, this was indeed "holy ground."

"this insensate stone"

Visitors began arriving in Gettysburg almost as soon as the smoke of battle had cleared. Initially many came seeking information about loved ones killed or wounded during the fighting. Others were drawn by a morbid curiosity to view the carnage. Moreover Gettysburg was the only major battle fought on Northern soil and therefore, to which Northern citizens had access.

What they found when they arrived was not a well cared for national park-there was no park-just thousands of acres of war torn land, including the town itself, over which two great armies had fought bitterly for three days. The sights and stench were almost overwhelming. Shattered buildings covered the landscape, thousands of wounded filled churches, town buildings, private homes, barns, even tents. The carcasses of uncountable hundreds of horses and mules lay rotting in the hot July sun. The odor of death permeated the air.

Despite this chaos, within two weeks of the end of the fighting David McConaughy, a Gettysburg lawyer, began the long, still ongoing effort to preserve this historic ground. By August some semblance of order had developed and McConaughy, with amazing foresight, had purchased Steven's Knoll, much of East Cemetery Hill, the west face of Little Round Top and part of Culp's Hill. It was his firm belief that " 'there could be no more fitting and expressive memorial of the heroic valor and signal triumphs of our Army on the 1st, 2nd, and 3rd, of July, 1863, than the battlefield itself, with its natural and artificial defenses preserved and perpetuated in the exact form and conditions as they were in during the battle' " (1)

In a letter of July 25, 1863, McConaughy had informed Pennsylvania governor Andrew Curtin that he had purchased "all the land on Cemetery Hill which encircles the Evergreen Cemetery Grounds... .In doing so I have had two purposes, one to enlarge the area of our Cemetery...and (2) to secure so as to be held in perpetuity the most interesting portions of the illustrious Battlefield that we may retain them in the actual form & condition they were in during the battle, the most eloquent memorials of those glorious struggles and triumphs."(2) McConaughy was president of the Evergreen Cemetery Association and thus had more than a passing interest in where the Union dead would be buried. It was also made clear that the intention was to honor only the Union forces. The Confederates were, after all, the enemy and therefore the land they had occupied was ignored for years to come.

On July 24, 1863, the day before McConaughy's letter, David Wills, another Gettysburg attorney, had written the governor urging "the propriety" and "necessity" of a "burial ground" at Gettysburg for proper honoring of the Union dead. " 'There is one spot very desirable for this purpose' " he wrote. " 'It is the elevated piece of ground on the Baltimore turnpike, opposite the (Evergreen) Cemetery.' "(3) Wills had already ascertained that the land could be purchased and urged that Pennsylvania buy it immediately. Governor Curtin, who had visited the battlefield two weeks before receiving Wills' letter, quickly gave approval. He appointed Wills " 'agent of the Commonwealth and authorized him to begin correspondence with the governors of the other northern states whose soldiers had been killed in battle and whose bodies were buried on the battlefield.' " (4) It was expected the other states would share in the anticipated expenses of such a venture.

However, McConaughy was one step ahead of Wills and when the latter looked into acquiring the land he had selected he was dismayed to find that McConaughy had already purchased it, planning to preserve intact the defenses on East Cemetery Hill. In addition, McConaughy intended that the Union dead should be buried on ground owned by the existing cemetery association. It took considerable negotiating before the Association agreed to sell Wills 12 acres of its land adjoining the civilian cemetery. Furthermore, the sales agreement stipulated that " 'an open railing enclosure of ordinary height be made and maintained by the State, or states interested, upon the division lines between said lands and the grounds of Evergreen Cemetery.' "(5) Soon after securing the Evergreen parcel Wills also purchased an additional five acres adjoining the original 12 acres creating what is now the National Cemetery. He later reported to Governor Curtin that 15 of the 17 governors contacted had responded favorably, adding that in accordance with Curtin's directions, the land was to be paid for, and the title held by, the state of Pennsylvania.

While the cemetery matter was being resolved McConaughy called for public support in his endeavor to preserve the battleground and received enthusiastic replies from 26 fellow townsmen who organized under McConaughy's leadership on September 15, 1863. The *Adams Sentinel* reported that " 'The natural and artificial defenses which are thus to be secured from the vandalism of avarice, and saved from destruction for mere selfish and practical considerations in individual owners, these scenes of conflict, which are thus to be preserved in the precise form and condition they bore in the hours of battle, have become historic and destined to an immortality of fame, among the great places and events of the world's history.' "(6) Yet not even the most farsighted of editors could imagine just how true those words would proved to be.

Meanwhile, all was not congenial between Wills and McConaughy as indicated in excerpts from Wills' letter to Governor Curtin a few months later:

"My dear sir: I have given the subject of the projected 'Gettysburg Battle Field Memorial Association' more consideration since you spoke to me about it at Washington, and since my return have been quietly making more inquiries into its designs and who are its projectors. In the first place, I think the whole project is visionary and impracticable. The breastworks proposed to be preserved on Culp's Hill are made of wood and therefore perishable. Many of them have already been torn up and cut into wood and rails, and what may be left will rot away in a few years. The earthen breastworks between Culp's Hill and Cemetery Hill have already been very much defaced. They were made, first by piling up rails and then throwing up earth on top. The farmers have in most instances dug out their rails and the effects of the rains have settled the earth very much. The stone walls built on Little Round Top are imperishable and I may add indestructible. Little Round Top is a steep, barren, hill of rocks and stones, & the stone defenses on it will never be disturbed. They are almost inaccessible, and the rocks and stone more accessible for a mile all around will meet the demands of the community for all purposes for centuries. ...Therefore, I say, the scheme is part visionary and impracticable and in part entirely useless. Mr. McConoughy (sic)is the sole projector of it. ...Thus it is, ...knowing him as well as I do (and probably you know his character also) I cannot fail to draw the conclusion that he originated the project and is endeavoring to carry it out for a selfish and mercenary purpose. ...I think the public should understand that they are not contributing in any way whatever to the Soldiers' National Cemetery when contributing to this 'Battlefield Memorial Association.' "(7)

Wills letter was one of the early indications of the ongoing controversies that continue to dog efforts to "protect and preserve" the battlefield.

Despite Wills' comments, on April 30, 1864 the Pennsylvania legislature granted a charter to the Gettysburg Battlefield Memorial Association to "...hold, and preserve the battlegrounds of Gettysburg...with the natural and artificial defenses, as they were at the time of said battle, and by such perpetuation and such memorial structures as a generous and patriotic people may aid to erect..."(8) By June 1864 the Gettysburg Battlefield Memorial Association had secured ownership of 70 acres but by 1867, hampered by lack of money and dwindling enthusiasm, the Association had managed to protect only an additional 70 acres although this did include the woodlot where Union General John Reynolds had been killed on July 1, 1863.

Maps played, and still play, an important part in understanding the battle action as it unfolded, and they also played a major roll in later land purchases. John Bachelder, an amateur historian, had visited the battlefield shortly after the battle, spending over three months studying and mapping the land over which the two armies had clashed and, whenever possible, interviewing wounded troops who had fought here. In 1864 he published an isometric map of the battlefield that was well received by Union officers including General Winfield S. Hancock, commander of the 2nd Corps at Gettysburg. Other maps were subsequently made, most notably the Warren map, the creation of which was supervised by General Gouvenor K. Warren, an engineering officer who fought in the Union defenses on Little Round Top. It is this map which today is considered the most accurate and detailed map of the battlefield of 1863.

In 1873 Bachelder, setting aside his maps, published a visitor's guidebook, "What to See and Do In Gettysburg." Predating modern tour books by many years, Bachelder included in his guidebook recommendations on how to reach the town and where to stay once here. He also reported, " ' no material changes had been made on the field.' "(9) There had been some alteration of fence lines and orchards but since the greater part of the battle ground remained in the hands of private farmers the general appearance of the land had changed little and, at that time, no substantial changes were anticipated for the future. The expectation was that the land would continue to be farmland for generations to come. The one exception was the county fairgrounds built on what is now the Gettysburg Recreation Park and which, in 1863, was the position of Confederate General Pender's troops on July 2nd and 3rd.

Those visitors for whom Bachelder wrote his book were primarily veterans and their families who continued to come in growing numbers. Since many of the most important sites were accessible only on foot the GBMA decided, in 1881, to construct an avenue, to be known as Hancock Avenue, from Little Round Top along the Union battle line to the Taneytown Road. The proposed 60 foot wide road crossed the land of seven landowners all of whom asked more for the right-of-way than the Association was willing to pay. Therefore it invoked the power of condemnation granted in its charter and the cost issue was resolved by the court during the winter of 1881.

While limited funding slowed land acquisition, preservation too became a problem. As Wills had stated, breastworks and lunettes-the earthworks that protected artillery positions-had begun to erode. The process was hastened by farmers who removed the logs and rails from the breastworks for their own use. Although the Association did manage to restore those on Culp's Hill, time continued to take its toll as logs rotted and soil eroded, until now only traces remain of the original defenses. (It is interesting to note that during the reconstruction of the breastworks Association members erected "guide boards", the earliest interpretive markers on the battlefield.)

Despite its best efforts to gain additional funding and increase interest in preserving the battlefield the GBMA was faltering, a fact not lost on John Vanderslice who had organized a highly successful Grand Army of the Republic encampment at Gettysburg in 1878. Convinced that veterans of the GAR could infuse the Association with new life he encouraged friends to purchase stock in the GBMA with a view to gaining control. This accomplished a change in the leadership was inevitable and David McConaughy was one of those voted off the Association Board of Directors. Steps were immediately taken to increase GBMA activity. A committee was formed to " 'solicit appropriations from the states to purchase additional land...' "(10) The results of these efforts enabled the GBMA to purchase not only the Klingle farm, Weikert farm and part of the Wheatfield, but also land over which these properties could be reached. The GBMA also published a pamphlet which stated emphatically that " 'its aims and purposes are NATIONAL with a membership widely scattered over different states.' "(11)

Although its members recognized that an understanding of the events of July 1863 required that the battle lines of both armies be interpreted the charter of the GBMA did not permit it to acquire land that had been occupied by the Confederate army. The Association was also aware that there were growing threats to this critical area of battle ground and so, in 1890, steps were taken to persuade Congress to purchase the endangered land. The argument was made that it was virtually impossible to explain how the Union army had defended its position against the enemy when no one could say exactly where the Confederates had been. The effort to secure government involvement gained added momentum with the announced intention of one group of entrepreneurs to construct an electric trolley on the battlefield, a project that threatened a vast section of the most historic ground. Unable to halt this construction on its own the GBMA turned to the federal government for help. It was not until 1895, following the agreement to transfer GBMA holdings, and supervision of the field, to a federally appointed Battlefield Commission that the government initiated condemnation proceedings against the trolley company. And it was not until 1896 that the case was finally resolved when the U.S. Supreme Court ruled that the government did indeed have the right to protect historic land through condemnation, a landmark decision for the future of the park.

By 1894 the GBMA held title to over 500 acres of land and had laid out 17 miles of road along Union battle lines, much of it separated from private lands by barbed wire. However "road" is really a misnomer. What the Association had created were actually a series of, often muddy, trails suitable at best for horse and buggy.

In 1893, in response to GBMA pleas, Congress had authorized a three man commission and allocated $125,000 to locate, survey, and purchase, the battle lines of both armies and it was this commission which later was involved in the eventual proceedings against the electric trolley company. The original commission members were John Bachelder, William Forney, a former member of the Confederate army who was wounded six times at Gettysburg, and Lt.Col. John P. Nicholson who had served with the 28th Pennsylvania Volunteers.

By the mid-1890's the Association decided it was in the best interest of preservation to turn over to the federal government the land that had already been preserved with the hope that additional land could be acquired more easily using government resources. In late 1895 the GBMA board voted to abolish the organization and in February 1896 deeded its 522 acres to the U.S. War Department. The land thus acquired was designated the Gettysburg National Military Park and its care and further development rested with the federally appointed Gettysburg National Park Commission consisting of the three men who had already been given the responsibility of protecting the battle lines of the two armies. The commission reported annually to the Secretary of War.

Union veterans had periodically held reunions at Gettysburg but with limited success until 1878 when the Pennsylvania Grand Army of the Republic held its first encampment on East Cemetery Hill. At this reunion GAR veterans placed a monument on Little Round Top to mark the spot where Colonel Strong Vincent, a brigade commander in the Union 5th Corps, had been killed during the defense of that position. A second monument was placed on Houck's Ridge across from Little Round Top where Colonel Fred Taylor, of the 13th Pennsylvania reserves, fell mortally wounded.

These were the first monuments erected outside of the National Cemetery and were soon followed by the 2nd Massachusetts Infantry monument placed by those veterans near Spangler's Spring where they fought on July 3rd. This seemed to open the floodgates with the result that 320 monuments, honoring Union troops, had been placed on the battlefield by 1895. The veterans considered the battlefield to be an extension of the National Cemetery knowing that some of their comrades could never be found to be interred with their fellow soldiers in that final resting place. Therefore they intended that the monuments placed on the field serve to honor them all as well as those who had fallen on other battlefields beyond Gettysburg.

The Gettysburg National Military Park has within its boundaries over 1879 monuments, more than any other Civil War battlefield. Although various states have continued to erect monuments to their soldiers who fought here, it is the regimental monuments erected by the veterans themselves that speak most eloquently. The magnitude of the Union victory here was important to those veterans. Here, they believed, they had stemmed the tide of the Confederacy. For them Gettysburg was the defining moment of the war and so it was here that they chose to honor their comrades fallen not only at Gettysburg but in the many other battles inscribed on their regimental monuments. Lieutenant Charles Fuller, speaking at the dedication of the 61st New York monument July 1, 1889, expressed it thus, " '(this) has become the place of all places in regard to the War of the Rebellion.' "(12)

Indicative of the Union veterans beliefs that the memorials here were to honor more than just the Gettysburg dead were words spoken by Corporal John Vanderslice speaking at the dedication of the 8th Pennsylvania Cavalry monument September 1, 1890, " 'Let us hope that in coming generations those who come to this field looking upon these monuments, will be reminded that they are memorials of the services, sufferings and sacrifices of men who fought not for conquest or empire, but of men who endured hardship, encountered perils and were willing to offer their lives upon their country's alter. ...Reminded of the priceless ransom given here and on other fields... .' "(13)

At other dedications the sentiments of the veterans of Gettysburg were expressed with equal passion. Dedicating the 2nd Pennsylvania Cavalry monument on September 11, 1889, Captain Albert Seip said in his remarks, " 'And now what does this monument mean? It symbolizes the buried youth and broken-down health of brave men who willingly offered up their lives that the Nation might live.' "(14)

Lieutenant Oliver W. Norton, at the dedication of the 82nd Pennsylvania Volunteers monument, also on September 11, 1889, declared " ' This place is holy ground.' "(15)

And the words of Corporal James Tanner of the 40th New York at their dedication ceremony July 1, 1888 " 'When you and I have long been dust and ashes this insensate stone, until it shall by the actions of time be reduced to the elements, will tell all people the story of those who held life so cheap and country so dear that they cheerfully flung away life for country.' "(16)

Among the many military statues and memorials erected during this time there stands one dedicated to the only civilian who participated in the battle. Too old to enlist even at the beginning of the war, John Burns was not about to be left out of the battle which threatened his home. As the Confederates advanced along the Chambersburg Pike on July 1 Burns took his flintlock musket and headed toward the fighting west of town. In tribute to the old hero General Abner Doubleday wrote, " 'My thanks are specially due to John Burns who, although over 70 years of age, shouldered his musket and offered his services to Colonel Wister of the 150th Pennsylvania Volunteers. Colonel Wister advised him to fight in the woods as there was more shelter there, but he preferred to join our line of skirmishers in the open field. When the troops retired he fought with the Iron Brigade. He was wounded in three places.' "(17) Although some of the Union troops thought Burns had been killed, he survived his wounds and died in Gettysburg in 1893. His bronze statue, with General Doubleday's words as part of the inscription, was placed near where Burns fought on what is now Stone Avenue, not far from the present day west end guide station.

Most Confederate veterans, quite naturally, chose to honor their comrades with memorials on Southern soil although today many believe that some of the most beautiful monuments at Gettysburg are those of the Southern states honoring their soldiers who fought here.

Fearing that the battlefield would become overwhelmed as more and more monuments were added the GBMA, in 1885, required every unit to mark the flanks of their position wherever possible. In 1887 every regiment and battery had to place its first monument where they had been positioned in the Union's general line of battle which, once established on Cemetery Ridge, had assumed a basic stability. Advanced position markers could only be placed once this initial requirement had been met. Yet by 1888 almost 200 monuments had been erected to mark Union positions, with many more to come.

Other than the monuments there were few changes to the battlefield landscape in the 1800's because of the rural nature of Adams County and its slow growth in population. Those changes that did occur were usually related to farming activities but nature itself had significantly altered the appearance of some of the more important features of the battlefield.

Despite efforts by the GBMA Little Round Top became covered with trees and brush obliterating many of its crucial features. This led John Bachelder to complain that the growth had significantly changed the character of that section of the field. The same was true of Culp's Hill where large trees, shattered by gunfire, had died and fallen, to be replaced by thick undergrowth not present during the battle. The Association managed to clear Little Round Top but limited funds made it impossible for the work to continue on other sections of the battlefield. Today Little Round Top, which still requires periodic clearing, looks virtually the same as it did during the battle but the 1863 openness of Culp's Hill has yet to be restored. In addition, vegetation growing unchecked in other areas of the battlefield has significantly altered important aspects of the terrain.

With an ever-increasing stream of visitors the possibilities seemed endless for new business ventures, especially as the name "Gettysburg" gained further national prominence following the dedication of the National Cemetery and Lincoln's appearance here. Entrepreneurs were quick to recognize the profitability of certain enterprises, particularly those which catered to the constantly arriving visitors, and businesses quickly sprang up to take advantage of this new source of revenue.

For years prior to the Civil War a small brick tavern, the Wagon Hotel, stood at the intersection of the Baltimore Pike and the Emmitsburg Road (Steinwehr Avenue). In 1893 the hotel was purchased by Adam Braunreiter, a German immigrant then living in Baltimore, Maryland who built a larger structure in front of, and attached to, the old tavern. He was successful from the outset but early in 1895 he returned to Germany because of ill health while his wife and four children remained in Gettysburg to operate the business. Braunreiter, still in ill health, returned to Gettysburg in July of that same year and died a month later. Following his death his wife put the business up for sale but just before the new owner was to make his first payment the hotel burned to the ground. Left with a ruined, unsalable building and the need to support her children, Mrs. Braunreiter decided to rebuild the structure and upon its completion in 1896 named it the Battlefield Hotel. It flourished under the management of this determined lady for 26 years after which it saw a succession of different owners until 1949, when the hotel was razed to make way for the blacktop entrance to a service station being built next to the old hotel site.

Among the earliest ventures seeking to take advantage of the region's new fame was the Katalysine Springs Hotel, more commonly known simply as the Springs Hotel. Situated just south of U.S. 30 at the western edge of the present national park boundary, the hotel, which no longer exists, had a major impact on both the battlefield and the town.

Prior to the war the spring itself was owned by Charles C. McClean, a Presbyterian minister who was convinced that the waters had medicinal properties. However, unable to interest anyone else in the financial possibilities of the spring, he sold the property and moved away from the area before the war began.

During the battle the spring, located near the present Gettysburg Country Club swimming pool, was used by Confederate soldiers. According to one report, " 'The wounded who dragged themselves to the spring to slake their thirst and bathe their wounds, found the water possessed wonderful healing virtues.' "(18), although before discovering those "healing virtues" the soldiers thought the water had been poisoned because of its taste.

In 1868 Emanuel Harmon, owner of the spring, formed the Gettysburg Lithic Springs Association, intending to bottle and sell the water commercially. Later that year the organization expanded to become the Gettysburg Katalysine Springs Association which then purchased five acres of land, including the spring, from Harmon and immediately began construction of a large hotel on the property. The Springs Hotel had about 200 rooms, cost $80,000 to build, and occupied land now owned by the Gettysburg Country Club. The hotel, located just west of Willoughby Run and about 300 yards south of the Chambersburg Pike (U.S.30), continued in operation until December 1917 when it was destroyed by fire.

Katalysine Springs Hotel   GNMP

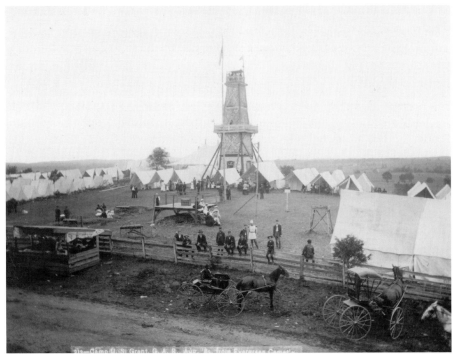

First Observation tower - East Cemetery Hill showing GAR encapment "Camp Grant" - 1885 GNMP

To solve the problem of transporting guests to the hotel from the train station in Gettysburg the hotel company proposed to construct a horse drawn railway connecting the two. For this purpose it purchased, according to one report, " '...all the land from Willoughby Run to Gettysburg between the Chambersburg Pike and the Hagerstown (Fairfield) Road, excepting the Lutheran Theological Seminary property...' "(19)

In describing the anticipated railway the Gettysburg Compiler declared in October 1868, "The railway will be laid down in a broad avenue which could doubtless become one of the handsomest thoroughfares in the county."(20) In November 1868 the paper stated that, "The road will start at the Passenger Depot (on Carlisle Street), run up Carlisle Street to the square, thence in a straight line to the foot of the Seminary grounds where a slight curve to the south of the President's house will be made, thence direct to the Katalysine Spring."(21) Two bridges, one across Stevens Run (locally now known as the Tiber) in town near the former Meade School building, and one across Willoughby Run just east of the hotel, were constructed to carry the railway across these two streams. Because there was considerable local interest in the project the press provided frequent updates as noted in a *Compiler* November article which began, "The work upon the Gettysburg Springs Street Railway is progressing finely."(22)

Later in the history of the town, that portion of the roadway from where U.S.30 bends sharply to the right to the intersection of what is now Seminary Avenue, became the present day Springs Avenue. Although the section of the railway right-of-way through the Seminary grounds is no longer visible, part of the old trace, from the west edge of the Seminary property to the east side of Reynolds Avenue can still be seen. On the west side of Reynolds Avenue the present Meredith Avenue follows another portion of the trace, while the bridge abutments over Willoughby Run still stand.

As a result of visitor interest in seeing, and purchasing, artifacts from the battlefield a number of relic shop/museums sprang up both in town and on the battlefield itself. Eventually the most extensive collection was owned by John Rosensteel. Portions of his collection, and that of his nephew George, are included in the current collection on display by the National Park Service in the park's Visitor Center.

Following the battle young John, then 13 years old, worked on a burial detail in the Spangler's Spring area. His interest in collecting battle artifacts began when he buried a Confederate soldier and kept the young man's rifle as a souvenir. In 1882, having by then purchased much of the land in the Round Top area, John built a house (since removed) on the north slope of Little Round Top. In 1885, to house his extensive and growing collection, he built the Round Top Museum. This too was on Little Round Top northeast of the intersection of Wheatfield Road and Sedgwick Avenue. Finally, in the late 1880's he built a small cottage near the Sedgewick monument for his hired hand, a structure which later served as a home for John's nephew George Rosensteel and his wife until the couple moved into the second floor of the museum building. The house is no longer standing but a carriage house built at about the same time still exists south of the Sedgwick monument. Some years later, in 1982, after being purchased by the National Park Service, the museum itself was torn down.

The museum building was large enough to accommodate not only the Rosensteel collection but also became the scene of group picnics and organization dinners for the local populace. Because of the facilities available, including a dance floor, the "museum" became a popular gathering spot for townspeople. Round Top Park, as the area was known even before Rosensteel purchased the land, could be reached by foot, horseback, horse drawn (and later electric) trolley, and the steam railroad which ran across the battlefield terminating just beyond the back, or east side of Little Round Top. At about the same time Round Top School was built, possibly to serve the little settlement, known as Sedgwick Post Office, which had grown up at the intersection of the Wheatfield and Taneytown roads. John Rosensteel later converted that building into a cottage, still standing, when it was no longer needed as a school.

He also became the owner of much of what is still known today as Zeigler's Grove, a crucial section of the Union battle line during the Confederate charge on July 3, 1863. In 1921 he sold a portion of this land to his nephew George urging him to build his own museum at the intersection of the Taneytown Road and Hancock Avenue, which at the time ended just across from the National Cemetery. In the early 1960's that section of Hancock Avenue adjacent to the museum was eliminated during the construction of the Cyclorama building and its parking lot.

When the Granite School building, located east of the battlefield on what is still called Granite School House Lane, was put up for sale George Rosensteel bought and dismantled it, using the foundation of the school in the construction of his new Gettysburg National Museum. Built in 1921 this building, which now serves as the park Visitor Center, eventually housed the combined collections of John and George Rosensteel among others, and has been added to 14 times since its construction. The land now used as the Visitor Center parking lot had been a clay quarry with adjacent tile and brickyard after the war, and became the town dump when the quarry ceased operations. For this reason whenever excavations are necessary in this area articles thrown in the dump are often exposed and small sinkholes periodically appear because of the irregular filling of the site.

About the same time that John Rosensteel was buying land on, and near, Little Round Top William Tipton, a local photographer, was buying land in the Devil's Den area in anticipation of the construction of the electric trolley which would bring visitors from the town to the battlefield. Tipton also built a restaurant and refreshment stand and, to take advantage of his renown as a photographer, included a photo studio and dark room in his building. By so doing Tipton offered visitors the opportunity to have their picture taken among the rocks of this famous portion of the battlefield. In 1901 the "Tipton Tract", as it had become known, was purchased by the government and the building, which was located near the site of the present comfort station, was relocated to Warren Avenue and later torn down.

A second, much smaller, relic shop was owned by David "Davey" Weikert, a war veteran who had become disabled after returning to civilian life. Located between the two Round Tops, it had been there since the days of the Gettysburg Battlefield Memorial Association. However in the early 1900's Warren Avenue was realigned and Weikert, by then in failing health, was refused permission to relocate when the new avenue was constructed through his site.

Private museums, usually as a part of souvenir shops, continued to dot the battlefield for decades. The Shields Museum/Refreshment Stand was one of the last to go. Situated on U.S. 30 directly across from the west end guide station and only a few feet from the Reynolds statue, it was bought by the government and the building removed in the late 1970's.

Strange as it may seem a railroad and an electric trolley line also played a part in the evolution of the battlefield in the late 1800's although little evidence remains today of either.

After the war the railroad to Gettysburg had been extended on westward using the unfinished cut through Oak Ridge that had played such a significant part in the battle on July 1, 1863. This construction meant easier access to the town although visitors could still only reach the battlefield itself on foot, horseback or horse drawn carriage. All of that changed in 1884. The Gettysburg and Harrisburg Railroad Company, formed in 1882, had constructed a line from about Hunter's Run in Cumberland county, south to Gettysburg. In 1884 a spur of this line, locally called the Little Round Top Railroad, cut off from the G & H tracks just east of the present day post office, continued south through what is now the Recreation Park, brushed the western edge of the modern Colt Park development, and entered the current national park just north of the site of the Bliss house and barn (which were destroyed during the battle and never rebuilt). Keen eyed visitors may still be able to pick out the trace of the old railroad bed just at the edge of the battlefield. From the Bliss house site the tracks ran southeast, crossing the Emmitsburg Road north of the Codori house, passed to the west of the Angle and the Pennsylvania monu-

Davey Weikert's souvenir stand   *GNMP*

Electric trolley on Baltimore Pike - National Cemetery entrance in background   *GNMP*

ment, and continued into a wooded area near the Sedgwick monument where some of the ties which supported the rails are still visible today. The line then crossed Wheatfield Road just west of the intersection with the Taneytown Road and ended at the rear of Little Round Top.

Until 1895 it was frequently used to carry both visitors and townspeople to Round Top Park a popular picnic area near the famous battlefield landmark. At one time plans were developed to extend this rail line as far as Westminster, Maryland but this extension was never constructed. The railroad continued to operate during World War I when men and materiel were transported into the Army training camp established on the Gettysburg battlefield. But its use dwindled after the war and the railroad was abandoned in 1944 with the right-of-way deeded to Gettysburg National Military Park.

There appears to have been little controversy over construction of the steam railroad due in part perhaps to the topography over which the rail bed was constructed. The land was flat, with few rocky obstacles along the route chosen by the G & H Railroad and therefore little dramatic change was made in the battle area landscape. Not so with another railway project however when, in 1893, a controversy erupted over exploitation of the battlefield which made all earlier disagreements pale by comparison.

Initially, along with the steam railroad, a horse drawn trolley carried visitors to the scene of the fighting, but in 1891 the Gettysburg Electric Railway was incorporated with the intention of replacing the horse drawn conveyances. Construction of a trolley line through Devil's Den, the Valley of Death, and Cemetery Ridge, began in April 1893. In May of the same year the Gettysburg Battlefield Commission tried to stop construction, charging that it would interfere with the preservation of historic landmarks, as indeed it did. But since construction was being done over private lands the commission was unsuccessful in its efforts and was forced to bring condemnation proceedings against the company. This lawsuit would not be resolved until 1896, a year after the Gettysburg Battlefield Memorial Association had voted to turn its holdings over to the federal government.

When blasting was done to create a roadbed through several sensitive areas of the battlefield opponents of the project were vehement in their protests. The *Philadelphia Ledger* stated, "The damage already committed by the electric road is very great and can never be repaired, but the present desecration is but the commencement of what may be done if this company is allowed to invade other sections of the battlefield. Is it not practicable to stop this wanton destruction of one of the most important historical spots in the country until the Government can decide its duty and its powers? Every hour the most flagrant depredations are committed which can never be repaired."(23)

In the *Press* of July 9, 1893 another protestor, perhaps reflecting even then a skepticism about the Congress, wrote in disgust, " ' If there is a bill introduced in Congress that will in any way interfere with the avaricious designs of the trolley company it will be sure of opposition. Already one of the Washington papers has taken occasion to discredit the damage done by the trolley company and to represent that corporation in the light of a great benefactor.' "(24)

Although vociferous in their criticism opponents were unable to alter the situation. The company refused to halt construction and thus began a legal battle of several years duration. The term "vandals" was frequently used by those opposing the electric trolley when referring to the owners of the line. One editorial of the day stated, "Do the people of Gettysburg realize that they are killing the goose that laid the golden egg when they permit an electric road to spoil the field? If people find that the battlefield has been destroyed there will be no more reunions there and the people who make money by entertaining visitors will find themselves cut off. It might be all right to give visitors a cheap trip across the field, but they'll find that cheap travelers are not the kind they want and anyhow, anybody who cares enough about the place to visit it will have enough money to get over the field without riding cheaply on a railroad that destroys the place."(25) Despite all the opposition the electric railroad was partially opened in July 1893 with the entire line in operation by May 1894.

However, thanks to the resolve of members of the 72nd Pennsylvania Volunteer Regiment the trolley company was forced to lease a portion of the steam railroad line in order to complete a circuit of the battlefield. The 72nd owned a piece of ground 30 feet square near the Bloody Angle on which they intended to erect a regimental monument. Surveys called for the trolley line to run directly through this small section of ground but the 72nd adamantly refused to either sell or grant a right-of-way. An article dealing with the situation in the *Evening Star* of May 27, 1893 stated, "That little piece of ground is now absolutely necessary to the trolley people or their road cannot be built and the trustees of the property for the Seventy Second Regiment declare that they will not sell or lease it to the trolley people for any sum."(26)

As a result, in 1894, the new company entered into an agreement with the Gettysburg and Harrisburg (steam) Railroad to use a portion of the G & H tracks leading to Little Round Top. However objection was raised by the Gettysburg Battlefield Memorial Association when the electric railroad company attempted to erect poles for their trolley near the Angle and in September 1895 the G & H Railroad, by then owned by the Reading Railroad, took up about 200 feet of track hitherto used by the electric trolley line, thus effectively ending its use of the steam railroad tracks to Little Round Top.

In 1895 E.M. Hoffer, president of the Gettysburg Electric Railway Company, sold his interest in the company which elicited this comment in the *Star and Sentinel,* "A new ordinance will be required and that will give the town a plain chance to insist that the company shall make proper repairs on the streets occupied, shall pay a reasonable tax on cars and poles, shall make a prescribed rate of speed and at a fixed rate of fare and that the cars shall run on every secular day of the year instead of at the pleasure of the company. Those friends of the Christian Sabbath who have been grieved at the ostentatious desecration of its sanctity during the last two summers will also have a chance to appeal to Council for protection – if they think it worth the effort."(27)

Finally in January 1896 the U.S. Supreme Court ruled that the government did indeed have the right to condemn private lands to preserve land of historic significance, a decision which, along with the advent of the automobile, ultimately led to the demise of the trolley company. Prior to the Supreme Court's decision a lower court had ruled against the Battlefield Commission, but upon hearing the government's appeal the High Court upheld the dissenting opinion of one of the lower court judges who wrote, " 'The battle was a great lesson in military science – the greatest ever taught on this Continent at least – a most important illustration in strategy and the art of war. That it may be fully understood and appreciated hereafter it is necessary to do just what is proposed – preserve the battlefield in its original condition, mark the positions and movement of the troops and the different arms of the service at the various stages of the battle, so that it may be seen as upon a great chart precisely how the battle was fought. The Government proposes to perpetuate and secure this lesson for the sake of those who at present constitute its armies, as well as to those who will hereafter constitute them.' "(28)

During its existence the electric trolley had two stations in the town of Gettysburg, one at the junction of Carlisle Street and Railroad Street where the Western Maryland station still stands. The other was located at the junction of North Washington Street and Railroad Street where the former Reading Railroad station now serves as the Gettysburg Railroad ticket office for tourist excursions to Cumberland county over the old G & H tracks.

In town the trolley line ran from the Carlisle Street station through the town square, then followed Baltimore Street and subsequently the Baltimore Pike, to the town limits and eventually joined the G & H tracks to reach Little Round Top. The other section of the line extended from the Washington Street station south on Washington Street and then Steinwehr Avenue to the town limits. From there it ran along the Emmitsburg Road to the vicinity of the Peach Orchard where it turned into the battlefield, running parallel to Wheatfield Road for a short distance before turning south across open fields into the wooded area west of the Wheatfield. The line then made a semi-circle around the Wheatfield and turned east through a portion of the Devil's Den area before turning north across the face of Little Round Top, eventually reaching what is today the intersection of Wheatfield Road and Sedgwick Avenue. When the Reading Railroad, which had taken over the G & H Railroad, withdrew permission for the electric trolley to use its roadbed in 1895 the trolley company used its own Emmitsburg Road line to Little Round Top and back for the trip.

A trace of the old electric trolley roadbed is still evident on the west face of Little Round Top. Except for this obvious section and one section of what is now a hiking trail west of Devil's Den there is little to mark its existence. However the general configuration of both the electric trolley line and the steam railroad can be located by cinders which were used in the construction of their roadbeds. In the open fields traces of the old roadbeds can still be found in their general locations despite extensive agricultural activities on the land over which they were built, but the dispute over the trolley line was only a precursor of controversies yet to come.

Shields Museum on U.S. 30   GNMP

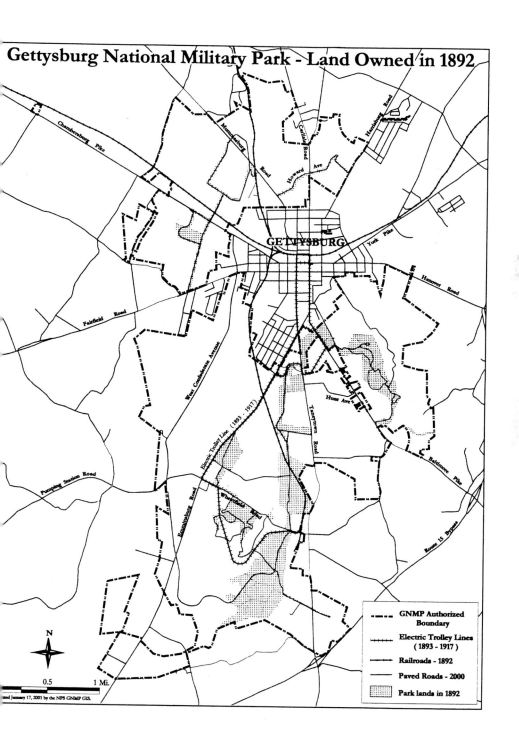

Gettysburg National Military Park - Land Owned in 1892

– · · – · ·	GNMP Authorized Boundary
+++++	Electric Trolley Lines (1893 - 1917)
——•——	Railroads - 1892
——	Paved Roads - 2000
░░░	Park lands in 1892

0.5   1 Mi.

Created January 17, 2001 by the NPS GNMP GIS.

"reasonable doubts"

With the federal establishment of Gettysburg National Military Park in 1895, and the transfer of land from the Gettysburg Battlefield Memorial Association to the War Department in 1896, came a change in the approach to managing the battlefield, securing additional land, and, almost immediately, a flurry of activity which had a major effect on the appearance of the battlefield. All of this was done under the direction of the Gettysburg Battlefield Commission, which had been appointed in 1893 to assist the struggling Gettysburg Battlefield Memorial Association. The Commission assumed official oversight of the battlefield when the land was deeded to the federal government three years later.

Some of the most immediate changes were also some of the most visible. Many of the dirt roads created by the Association were replaced with Telford avenues. Although this process is no longer in use it was a highly durable surface and in some sections of the battlefield it still exists under the modern asphalt surface of current park avenues. In January 1896 the *Star and Sentinel* described a Telford surface as, "A foundation pavement of 8 inch wedge-like stones set on edge and well kapped, and chinked; on this 4 inches of stone 1½ inch in size, then a slight layer of clay as a binder; and finally a top dressing of one or two inches of quarter inch stone screening. The whole is then rolled with a roller weighing 14 tons."(1) To house and maintain this sizable equipment a brick building was constructed at the corner of Pleasonton Avenue and the Taneytown Road in the early 1900's. Appropriately named the "Roller Building" it continues to house maintenance facilities for the park. During the construction of the roads two stone bridges were also built over Plum Run. Made of Gettysburg granite, 6 inch steel bars and 3-inch oak planking both they, and the roads, were obviously intended to last as indeed they have although the oak planking on the bridges has been replaced with a paved surface.

Simultaneously with road and bridge construction five iron observation towers were being erected on the battlefield. Built by the Variety Iron Works of Cleveland, Ohio, they ranged in height from 60 to 75 feet. The towers built on Culp's hill and on Big Round Top marked the approximate flanks of the Union army while the ones on Oak Ridge and at the intersection of West Confederate Avenue and the Millerstown Road indicated the general

Telford type road construction-Pleasonton Ave. Base stones were set by hand for smooth surface. Finished section in distance. GNMP

Rugg's Battery showing original cast iron markers and ammunition pyramid GNMP

extent of the original Confederate lines. A fifth tower was erected in Zeigler's Grove near the site where the Cyclorama building was built in 1961. Later the towers in Zeigler's Grove and on Big Round Top were removed and the one on Oak Ridge reduced in height. The "Eisenhower" tower, so named because of its proximity to the late president's farm, and the Culp's Hill tower, remain at their original height and are still in use as is the lowered tower on Oak Ridge.

About the same time the wooden carriages of cannon placed to mark artillery positions had begun to deteriorate. By the late 1800's they were gradually replaced with replicas made of cast iron, which were then attached to the granite foundation stones still visible today. Stacks of ammunition appropriate to the type of cannon in the battery were placed beside the carriages but it has since been necessary to remove these because so many were being stolen. Bronze plaques were also placed on polished granite bases throughout the battlefield to aid in understanding the movements of the armies. Plaques with square bases represent Union positions; those with round bases denote Confederate army lines. In addition, upright cannon tubes were placed throughout the battlefield and surrounding areas to mark the locations of the headquarters of the various generals.

Fencing too received attention from the busy Commission. Stone fences present during the battle were rebuilt, and pipe-rail fencing was constructed along the avenues to indicate government ownership of the land enclosed. Although many stone fences still exist the pipe-rail fencing, which one local paper had called "strong and handsome", has been removed. However there are now plans to restore this fencing at appropriate locations.

Nor did the Commission hesitate to set new rules for the park when it deemed them necessary. In August 1897 bicyclists, or as then termed, "wheelmen", in town blackened one eye to protest rules for riding in the park which they felt were unfair and gave the wheelmen a "black eye." In part the rules were:

II. Every machine must be provided with a bell…and shall be distinctly heard at a distance of 30 yards, sleigh bells, large gong bells and continuously ringing bells being inadmissible.

III. Every machine while in motion must have a lighted lamp after dark. Chinese lanterns are not permitted.

V. No more than 2 machines shall be ridden abreast

VI. Riding crosswise and curving to and fro are strictly prohibited..

VII. Bicycle coasting within the limits of the Park is prohibited and the rider must not take hands off handles.

VIII. In any case where a bicycle meets or overtakes any horse which may become restive such bicyclists shall take every precaution to avoid danger.

X.   Blowing of horns, playing of musical instruments, shades or awnings attached in any way to a bicycle is forbidden.

XIII. Parties unable to ride wheels safely will not be permitted to learn on the Park drives but must confine themselves to the place indicated by the Commission for practice riding."(2)

After having listed all 14 rules the paper observed, "We can't see any good reason why the Gettysburg wheelmen should object to the above rules…looking at it as a wheelman and disinterested party, we do not see how the rules could be improved upon to meet the necessity and protection of all concerned. They are wise provisions."(3)

Not everyone greeted the new national park with enthusiasm. Even the two local newspapers took differing views. The *Star and Sentinel* welcomed the Congressional action but the *Gettysburg Compiler* was less enthusiastic as an editorial in the May 14, 1895 issue indicates: "There are in Gettysburg and Adams county many people, a vast majority perhaps, who have reasonable doubts as to the benefit which the National Park may bring to our town and vicinity."(4) The next week this statement appeared in the same paper, "Gettysburg will gladly welcome any institution that will help its business and it may be that the National Park will have that effect—to deny it is not our purpose but the conditions are such as to give rise to *reasonable* doubts."(5) This article elicited this scornful editorial in the *Philadelphia Inquirer*, as quoted in the *Compiler.* "The Gettysburg Compiler makes the remarkable statement that a vast majority of the people of Gettysburg have reasonable doubts as to whether a national Park is going to be a benefit to the town and vicinity. It is so incomprehensible that any such feeling should exist that the Inquirer takes the liberty of questioning the Compiler's statement. So many of the people of Gettysburg have lived off the battlefield for so many years that it is to be presumed that they know which way their interest lies."(6)

While the debate in the press continued the Battlefield Commission went on with its work. By 1898 wear and tear on the avenues was becoming a source of serious concern as the restrictions published in the *Star and Sentinel* of March 1, 1898 indicated. "Our liverymen and others have received notice that hereafter wagons carrying tourists over the avenues of the Gettysburg National Military Park will be obliged to have tires of the following width on their vehicles: 1 or 2 horse wagons, 6 people—1½ inches; 2 horse wagons, 8 people—1¾ inches; 2 horse wagons, 10 people—2 inches; 2 horse wagons, 12 people—2¼ inches; 4 horse wagons—2¾ inches. We understand that most of our livery men will have to change some of their tires to comply with the order."(7) What penalty, if any, would be imposed on those who failed to comply is not stated.

An 1898 "Military Avenues" report to the War Department by the Commission offers further evidence of the continuing effort to establish suitable avenues throughout the park. "Since the last report an avenue along the battle line of the First Corps on the field of the first day's Battle has been constructed. It is about a mile and 2/3 long, 20 feet wide, and made on the Telford plan in a most substantial manner. The main section is called Reynolds Avenue, but with the approval of the Secretary of War three minor sections have been named, respectively, Wadsworth, Doubleday and Robinson Avenues."(8) Those avenues still exist today and carry a significant amount of traffic. Wadsworth Avenue leaves Reynolds Avenue to the right at the first "T" intersection. As this avenue makes a left turn on Oak Ridge it becomes Doubleday Avenue which runs along the crest of Oak Ridge. At the observation tower Robinson Avenue cuts off from Doubleday and winds down the slope to connect with the Mummasburg Road at the railroad crossing.

Once the federal government took over the battlefield, land speculators rapidly began buying up land expecting to reap fortunes reselling it to the Battlefield Commission at greatly inflated prices. Their activities were the subject of a stinging article in *The Press* of March 4, 1898. "The Gettysburg National Park Commission…has been hampered in an unexpected manner from the beginning. A…swinish invader appeared in the form of land speculation. A syndicate went ahead of the commission buying up battlefield land at $35 an acre and proposing to sell it to the Government for $400 an acre. This attempt to swindle cannot succeed with the present commission… . The men who would make the Gettysburg battleground a field for speculation are in point of morals a species of ghoul."(9)

But the Commission was not without its critics. As the number of monuments on the battlefield grew so did criticism. In the September 1895 issue of the magazine *Century*, in turn quoted in the September 10, 1895 issue of the *Star and Sentinel*, one writer declared, "It is probably within the fact to say that there are not four pieces of good sculpture on the battlefield of Gettysburg including the beautiful and appropriate Celtic Cross which marks the position of a body of Irish troops. There are a few unobtrusive pieces of natural rock which fittingly express willing sacrifice or unyielding valor; but for the most part that beautiful field—the chosen valley for the nation's salvation—has become for lack of co-ordination in planning and good taste in execution an unsightly collection of tombstones… ."(10) In defense of the Commission the *Star and Sentinel* replied, "It is true there is much inferior work on the field and much money has been wasted on memorials that are inappropriate and inartistic, but the Government Commissioners are in no wise responsible for these mistakes. They must be placed on the several State Commissioners… . This critic must also remember that the marking of the Gettysburg field has been a steady growth through twenty years and the originators of the scheme had not the faintest idea that their efforts would finally result in such a comprehensive result as a National Park."(11)

Undeterred by criticism, units which had fought at Gettysburg continued to place their monuments on the battlefield. Now that Confederate lines were also coming under protection Louisiana veterans, appointed by the governor of that state, visited the battlefield in 1894 and marked the position of five different units. "The Southerners were high in their praise of the courtesy of the Government Commissioners" reported the *Star and Sentinel, "* and declared that the other states that were represented in the Army of Northern Virginia will now proceed to send committees to cooperate in the work being done here."(12)

As the Battlefield Commission continued its efforts to purchase land it also continued to face the problem of not only outside speculators but local landowners asking astronomical prices for their holdings, continuing a trend reported in 1899 when seven landowners held out for higher prices. One particularly important piece of land was the 13 acres owned by photographer William Tipton located between Big Round Top and Devil's Den. Included in Tipton's holdings were a "dancing pavilion and eating house"(13) patronized by local citizens as well as visitors. Tipton refused to consider anything close to the Commission offer, claiming that any evaluation of the land should include profits—about $3000 per year—derived from the business operated on that land. Finally the Commission initiated condemnation proceedings and at a court hearing witnesses for Tipton placed a value of between $20,000 and $30,000 on the property. However the jury apparently failed to be convinced by the testimony and awarded Tipton the sum of $6,150, which he accepted in November of 1901 after threatening to appeal the award. The buildings were removed the following spring.

By 1900 tourism was a fact of life in Gettysburg. One newspaper observed, "A striking proof of the great and general interest by the people with reference to this battlefield...that having caused a record to be kept...it was found that about 9000 vehicles, carrying 30,000 tourists, passed over Hancock Avenue in a single month."(14)

It was this growing interest which raised alarm among some of the local residents and resulted in a "Sabbath Association" convention being held at Christ Lutheran Church on Chambersburg Street. Among the resolutions unanimously adopted during this two-day meeting was one that read: "That as citizens of Gettysburg in Convention assembled, we do hereby earnestly petition the officials of the Philadelphia and Reading, and Western Maryland railroads, that they do not carry excursions to Gettysburg on the Lord's Day. We also request the management of the Gettysburg Trolley Railroad to sus-

Pipe rail fence. Restored stone fence in distance   GNMP

GROUND PLAN OF MEMORIAL
to be placed on the field of Pickett's charge

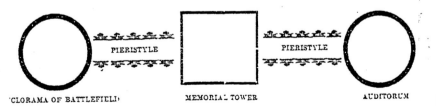

From the Philadelphia Ledger *as reported by the* Star and Sentinel *(Gettysburg) August 29, 1899.*

pend the running of its cars on the Lord's Day, commonly called Sunday, and that we request the Town Council of Gettysburg to enact a law in harmony with the law of the State, forbidding the desecration of the Sabbath within the borough..."(15)

In 1899 the Grand Army of the Republic encampment in Philadelphia was presented with a plan for a memorial building on the battlefield. James Huston had produced a drawing that showed a central tower, flanked by two circular buildings connected to the tower by walkways. "The central tower is planned to be 300 feet high and 50 feet in diameter at the base," reported the *Star and Sentinel.* One of the two side buildings would house the Cyclorama painting (then privately owned) the other would contain a 6000 seat auditorium. "It is proposed to erect the memorial on the level meadow over which Pickett and his men, with a valor that was sublime, charged against the desperate fire and gallant defense of the Union troops."(16). However the necessary funds were never raised, for which many historians are doubtless more than a bit grateful.

Despite the outcome of the Tipton land condemnation it failed to deter other landowners from demanding exorbitant prices for their holdings. In 1904 the Battlefield Commission attempted to purchase the famous Peach Orchard but the owner of the 11½ acres claimed it was worth $400 per acre or $4600 because of both its agricultural and historic value. Believing the price too high the Commission, which usually paid around $75 per acre for woods and $100 per acre for open land, again sought a court judgment to determine a fair price for the orchard. Citizens from the county testified on both sides of the issue and the jury's verdict was that the land was worth $1341.70 or $116.67 per acre, which the Commission paid.

But controversy continued to follow actions both in land acquisition and monument design even when the Battlefield Commission played only a secondary role. For the local citizens a particular bone of contention was the accepted design and location of the Pennsylvania state monument. In 1907 a commission had been authorized by the Pennsylvania legislature for the purpose of selecting a design and site for a monument to honor the Pennsylvania troops who fought here. This state commission selected the site on which the monument now rests but the selection was greeted with howls of protest from the community. The October 28, 1908 *Gettysburg Compiler* complained, "They paid no attention to the unanimous voice of Gettysburg for a building."(17) Earlier another article in the same paper stated, "The great demand of the patriot, visitor and military student was a memorial structure within the borough, accessible in the evening for visitation and study. The hope of the citizens was for an enclosed memorial which would contain trophies of war, military records, a military museum, a structure that might be richly adorned architecturally."(18) One site suggested for this building was the center square of Gettysburg, a location also favored by several designers hoping to build the Pennsylvania memorial. Given the traffic situation in Gettysburg today the public may be thankful that the Pennsylvania Monument Commission held to its original decision to place the monument on the battlefield although obviously neither the choice of site nor the design was greeted with anything near unanimous approval. Begun in the fall of 1907, the Pennsylvania monument was dedicated with much ceremony in September 1910.

Another proposal, which raised an even greater storm of protest by, among others, members of the Grand Army of the Republic, was the suggested memorial to Confederate General Robert E. Lee. Although by this time the "memorialization" of the battlefield through monuments and markers had been under way for some time and portions of the Confederate battle line had already been protected, the suggestion that Lee might be honored on the battlefield caused many Union veterans to react in anger. Union veteran Major William H.Lambert wrote, "I think we can safely wait until Virginia erects a statue to Abraham Lincoln...before erecting one to Lee at Gettysburg."(19) General Louis Wagner declared, "Either we were right or they were. If we were right there is no reason why they should be glorified. I am opposed to placing the statue of any rebel general on the battlefield of Gettysburg."(20) The *Public Ledger-Philadelphia Times* of January 24, 1903 reported a resolution passed by GAR posts 2 and 19 in that city, which read in part:

"What Gettysburg is we and our comrades have made it. The glory, the fame, the sentiment that cluster around the very name of Gettysburg whenever spoken either in this land or in a foreign land is all ours and to the memory of our fallen comrades...Resolved, that we appeal to the Senators and Representatives in the legislature of our state to defeat this insult to the memory of our dead defenders, whether Pennsylvanian or not, and to those living who gave their energies and the best efforts of their youth to overthrow the man whose statue it is proposed to place in honor upon the soil he desecrated and which the blood of our comrades made sacred."(21)

Despite these protests the base of the monument was erected in 1910, the same year that construction was completed on the Pennsylvania monument. However, it was another seven years before the controversy over Lee and the Confederate flag would be resolved and the bronze work on the memorial completed. Today the Pennsylvania monument and the Virginia monument, adorned by the statue of General Lee, are among the most visited memorials on the battlefield.

By the 1900's local commercialism had become rampant even within the national park itself, but in July 1905 the Battlefield Commission took steps to remedy the situation as much as possible. Advertising signs had long been banned on the battlefield avenues and now the Commission began the removal of all advertising signs on the state roads that transected the park. Signs that could not be removed were painted over and the advertising obliterated. According to the *Gettysburg Times* "Hundreds of signs advertising automobile oils, tires and many other supplies were removed on Wednesday.... On many of the rail fences paint had been used by local firms to advertise their wares or their places of business. Paint, as nearly the color of wood as could be secured, is being used to obliterate these advertisements and when the work is completed not one sign will appear."(22)

During this same period changes on the battlefield could be considered slow but steady. However the entry of the United States into World War I had a major impact on the park. Of all the intrusions which have affected the Gettysburg battlefield through the years the largest although not the longest lasting, was the U.S. Army training facility established in 1917 and generally referred to now as Camp Colt.

In 1896, after all the land then preserved as part of the battlefield had been deeded to the U.S. War Department, the Pennsylvania National Guard began spending a week each year training on the battlefield, erecting tents, digging entrenchments and engaging in mock battles. While doing this the Guard also put up a number of more or less permanent structures between the Angle and the Emmitsburg Road. Their maneuvers covered the land where the Gettysburg Hospital now stands and included all of the area where Pickett's and Pettigrew's men made their gallant charge on July 3, 1863. Beginning in the early 1900's U.S. Army regulars also carried out training exercises on portions of the battlefield and its use, for military training purposes continues today although in a less invasive manner. Annually over 9000 military personnel from U.S. bases, and officers from many foreign countries, study terrain and tactics on the battlefield. Students from the various U.S. military academies make annual field trips here and the U.S. Army War College in Carlisle, Pa. makes extensive use of the battlefield as part of its officers' training program.

Given the early use of the battlefield as a training ground it was natural that when the United States became involved in World War I, Gettysburg was selected as one of the Army's training sites. On May 17, 1917 an article in the *Gettysburg Compiler* stated, "A camp here seemed to be at a most available point with good rail accommodations. It had always proved a most healthy site for the camping of National Guard and Regulars. There has always been a sufficient supply of good pure water and the natural characteristics of the place have always recommended Gettysburg for training and maneuver purposes."(23)

However, it was the presence of the steam railroad that made the site

Camp Colt as seen from the Spangler house   GNMP

Camp Colt looking toward the Spangler house   GNMP

a particularly desirable one. Connected with the main rail line through the town, this spur line across the battlefield provided rail transportation to the training camp throughout the war and provided an easy and efficient means of bringing both men and materiel to an area which still more closely resembled the small town and farmland of 1863 than today's modern borough and national park.

In 1917 the camp was used as an infantry training site and following the Army custom at that time it had no specific name but was simply referred to as the U.S. Army camp at Gettysburg. Not until 1918, when a Tank Corps training ground replaced the one used by the infantry, was it given the name of Camp Colt in honor of Samuel Colt, inventor of the Colt revolver. The Colt Park development of today takes its name from the Tank Corps training camp, a portion of which covered much of the land now occupied by housing.

From the initial contingent of about 4000 men the infantry camp eventually grew to hold 8000 soldiers, roughly the same as the current popu-lation of Gettysburg borough. To provide for the needs of the trainees, sewer and water lines were laid throughout the camp. Water was supplied from lines running into Marsh Creek about three miles southeast of town and six infantry regiments—the 4th, 7th, 58th, 59th, 60th, and 61st—received training on the battlefield. Three regiments were stationed east of the Emmitsburg Road, one was on the west side of this same road as were the bakery, hospital and motor ambulance pool. The remaining two regiments were located in the area of the present day Recreation Park and adjacent to the future Colt Park. The horses used by all regiments were stabled near the location of the current Rite Aid Pharmacy and, for the benefit of the officers, a small swimming pool was con-structed just west of the High Water Mark.

At its assigned location each regiment was provided with 15 to 16 wooden barracks and at least two regiments had their own sewage facilities that emptied into creeks on the battlefield. Although the regiments had barracks, tents were also commonplace as old photographs reveal. However no struc-tures were suitable for winter quarters and so by October 25, 1917 the first infantry regiments had been transferred to other locations and by November 26 all but a small detachment had left the Gettysburg camp.

Even in those days there is an indication that the protection of monu-ments on the battlefield was a concern as indicated by a letter from the com-manding officer of the 61st U.S. Infantry who wrote to the Battlefield Com-mission, "…every effort will be made by myself to see that the enlisted men of the 61st infantry do not molest in any way, the monuments, trees, shrubbery, woods, etc. of the Gettysburg National Park."(24)

With the departure of the infantry in November 1917 the camp stood idle throughout the winter but in March 1918 the camp was reopened as a training ground for the Tank Corps and at this time received its name of "Camp Colt." Although the government owned the land some of it had been leased to local residents for farming operations. However, in order to accommodate the needs of Camp Colt 126 acres of land at the southwest end of town were leased back from the farmers including over 100 acres of the Codori farm, 10 acres of the Klingle farm and 6 acres near the Brien house. With the opening of the camp, training facilities were moved to Gettysburg from Camp Meade in Maryland and over the ensuing months nearly 9000 men went through training at Camp Colt although only two tanks were ever brought there. Additional construction supplemented that erected by the Infantry in 1917. However, a number of officers, including the commanding officer, Captain Dwight D. Eisenhower, resided in town. As before, the camp was not suitable for winter quarters so by October 1918 most of the men had been transferred to other training sites. The signing of the Armistice on November 11, 1918, ending World War I, ended the need for Camp Colt and it was completely abandoned on November 17, 1918.

The closing of Camp Colt left the Battlefield Commission with a vexing problem. Throughout the months that the camp had been used as a training site, for both infantry and the Tank Corps, heavy truck traffic moved constantly over the Emmitsburg Road doing major damage to the road, which could not withstand that kind of pounding. As a result the Battlefield Commission asked that the Army assist in repairing the damage and the 1920 Commission report to the War Department stated, "At the request of Major D.D. Eisenhower, U.S.A. Commander of Camp Colt, and in consultation with Captain F.B. Moore, Quartermaster, an agreement was made with the Gettysburg National Military Park Commission to rebuild about one mile of the Emmitsburg Road... ." The Commission was to pay $5,760 as its part of the total cost and work was to be completed by December 31, 1918.

The report continued, "The work went very well until the Armistice was signed in November as the Quartermaster's part of the work was being done with Army trucks and enlisted men from the guard house. There was trouble after that in having the hauling and spreading done... . The agreement was never completed, consequently the National Park Commission was obliged to hire trucks and employ labor to finish the work..."(25) Total cost to the Commission was $7,372.57.

There was also the matter of cleaning up the training grounds and the 1920 report stated, "On May 24, 1919 the camp equipment—buildings, drains, sewer lines and water pipes were sold at auction to Lewis Wrecking Company of Chicago, Ill. As part of the sales agreement the firm was given 6 months for removal of all equipment and restoration of the land as far as practical to its original condition." However, the Commission continued, "We regret to report as yet nothing has been done along the lines of restoration of this most interesting part of the field. A large area remains covered with the debris of the camp, several miles of Tarvia cover the roads, and deep drains, running in all directions mar the different areas."(26)

Nor were Camp Colt and its predecessor the only wartime intrusions on the battlefield. During the summers of 1917 and 1918 Gettysburg school students were given plots of land, primarily on Cemetery Hill, ranging in size from a few square feet to almost an acre, for cultivation of "War Gardens." Not only were the students expected to raise food on these plots for their families and others but they were also required to submit a report of their work to the chairman of the Battlefield Commission at the end of each growing season.

Despite numerous setbacks the situation on the battlefield gradually returned to normal. The Camp Colt site was eventually cleaned up, although long after the original deadline, roads were repaired, war gardens became a thing of the past and the Battlefield Commission was able to get on with its task of preserving and protecting this "holy ground."

50th reunion encampment along Emmitsburg Road   GNMP

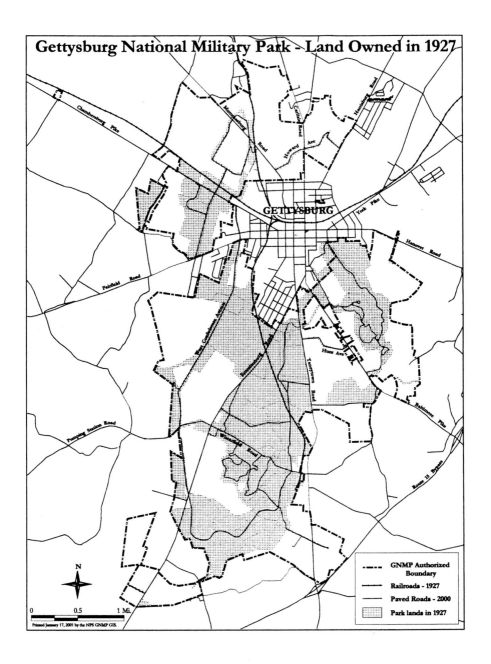

Gettysburg National Military Park - Land Owned in 1927

"our hands are tied"

Although World War I slowed battlefield development significantly and the Depression did likewise, concern over preservation of battle land did not disappear entirely. By the mid-1930's it had again become a major issue as more and more land over which the battle had been fought was sold for development. Moreover some aspects of the management of Gettysburg National Military Park were altered in 1933 when responsibility for the park, which by this time contained 1723 monuments and 23.2 miles of roads on just over 2500 acres, was transferred from the War Department to the Department of the Interior and the National Park Service.

NPS administrators took the view that one of its primary missions was preservation of park land which, in their minds, meant soil conservation. Therefore, in keeping with the changing agricultural practices of the time, "NPS began an active campaign to remove historic fences, combine fields, drain wetlands and remove boulders."(1), all to accommodate the large farm machinery needed to maintain a viable agricultural industry within the park. Woodlands grew up on formerly open land not suitable for farming and con-tour plowing changed both the appearance and topography of many fields.

The NPS found that it was also necessary to rethink land acquisition policies. In the formative years of the park priority was given to securing lands encompassing the actual Union and Confederate battle lines. Most of the remaining land at that time was still agricultural in nature and the assumption had been that the private landowners would continue to farm and in so doing protect the landscape itself. However by the 1920's and '30's this was no longer true. Development was beginning to encroach upon historically signif-icant land as later generations of farmers were sought out by private and com-mercial developers and offered prices for their properties which the owners felt unable to refuse. So it was that the NPS found itself faced with the necessity of purchasing land other than the battle lines themselves in order to protect the historic integrity of the battlefield, a task made more difficult because Con-gress had never set official park boundaries.

When Gettysburg National Military Park was officially established by the federal government in 1895 a map drawn by Union General Daniel Sick-les, who commanded the 3rd Corps at Gettysburg in 1863, had been accepted as a de facto map of the park limits. Interpretation of this map provided for an aggregate area of "15,360 acres." (2) This situation continued until the early 1970's when the U.S. Senate requested that more specific boundaries be established in a "boundary understanding" which was intended to be permanent. In June 1974 the Senate Appropriations Committee accepted the Park Service recommendations to protect 3,874 acres and eliminate the Sickles map as marking the official park boundary. In accepting the NPS proposals the sub-committee involved stated, "implicit in this approval is the firm understanding that the depicted boundaries will not be subject to change in the future except for substantial and compelling reasons that are not now apparent."(3) By 1986 those "substantial and compelling reasons" were fast becoming apparent.

While changes were going on outside the park, changes were going on inside the park as well. The advent of the automobile and increasing use of buses required changes in the road system in the interest of safety. Hairpin curves on Little Round Top, and others on Culp's Hill, were eliminated and two dangerous sections of road were removed. When concerns were voiced about the historical significance of the sections to be replaced the *Gettysburg Times* reported, "It was explained that the curves to be eliminated do not follow the original battle lines and by their elimination the historical value of the park will in no way be marred."(4) Another article described the changes, "The Little Round Top by-pass, a stretch of .388 of a mile, will begin at Rosensteels (on the west side of Little Round Top) and run in an almost straight line over the hill, northeast of the present guard's station there (since removed), joining Sykes Avenue on the opposite side of the slope. The new road of .434 of a mile on Culp's Hill will encircle the observation tower and will eliminate curves on Slocum Avenue on both sides of the slope."(5)

In 1934 a sign of the times was evident when the local paper reported new park regulations announced by Superintendent McConaghie, "There will be no beer parties on the Gettysburg battlefield, the speed limit will be increased from 10 to 20 miles per hour and two uniformed motorcycle policemen will patrol the battlefield to enforce park regulations." The paper continued, "The 'no beer party' order recalled to the minds of many old timers of Gettysburg how a group of men would take a number of bottles of beer, a basket of sandwiches, and drive out to Spangler's Spring late in the evening for some 'quiet entertainment' "(6) Times have not changed much since then despite the regulations.

As the nation struggled to recover from the Depression intrusion on the battlefield continued to be a fact of life. The government owned the land and could do with it as it wished. Preservation became secondary to utilization. This attitude led to the selection of the park as the location of two Civilian Conservation Corps camps to house "Forest Units", men who would work on various government funded projects both on the battlefield and throughout the area. The camps were opened in 1933 and organized on the pattern of military units complete with officers.

Camp 1, located in Pitzer's Woods, reached a total strength of 214 men at its peak. It consisted of five barracks, a mess hall, shower room, latrine, garage, hospital, gasoline supply house, forestry building, recreation hall and two buildings for officers quarters. Camp 2, situated in McMillen Woods further north on West Confederate Avenue, was of a similar size, housing 215 men and officers. The *Gettysburg Times* proudly reported that Camp 1, "...was rated the best in sub-district number eight and according to advices from Baltimore was in line for first place ranking in the Third Corps area." (7) The men enlisted for a six month period after which it was hoped that they would be able to find permanent employment elsewhere.

Most of the work done by CCC men was in local communities outside of the park. However they also were engaged in repair and replacement of stone fencing and rehabilitation of farm lanes within the park. When government officials indicated that the camps might be closed in 1934 pleas from local residents, benefiting from the work being done, kept them open. Camp 1 was finally abandoned in April 1937 and the buildings razed soon after. Camp 2 remained active for another six months but by the end of the year it too was closed although the buildings were left in place and would play a part in another intrusion on the battlefield a few years later.

In 1934 a separate government program enabled the park to construct a steel and concrete bridge (since replaced) on Reynolds Avenue over the railroad cut. In addition two entrance stations were constructed, one located at the west side of the park on U.S. 30 across from the Reynolds statue, the second at the south end of the battlefield across from what is now a portion of the Eisenhower farm. The buildings were designed to serve as battlefield guide stations, information centers, and comfort facilities. They remain in place today although only the station on U.S. 30 continues in active service for guides.

That same year Congress appropriated $13,000 for the badly needed repair and restoration of buildings which existed on the battlefield in 1863 and were now included within park boundaries. Among these were the McPherson barn, Meade's headquarters, and homes and buildings on the Culp, Brien, Biggs, Hummelbaugh, Weikert, Codori, Klingle, Wentz, Bushman, and Slyder farms. Despite this impressive list of holdings much of the 1863 battle ground remained in private hands.

As local landowners showed dwindling interest in preserving land over which the battle had been fought citizens living elsewhere expressed growing concern. In May 1937 Richard Little, a frequent visitor to the battlefield,

Overturned CCC truck - caused by speeding on park road   GNMP

Rosensteel Cottage on Sedgewick Avenue. General Sedgwick statue at left - 1940   GNMP

wrote a 10 page letter to then Secretary of the Interior Harold Ickes. After a lengthy discussion of battlefield roads Little continued, "I was much disturbed on this last visit to Gettysburg to see the nuisances, which indeed existed before on a smaller scale, have increased beyond belief. Two immense automobile dumps are now on the battlefield... . Now a visitor sees only piles of dismantled, half-burned, ruined automobiles, on what was once the position of a portion of Ewell's artillery." Referring to the city garbage dump he wrote, "(what) seems to me absolutely inexcusable is the burning of city garbage on that part of the battlefield at the foot of East Cemetery Hill... . The smoke from the burning garbage was so dense I could hardly make out the inscriptions on the monuments. Naturally the smoke has an acrid, nauseous odor."

He went on to describe the Rose farm as "...quite a large piece of property at one time, but I've seen it whittled away to gas station owners, truck farmers, tourist cabin and bungalow builders year after year until now only the old stone house, the mammoth end walls of the barn, and about fifty acres of land remain."(8) Mr. Little went on for another four pages listing intrusive changes that he had observed on the battlefield. Were he to return today it would no doubt please him greatly to find that much has changed for the better. The junkyards and garbage dump are gone and the Rose farm has not only been preserved and partially restored but presently serves as a residence for park personnel. However not all of the "nuisances" noted by Mr. Little have been removed and some, not anticipated in his letter, have arisen.

In 1937 a major, and appropriate, addition to the battlefield was heralded when Pennsylvania state senator John Rice, a Gettysburg resident, introduced a bill in the Pennsylvania legislature to create, "the Gettysburg Peace Memorial fund, for the purpose of building an eternal light peace memorial on the battlefield at Gettysburg." In its article reporting on Senator Rice's action the *Gettysburg Compiler* added that the monument "may be erected on Big Round Top on the spot where the observation tower now stands."(9) Rice hoped to interest other states in the project (he did) and to have the memorial dedicated during the 75th reunion of Civil War veterans in Gettysburg, scheduled for July 1938.

By September 1937 the design for the memorial had been selected and the agreed upon site changed from Big Round Top to 35 acres along the Mummasburg Road purchased expressly for that purpose by the Pennsylvania commission headed by Senator Rice. It was also announced that President Franklin D. Roosevelt had tentatively accepted an invitation to dedicate the memorial on July 3. The date was especially significant since the ages of the veterans who would be returning to observe the 75th anniversary of the battle made it a certainty that this would be the last great encampment for the men who had fought at Gettysburg.

It also became an enormous spectacle, including not only more than 2000 Civil War veterans but veterans of the Spanish-American War and World War I, along with 3000 regular Army troops, the U.S. Army Air Force, 300 motorcycle police, the National Guard, and hundreds of dignitaries and other participants.

The Civil War veterans were housed on the fields of the first day's battle. The camp reached from the intersection of Howard Avenue and the Biglerville Road (Carlisle Street extended) across the Mummasburg Road, and spread on to Lincoln Avenue and the edge of the Gettysburg College campus. Union veterans were housed between the Biglerville and Mummasburg roads while Confederate veteran housing stretched from the Mummasburg Road to beyond West Broadway in town. Each veteran had his own tent shared by an attendant, and each tent had a wooden floor, rug, 2 beds, electric lights, bedding, chairs, screen doors and mosquito netting. Water and sewer lines were laid, wooden sidewalks constructed, street lights were installed and water fountains with underground cooling systems were placed throughout the camps as were latrines. There can be little doubt that many of the veterans must have compared these conditions with those they suffered through in 1863. Because the memorial was meant to honor men who had fought in all wars those men who had seen military service in the Spanish-American War and World War I also participated although they were housed elsewhere.

In addition to the veterans camp another for the motorcycle police adjoined the college football field, a Pennsylvania National Guard camp was placed at the foot of Oak Ridge and the 3000 regular Army troops were encamped on the old Camp Colt site between the Emmitsburg Road and West Confederate Avenue. Their camp extended north through the present Colt Park and Gettysburg Hospital grounds to the Catholic cemetery on West High Street.

The entire program, attended by an estimated 200,000 people, lasted for four days, from July 1 through July 4, although the dedication itself took place on July 3. A description of the anticipated program included a very non-Civil War event. "On the night of July 3 at dusk the G.H.Q. air force will simulate an attack on Gettysburg with 48 planes including six 'Flying Fortresses'. Anti-aircraft guns with searchlights will 'defend' Gettysburg."(10) The final day was given over, according to one paper, to "a gigantic military demonstration on Monday, July 4, by the United States Army, to be followed in the evening by a 2 hour fireworks display... ."(11) Although President Roosevelt was easily the outstanding figure at the dedication ceremonies it was the old veterans themselves who were the center of attention throughout most of the four days as they participated in what local papers described as their "Final Reunion".

Hancock Avenue entrance from Taneytown Road   GNMP

Aerial view - 75th reunion encampment. Howard Ave. runs L to R   GNMP

Despite the impetus for preservation provided by the great celebration of July 1938 commercial and other interests continued to threaten the further protection of the battlefield. In his November 1938 reply to a letter complaining about the condition of the battlefield Superintendent James R. McConaghie described a major part of the problem, "Construction of houses, cabin camps(motels), and private museums, not to mention the automobile wrecking yards on the Baltimore Pike and Taneytown Road, continues on battle grounds, but on private property adjoining Park lands. Recently, upon persistent complaints by Park authorities, two city garbage dumps, which were located on ground adjoining Park property, were closed by the State Department of Health authorities as public nuisances. As the Park cannot obtain funds for the purchase of certain properties which are absolutely essential for the preservation of historical values…our hands are tied and private developments continue."(12)

And continue they did. Coster Avenue is a little known piece of the battlefield seldom visited by the general public but which, in 1940, was central to the problem increasingly faced by the park. Its importance came to light in August when Joseph and Grace Codori of Gettysburg purchased the remaining 21 acres of an early farmstead intending to subdivide the property into building lots. As described by park historian Frederick Tilberg in a report to the NPS regional director later that month, "Coster Avenue, a government owned plot of land the width of a street and one city block in length, extends from Stratton Street…about one block's distance into the tract purchased by the Codoris… . The ground purchased by the Codoris is of real importance." Tilberg then described the advance of Union troops, under Colonel Coster, from Cemetery Hill in an effort to check the onrushing Confederate troops who were chasing the fleeing soldiers of the 11th Corps after the Union line north of the town had collapsed. Tilberg continued, "In this stand by Coster's brigade, perhaps as heavy loss of life took place as on any part of the field during the three days' struggle at Gettysburg." Then, in words that must have been wrenching for this devoted historian to write Tilberg continued, "Although the ground which is the subject of this purchase is of historical importance, it is felt that as it is entirely within the borough limits and adjacent to a residential section already developed, no attempt be made to forestall this development."(13) More supposedly "safe" battle ground had fallen to development.

In the mid-1940's war again left its imprint on the battlefield. This time Camp Colt was not resurrected nor was any other actual training camp constructed but at least 30 large groups of soldiers bivouacked there as they passed through Gettysburg on their way to other assignments, and parking for 2900 vehicles was provided on park avenues. Throughout the war, "Several training camps have sent units to Gettysburg and the sight of armed men skulking through the park shooting blanks from carbines or setting off flares has not been uncommon."(14) noted the *Gettysburg Times* in May 1945.

In March 1942 the old CCC Camp 2 had been closed, its usefulness as a storage site having come to an end. But it was reopened again in 1943 and occupied this time for training by an intelligence detachment from nearby Fort Ritchie in Maryland. While here the men of the unit renamed the facility Camp Sharpe in honor of the man who had served as Union General Meade's intelligence officer at Gettysburg in 1863. Over 200 men remained at Camp Sharpe until July 1944 after which it was converted to a prisoner of war camp.

In June of that year a group of 40 German prisoners of war had been brought to Gettysburg and housed temporarily in the Pennsylvania National Guard Armory on West Confederate Avenue. They were to prepare a prisoner of war camp on 15 acres of the Codori farm immediately south of the Home Sweet Home Motel on the Emmitsburg Road. At the camp a guard tower was located at each corner of the 400' x 600' site which was enclosed with a nine strand barbed wire fence. Tents for prisoners were within the enclosure while a headquarters building was located near the motel and 10 tents for housing guards were just to the south of the enclosure. As one report stated, "All construction, even to the design and layout of the sewage disposal plant was effected by prisoners of war... ."(15) The camp was designed to hold a minimum of 80 and a maximum of 400 prisoners, with 60 U.S. Army enlisted men and 5 officers in charge of the camp. About 400 men were housed there from July to November 1944. On July 4, inspired perhaps by Independence Day celebrations in town hours earlier, two of the prisoners managed to escape by crawling through a drain pipe leading under the Emmitsburg Road, but their freedom was short lived. They were captured a few hours later near the High Water mark. In January 1946 two other Germans escaped by crawling under the barbed wire at the corner of the grounds of Camp Sharpe which by then had been converted to an all-weather prisoner of war camp. Freedom for these men lasted a bit longer. They were not recaptured until four days later near Zora, Pa. on the Pennsylvania-Maryland state line, having not eaten for two days and "very badly scared", according to the newspaper report of the incident. "...statements made to the FBI...were to the effect that they had escaped because they liked America, wanted to see more of it, and hoped to reach a large city and stay in this country rather than return to Germany."(16) Zora had a population of less than 500.

While they were here the prisoners were put to work on local farms and in packing plants in an effort to harvest and preserve crops since manpower was in short supply. They were paid $1 per hour of which 90 cents went to the U.S. government for food and housing as well as supervision because each group of prisoners was accompanied by U.S. Army personnel at their place of work. The Emmitsburg Road site was not intended for winter use and so 200 prisoners were transferred to Camp Sharpe in November 1944 with the remainder relocated to other prisoner of war camps. At Camp Sharpe 50 acres were initially utilized, surrounded by perimeter fencing and a number of sentry boxes. Once the prisoners had settled into this new camp the tent camp on the Emmitsburg Road was dismantled.

Camp Sharpe was enlarged in July 1945 when another 350 prisoners were brought to Gettysburg and housed in tents on an additional 20 acres next to the original camp. This expansion was intended for use only during warm weather when the additional manpower was needed for farm and food processing work. Initially the War Deparment had not intended to create a year-round prisoner of war camp at Gettysburg but the shortage of labor in the area, especially on farms and in food processing plants, made prisoner of war labor necessary throughout the year and so the camp was upgraded to provide housing on a 12 month basis. The last of the prisoners of war left by April 1946 but while here they had provided labor for Adams, Cumberland, Franklin and York counties.

With the labor shortage still acute after the end of the war fruit growers and other farmers in the area asked the Emergency Farm Labor Office to see if it might be possible to use Camp Sharpe for the housing of seasonal labor during the 1946 growing season. Since the land was part of the national park but ownership of the buildings had been transferred to Penn State College(now University) in 1943, and the facilities had been used by the War Department from 1944-46, there was a great deal of correspondence involved before permission was finally given for Camp Sharpe to be used as a seasonal, or migrant, labor camp in 1946. A subsequent request to extend its use for 1947 was also granted after which the camp was closed and the buildings eventually removed.

Post war development of battle ground began again in earnest shortly after World War II ended. Early in 1947 a York contractor announced that he had purchased a portion of the William John farm adjacent to Queen Street and the hospital grounds. 25 new houses were to be built during the year with others added in the future. Meanwhile, in a theme all too familiar today, the developer asked the town to pave the streets surrounding the first phase of the development which was to be located just south of the present hospital and across South Washington Street from the rear of the Dobbin House. Johns Avenue was named for the owner of the old farm.

In September 1952 U.S. Senator Edward Martin of Pennsylvania inquired about the possibility of using 20 acres of government land between

Wainwright Avenue and East Confederate Avenue for construction of a new secondary school adjacent to the existing high school. After the not unusual legislative maneuvering, and lengthy negotiations, a bill was passed by Congress and signed by President Eisenhower which conveyed the 20 acre tract to the Gettysburg School District and added to the park a 29 acre parcel of historically very important land at the base of Culp's Hill and East Cemetery Hill.

By 1949 monument upkeep was creating some serious problems for the park and it had become evident that some of the limestone used to build the Peace Light memorial was failing. Rather than hardening with age, as the Bureau of Standards in Washington had assured the Peace Light Commission it would do, the limestone was actually disintegrating. Since the builder's guarantee had expired and the Commission no longer existed the NPS was left to deal with the problem. Eventually damaged sections of the limestone were replaced with granite of the same color at a cost of over $50,000.

The park was not alone in having difficulty securing land from private owners. In January 1949 officers of the local American Legion post urged federal action to purchase additional land for the National Cemetery. Although Congress gave its approval, as so often happens, no money was appropriated to buy the land. So, in 1951, frustrated by lack of federal funding, the Gettysburg post attempted to purchase the land with the intention of reselling it to the park when government funds became available. However one property owner not only refused to sell but stated through his attorney that he would fight any effort by the government to take the property through condemnation. It was not until the 1970's that the park was able to secure this and other critical property necessary to expand and protect the National Cemetery.

In 1936 the Advisory Board on National Parks, Historic Sites, Buildings and Monuments had declared the Cyclorama painting to be of national significance and the National Park Service purchased it from Jeremiah F. Hoover in 1941. The purchase agreement allowed the NPS to lease the land, on which the building housing the painting stood, from the Gettysburg Water Company for $2225 from 1941 to 1947, and required no rent thereafter for a period of 10 years. Later the site was donated to the park by the Water Company. As stated in the sales agreement Hoover was to receive $3000 annually "during his life, and thereafter to his wife during her life..." Charles H. Cobean, who was employed by Hoover at the time of the sale, was to receive "$600 per annum" as long as he was able to perform his "duties in connection with the maintenance and operation of the Cyclorama."(17)

Although round in shape to conform to the painting, the building lacked any type of temperature or humidity control and in fact was closed from November 1 to April 1 because of lack of heating. Kept in these unregulated conditions the painting was steadily deteriorating and the park administration

Original Cyclorama building - front view from Baltimore Pike   GNMP

Original Cylorama building-rear view showing Gettysburg reservoir (R) - restored artillery lunettes (L)
GNMP

realized that a new facility was essential if the painting was to be saved. In 1947-48 Congress appropriated "$10,000 for cleaning and preservation of the cyclorama"(18) and in 1948 the acting director of the NPS wrote, "We believe...the preservation of the Cyclorama painting is now assured if funds to erect a modern building...become available reasonably soon."(19)

But while the park was planning for its future it had to contend with interests which threatened its protection of the past. The battle of land acquisition was escalating rapidly and Senator John F. Kennedy had expressed his concern to the NPS. In her reply to the senator in April 1957 Acting Director Hillary A. Tolson wrote, "We are fully aware of and concerned about the encroachment on the historical battlefield at Gettysburg. ...even though we have endeavored to acquire certain various strategic parcels with the lands acquisition funds available to us, the asking prices are so far out of line with the appraised values we have been unable to negotiate successfully in these few instances."(20)

Kennedy's concern was well justified as an article by Robert Novak in the *Wall Street Journal* made clear. On January 8, 1959 he wrote, "A housing development and shopping center are planned in the area where the great Civil War Battle of Gettysburg began. A gas station and candy shop mark the line of Confederate General Longstreet's assault on Union troops. The scene of a fierce artillery duel is decorated by an auto graveyard and city garbage dump." Referring to the vigorous argument on both sides of the issue he went on, "The core of the conflict is this; The National Park Service, which maintains a national military park of 2,773 acres in the battlefield area, wants to buy up 680 additional acres... . The proposed Gettysburg acquisition would stymie at least two real estate developments and would doom a string of taverns, gas stations and motels crowded along historic Emmitsburg Road... ." Novak included this quote in his article, " 'We respect the battlefield' commented a vigorous young businessman who moved here 19 years ago, but you have to look at the human side. You have to consider the people who live here. We need industry and we need room to grow. And we have to have some place to live.' " The article continued by noting that some young businessmen, not native to the area, "view the battlefield as something of a barricade to progress."(21)

Yet ironically just two months after Novak's article appeared the Chamber of Commerce, the Retail Merchants Association, and the Travel Council, appealed to the townspeople to write their two U.S. senators requesting that $1,250,000 for the purchase of Civil War battlefield land, much of it destined for Gettysburg, be restored to the Department of the Interior budget from which it had been cut earlier. The restoration of funds was strongly opposed by Representative Michael Kirwan (D Ohio) who expressed an often heard argument, "We have enough land at Gettysburg. There is no use taking any more."(22)

Although by far the greatest public outcry was to save the battle ground other concerns were expressed as well. Despite the opinion of Representative Kirwan others made their voices heard in the *Columbus Dispatch (Ohio)*. "Monuments erected by the State of Ohio in the 1880's are now located along a National Park-owned 40 foot right of way across the threatened area which may be hemmed in by whatever buildings are erected there. The historic scene will then, of course, be obliterated... . The 8th Ohio's monument…was placed along the Emmitsburg Road at its main battle position. A motel has been erected behind it so that today the monument rests in the corner of the motel's front yard, making, you will agree, a rather unique lawn decoration."(23) Both the monument and the motel (Home Sweet Home) are still there.

On another section of the battlefield a monument to Company C of the Wisconsin sharpshooters was the subject of a protest by Representative Henry S. Reuss (D Wis) who wrote the owner of the Lee-Meade Inn asking that a billboard erected right next to the monument be removed. Owner Leroy C. Wayant replied, "In respect to the National Park Service and to the people of Wisconsin and to your request I will take the Lee-Meade sign down, for I think the park should be well kept and respected always."(24)

As the year went on voices on both sides of the preservation/development controversy became more strident. However both U.S. senators from Pennsylvania weighed in favoring restoration of the Department of the Interior funds as did U.S. Representative James Quigley whose district included Gettysburg. A strong proponent of purchasing additional land, Quigley had made a concerted effort to have the deleted funds restored. But he went beyond additional funding to urge zoning of areas adjacent to the battlefield as an additional way of protecting the historic ground. "Purchasing" he said, "is frightfully expensive, yet only partially effective. At Gettysburg it is not only necessary to correct past errors, it is essential that future ones be avoided. To this latter end I have a very positive answer: Zoning. I would hope that with a minimum of delay the supervisors of Cumberland Twp." (which borders by far the greatest area of the battlefield) "would enact into law an ordinance which provides zoning of the Battlefield area and territory adjacent thereto."(25)

But there was much more than a "minimum of delay". It was not until November 1990, more than 30 years later, that the township, despite fierce opposition even then, passed its first zoning law. The battle cry among residents of the township, and indeed in every township throughout the county, was "No one has a right to tell me what to do with MY land!"

Resistance to zoning of any type was widespread and vehement. One landowner spoke up at a public meeting saying, "I don't want anybody telling me which side of the road to put my mailbox on!"(26)

Lack of zoning exacerbated the problem of commercialization and in June 1959 "Fantasyland" a children's amusement park, was opened on the Taneytown Road diagonally across from Meade's headquarters. Owners Mr. and Mrs. Kenneth Dick had refused to halt construction and expressed their feelings in a letter to the editor of the *Gettysburg Times* "...We agree with Rep. Kirwan (D Ohio) who said, 'We have enough land at Gettysburg' ...We have used restraint in the location of our 'Fantasyland'. So must the government use this same restraint. After all Lincoln did not save this nation to have the government deny people their just rights.... So we...are exercising our inherent right, our great American privilege of going into business in this land of the free."(27)

At about the same time that "Fantasyland" opened the U.S. Senate restored $650,000 of deleted funds to the Department of the Interior for the purpose of purchasing battle ground at both the Manassas (Va) and Gettysburg battlefields although Gettysburg was scheduled to receive the lion's share. But there was a string attached to the appropriation that would prove fatal to Gettysburg's hopes. "The Committee recommends the allowance of $650,000 for the acquisition of such developed areas, which is not to be obligated until the Secretary of the Interior has reported...that the local governments have adopted adequate zoning regulations to assure against future development in these areas."(28) Manassas had zoning already in place but the townships adjoining Gettysburg National Military Park refused to enact the required zoning ordinances. As a result Gettysburg did not receive a penny.

Meanwhile other efforts to preserve battlefield land at Gettysburg were underway. Historians, many of them of the stature of Bruce Catton, spoke favorably on the matter. Cliff Arquette, a well known TV personality who himself had a museum in Gettysburg, sought supportive material for television use. The *Saturday Evening Post* carried an editorial favoring additional battlefield protection. From across the country private citizens in every walk of life urged that the battlefield be protected from development and decried commercialization of the famous site. But while the outpouring of support may have heartened the National Park Service it fell on the deaf ears of developers and local officials.

Although the county land north of the town had been the scene of a major Confederate attack on July 1, 1863 which broke the Union 11th Corps line and almost resulted in the defeat of the Union army, the county refused a National Park Service request that the land be donated to the park. In a letter replying to many who urged such action the county commissioners wrote,

"The County Institution District has no right under the law to hold land for the purpose of preserving the Gettysburg battlefield.... The Institution District cannot legally give this land away and can only sell it for the highest price obtainable.... If 80 acres of the county farm land in question become a part of the National Park they will be forever free of real estate taxes, but the county commissioners are willing to sell this land to the park if only the park would or could pay the fair purchase price."(29) The park, having no funds, had to stand by helplessly while developers made offers to the commissioners.

Baltimore contractor and developer Morton Klaus received an option from the Adams county commissioners to "buy the 33 acre plot of county land east of the Harrisburg Rd."(Bus. 15) "between the Eisenhower Elementary School and Radio Station WGET."(30) stated the *Gettysburg Times* of September 20, 1959. His plan included the construction of a supermarket on the land. This building and others today make up the North Gettysburg Shopping Center. County land on the west side of the Harrisburg Road surrounding Barlow's Knoll and extending across the Carlisle (Biglerville) Road was also slated to be sold. Clearly, when it came to protecting major portions of the battle ground the park's hands were still tied, by both the Congressional requirement of zoning and the sheer price of the land itself.

But public support for protection of the battlefield continued to grow and in November 1959 a local group, the Gettysburg BattlefieldPreservation Association, was formed which was to have a considerable role in the future of the park.

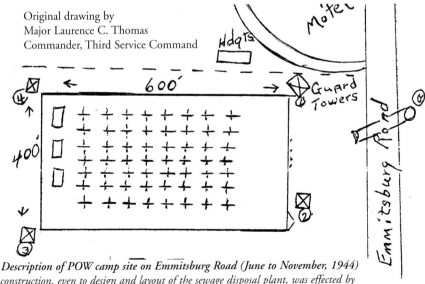

Description of POW camp site on Emmitsburg Road (June to November, 1944)
All construction, even to design and layout of the sewage disposal plant, was effected by prisoners of war
(Two escapees used tube under the highway to make their escape to the vicinity of the rock-wall at the High Water Mark, July 5, 1944.)

"an interested bystander"

From the 1960's on controversy concerning NPS actions at Gettysburg, rather than dwindling, continued to grow as commercial interests began to flex their considerable muscle. Local citizens who also resented the battlefield jumped into the fray, and there has been no peace at Gettysburg since then. The guns may be silent but the roar of battle continues.

As the decade opened the arguments continued to rage back and forth (and they still do), "Preserve this hallowed ground" vs "The government has enough land and we have a right to make a living." Local residents also resented the influence of "outsiders" in what Gettysburgians considered their personal business, while historians and ordinary citizens from beyond Adams county expressed dismay at what they believed was commercial desecration of a national shrine. Meanwhile the park, with little in the way of funds for land purchases, cast an anxious eye at land important to battlefield preservation but not yet protected.

By now tourists were coming to the battlefield in ever increasing numbers. In 1961 a new record was set as 1,711,491 people visited the park exceeding the 1,554,234 mark set in 1938 when the last great reunion of the Blue and Gray veterans took place during the 75th anniversary of the battle. As visitation increased so did commercialization as entrepreneurs sought to take advantage of the situation. It was this ever expanding commercialism which concerned the park and which gave rise to an editorial in the Rochester, N.Y. *Democrat-Chronicle*. Entitled "How to Mess Up a U.S. Shrine", the editorial read in part: "THE TOURIST season is almost with us, and it seems appropriate to note the latest of many examples of how America fouls its historic nest. This example is Gettysburg. 'We are fighting the second Battle of Gettysburg now' writes a former Rochestorian, a friend of this department who moved to near the historic spot. 'Commercialism threatens to take over the battlefield so that by 1963 you will have to hunt for the monuments between hotdog stands, motels and gift shops.' He enclosed newspaper stories and picture layouts from papers as far away as Washington. Shocking stuff. General George Meade's council headquarters now is within 100 yards of where a miniature golf course and a man-made fantasy land are planned. Souvenir shops, beer parlors, an auto junk yard, a housing subdivision, commer-

Aerial view of Emmitsburg Rd. & West Confederate Ave. circa 1950   GNMP

Intersection of Emmitsburg Rd. & West Confederate Ave. circa 1950   GNMP

cial establishments, and signs spatter the consecrated area where 160,000 men from the North and South fought a battle that helped determine the nation's course for all time to come. …Our sorrow at this mess is mixed with a measure of disbelief. Cannot our great, proud, free, rich, America somehow find the way to preserve such a heritage as this against desecration? Is this tragic commercialization inevitable? Cannot Congress help us to save a symbol of the very heritage of which it is part?"(1)

The loss of the $450,000 in federal funding earmarked for Gettysburg, because adjoining townships refused to enact Congressionally required protective zoning, was a severe blow. But in one fortunate transaction in August 1959 the park had been able to purchase an option on the Lee-Meade Inn across from the Rose farmhouse. Constructed in 1930, the Inn had been one of the objects of complaint in Mr. Little's letter of 1937. In 1960 the park exercised the option, sold the buildings, and restored that portion of the battlefield. Most of the bids received were for the cabins surrounding the Inn itself. These sold for between $60 and $525 dollars depending on the size of the cabins and the eagerness of the buyers to acquire them.

A prime example of the commercialism decried by the Rochester newspaper was the sale, reported in the *Gettysburg Times*, of a home "at the south end of Steinwehr Avenue near the new entrance to the Gettysburg battlefield, to Texaco, Inc. for $61,000. …The company plans to construct a gasoline station at that point."(2), and it did.

Another scathing article in *Parade* magazine in February 1960 expressed the feelings of many beyond the borders of Adams county, "While the nation honors Abraham Lincoln this week, a tawdry commercial war continues to wage over the site of his famous Gettysburg Address. For-profiteers are still invading the historical battlefield to the musical accompaniment of cash registers. Their monuments are beer parlors, souvenir stands, service stations and drive-ins, which stand alongside the sacred shrines honoring the Civil War dead. Where cannon once flashed neon signs now blink."(3)

On the other side of the opinion fence was Representative Michael Kirwan (D Ohio), obviously no friend of historic preservation, at least not at Gettysburg, who demanded, "Do not buy the land unless there is a zoning ordinance. If the people adjacent to it (the park) have no love for the shrine, why should we from other states?"(4) He apparently overlooked the appearance before a Senate committee, by Henry Sharf of Gettysburg urging Congress to provide the needed funds to buy the 118 acre Meals farm on the Mummasburg Road, the 80 acre Sherfy farm on the Emmitsburg Road, and the 55 acre Wolf farm near Devil's Den. Obviously not all local citizens viewed commercialization as a benefit.. Many realized that certain vital and threatened areas of battle ground were essential to the historic integrity of the park and so they did what Americans are very good at doing – they organized.

From the outset the Gettysburg Battlefield Preservation Association, officially chartered in November 1959, took a national approach to fund raising and wasted little time in getting its efforts underway. By April 1960 the group had mailed out 1000 "deeds" to individuals who had donated $1 or more to the GBPA's land acquisition fund. Each deed recognized ownership of one square foot of battle ground which the deed holder then agreed would be conveyed to the U.S. Government. Unencumbered by Congressional restrictions the GBPA's first outright purchase of land came in June 1960 when title to the 55 acre Wolf farm, adjoining Devil's Den, was transferred to the group. A second purchase followed five months later when an agreement was signed to buy the 118 acre Meals farm along the Mummasburg Road east of Oak Ridge. The price was $175,000, a far cry from the $100 per acre price paid for land by the Battlefield Commission 30 years earlier. Three houses already constructed and two additional building lots were excluded from the sale but since that time the lots and two of the houses have become park land and the houses removed. Only one house, across from some of the Gettysburg College playing fields, remains in private hands. At the first annual GBPA meeting in the fall of 1960 the president reported that over 45,000 donations had already been received from every state in the union. It wasn't easy but in its first year 173 acres of critical battle ground had been saved by the neophyte organization. In 1961 the GBPA received the Thomas Jefferson Community Program award for its efforts to purchase and protect battle ground land at Gettysburg, and funds continued to be received from citizens across the nation to keep up the work.

But local residents seemed less interested in historic preservation. The Leister home on the Baltimore Pike, a pre-Civil War house, was offered for sale in August 1962. According to the sale advertisement quoted in the *Gettysburg Times*, "This property adjoins the Cemetery Hill section of the battlefield and is one of the few remaining sites in the historical development area and has outstanding possibilities for museum, motel or other commercial purposes."(5) Although not sold at the time because the desired price was not reached, the property was later sold and a military museum constructed near the dwelling, which itself was retained as a home. The property is located just east of Cemetery Hill at the junction of Slocum Avenue and the Baltimore Pike.

Meanwhile the park itself was able to secure a vitally important piece of ground directly across from Meade's headquarters on the Taneytown Road. The *Gettysburg Times* reported that, "The ten acre property, assessed by the county at $2000, was sold to the National Wax Museum for $45,000. Earlier the Military Order of the Loyal Legion of the United States…offered $22,300 for the property with the intention of turning it over to the National Park."(6) But the offer was rejected as too low. The property was bounded by the National Cemetery, the Taneytown Road and Hunt Avenue, and the buyer intended to construct a wax museum on the land. However the NPS took legal action against the project and the U.S.District Court in Washington ruled that the 10 acres must be sold to the park by the National Civil War Wax Museum for a price of $55,000. Today the private residence still there is used as headquarters for the park protection staff and the Wax Museum is located on Steinwehr Avenue.

To the everlasting credit of the Loyal Legion they persisted in their efforts to protect battle ground and at the centennial celebration in 1963 presented to the park a 12 acre tract adjoining Reynolds and Buford Avenues. At that same ceremony the GBPA also presented to the park a deed covering 7½ acres of land on the first day's battle ground near Oak Ridge.

But while funding for the park and for the GBPA was hard to come by, one couple found the battlefield a source of unexpected wealth. During a visit to the field with his family, George Rapport of New York state found a package of moldy money, which was determined to be worth $49,000. After a year, no one having claimed it, Rapport was allowed to keep the money – minus income tax.

Another park milestone was reached when the new Visitor Center, today known as the Cyclorama building, was dedicated in 1962. Prior to its construction there was no visitor center on the battlefield. Park historian Frederick Tilberg wrote in one of his reports, "The Park Service maintains a museum on the second floor of the Post Office building (now the county library on Baltimore Street) where the services of Park historians are available for orientation talks over a relief model of the battlefield.... An information booth sponsored by the Retail Merchants Association of Gettysburg was placed on the town square last June and was operated about three months.... The booth was attended by volunteers... , had met with fine response, and has served approximately 30,000 visitors... ."(7) At the time the Rosensteel museum and electric map, located directly across from the National Cemetery, was still privately owned and it was obvious that an NPS visitor center on the battlefield was long overdue.

Built as part of NPS "Mission 66", the new building was intended to serve not only as a Visitor Center but one section was designed specifically to house the Cyclorama painting. The site of the building however was then, and continues to be, a point of controversy. Park historian Tilberg reported that the location best suited to "serve the various purposes of the Visitor Center was the 'location between Zeigler's Grove and the Emmitsburg Road.'"(8), (about 75 yards to the west of the present location). Ignoring this report and over many vigorous protests NPS Director Conrad Wirth decided that the structure would be built within Zeigler's Grove itself rather than the location recommended by Tilberg. Wirth made his decision despite the fact that Zeigler's Grove had been near the center of the Union line on July 2 and 3, 1863, a position critical to Union defenses, and was an historically important section of the battlefield. Before construction began the iron observation tower, erected in 1875, was removed, as was most of the grove of trees. Bulldozers cleared the land, altered the topography and a ravine to the north of the building was filled to create a parking lot thus obliterating that section of the original Union line.

Upon its completion one analysis of the building was expressed in a *Washington Star* editorial, "It may look like a gas tank but it's the best of all possible homes for Paul Phillipoteaux's cyclorama."(9) In general the writer approved of the facility. Intended for use as administrative offices, as well as a visitor center and home for the Cyclorama painting, it was only five years later that the number of visitors began to exceed the capacity of the building and the park was forced to begin considering other options for the future.

In 1950 President and Mrs. Dwight Eisenhower had purchased a 230 acre farm on the southwest edge of the battlefield along Waterworks (or Millerstown) Road, and in 1961 it became their retirement home. Once the announcement was made that the Eisenhowers would eventually be moving there the land rush was on. Excerpts from the park Administrative Record tell the tale. "On July 11, 1955 *Newsweek* described the effect of the Eisenhower home on Gettysburg. 'Four years ago, there were no modern motels near the stretch of U.S.15 (Emmitsburg Road) that passes within a half mile of the Eisenhower farm. Now there are six – four of them expanding – and more to come.... A candy chain (Stuckey's) is putting up a shop at Highway 15 and Waterworks Road, a drive-in theater was blocked when the government added the proposed site to its battlefield park, a restaurant is going up nearby.... Real estate prices have zoomed for miles around the President's home. One commercial lot, worth $15,000 three years ago, just sold for $65,000...'"(10) Real estate developers eyed the farms on either side of the Eisenhowers with unabashed glee but fortunately for the President and his family, to say nothing of the battlefield, W. Alton Jones, a good friend of the Eisenhowers, bought the two properties and in November 1962, following Jones' death both farms, one of 102 acres, the other of 162 acres, were transferred to the government. The three farms together now make up the Eisenhower National Historic Site. The move back to Gettysburg ended quite an odyssey for the one time commander of Camp Colt.

Also in November, but on a significantly smaller scale and little noticed by the public, the park was able to acquire an important 5 acre tract of land "along the Emmitsburg Road near its intersection with West Confederate Avenue."(11) With the house which stood there removed and the land restored, one more small, but historically important piece of battle ground had been preserved.

Early in the 1960's Congress had appropriated $450,000 for land acquisition at Gettysburg with an additional amount designated for the Manassas battlefield in Virginia. But the money came with the restriction that zoning had to be in place to protect against commercial encroachment before the money could be utilized. To the absolute frustration of both park officials and civilian preservationists both the town and Cumberland township refused to enact any such legislation. In fact in February 1960 the town council had decided that Gettysburg was not yet ready for a zoning ordinance although admitting the inevitability of zoning in the future. Council president Glenn Guise stated that it was his opinion "and the opinion of council" that "we are not ready for zoning."(12) It was not the last time this statement would be made. As a result of the lack of zoning the entire amount of Congressional funding was awarded to Manassas. This loss of federal money for local preservation was a severe blow to both historians and park administrators, and relegated them once more to the roll of "interested bystanders."

The 100th anniversary of the Battle of Gettysburg in 1963 saw no great veterans reunion, no Peace Light dedication, no encampment of thousands of veterans and regular Army troops. There was instead, a parade viewed by an estimated 55,000 people, a multitude of reenactments and historical pageants, the dedication of several state memorials, and speeches by former President Eisenhower, Vice-President Lyndon Johnson, and Pennsylvania governor William Scranton. Special concerts, films, and religious services rounded out the schedule of events. One enterprising citizen even wrote a poem of 56 four-line verses describing the battle in 1863. Largely because of the centennial, visitation to the battlefield totaled 2,041,378, the first time the two million mark had been reached.

In general the centennial celebration was well received, but not by all. An editorial in the *Cleveland Plain Dealer (Ohio)* called it, "A vulgar show at Gettysburg." The writer continued, "A lot of people have become mighty weary of all the fuss and bother about the centennial of the Civil War. They ask a highly pertinent question. They want to know why the dead can't be left alone. They doubt the wisdom of pageants, reenactments, wreath layings, parades. They see the Civil War as the greatest tragedy of American history. They do not see it as an occasion for fireworks, drum majorettes and fancy floats.... If the Battle of Gettysburg were to be fought today Pickett's men would be able to see one landmark over all others and squarely in the path of their march. It is a tall, neon landmark, crimson and bright. It says 'CAFETERIA."(13)

Lost among all the hoopla of the centennial was the construction of a much needed park facility. Prior to 1963 the park, despite increasing visitation, had no place to hold "campfire" programs so dear to the hearts of many national park visitors even today. But in January of that year $29,000 was allocated to construct an amphitheater in which historical films would be shown to visitors in the outdoor setting of the park. It was also expected that the facility would be used for other events, but what was certainly not anticipated was its use as a site for weddings. The inaugural "campfire" program, held in the summer of 1963, was attended by 2000 people including Governor George Wallace of Alabama. The guest list and number attending a wedding there in 1998 is not known but, in keeping with the location, the bride and groom set off in a horse drawn surrey.

The battlefield may have gained greater national attention because of the 100th anniversary of the battle but the park failed to gain significant funds for land purchases, which put it at a severe disadvantage when the officers of Evergreen Cemetery, which adjoins the National Cemetery on the east, decided to sell a 300' x 150' section of cemetery land, terming it a "commercial site". The land to be sold fronted the Taneytown Road just south of the National Cemetery and across the road from the new Visitor Center. According to the *Gettysburg Times* of July 22, 1964 the Park Service had been given an opportunity to buy the land in 1962 but the NPS offer was "far below the $70,000 price set by the association on the plot... . The cemetery association has no plans to offer the land to the Park Service as a gift, one officer said, explaining that the sale of this land is intended to bring in funds for...needed new buildings."(14)

Park Superintendent Kittridge Wing, noting that Congressional zoning requirements were still in effect, said that, "...present restrictions on land acquisition by the Park Service make it impossible for the Park Service to be anything other than an interested bystander."(15), a situation repeated with discouraging regularity. However circumstances changed and on August 18, 1964 the park purchased the plot for $49,500.

While all this was going on a new and more insidious problem, although already present to some degree, began to invade the park in a major way and it continues to grow in magnitude even today.

Vandalism raised its ugly head. In 1963 vandals toppled the 9 foot bronze statue of Major General G.K. Warren which had stood on Little Round Top since 1888. The statue, weighing several thousand pounds and fixed in place by metal pins, was found lying on the slope nearby. Park officials believed that it had been pulled over using a long rope attached to a car on Crawford Avenue at the base of the hill. During that same time period vandals also broke glass in the comfort stations, removed a caution blinker light from a construction barricade on Big Round Top, and threw piles of brush onto the roadways causing automobile accidents. The next year another wave of vandalism struck the park when park signs were removed, a bronze musket was taken from a statue on Reynolds Avenue, and a pyramid of 30 3-inch cannon balls was stolen. This latter action became so prevalent that park officials eventually removed all remaining pyramids in order to preserve them. In another incident Wheatfield Road was blocked when vandals pushed a cannon of the 5th Massachusetts battery off its foundation stones near the Peach Orchard and into the road. Just prior to the centennial celebration the glass fronts on eight large exhibition cases on the battlefield were broken and two of the cases badly damaged, while at about the same five "flasher lights", warning drivers of the construction at the new amphitheater, were destroyed.

Despite this senseless and destructive activity however, the primary focus of attention throughout the '60's was land protection: 20 acres of land saved here, another 12 acres saved there, as much as 100 acres in another location. But vast portions of what was once bloody battle ground fell to development including much of the 173 acres of county land north of the town where the early stages of Confederate General Ewell's assault raged on July 1, 1863. In 1960 the county sold 33 acres of this land along the Old Harrisburg Road for a shopping mall. Eventually 10½ acres along the Biglerville Road was sold to an automobile dealership, and 60 acres became the site of James Gettys Elementary School and the school district administrative offices. Despite its desire to protect this important part of the battlefield the park could only stand by as others assumed ownership – and developed – the historic ground.

In 1969 the draft of a new park master plan, today called a General Management Plan, was released to the public for review but it "would face an almost endless series of difficulties." (16) according to the park Administrative Record, in a monumental understatement. The Record also states that, "The planning effort would also be hindered by local political pressures. The Park Service needed the cooperation of local officials in terms of zoning for land protection, but some of these individuals viewed the park as a visible symbol of the federal presence that was limiting the residential and commercial development of the town."(17), development, it might be added, that was due in great part to the existence of the national park.

Despite one change after another to meet objections voiced by almost every facet, of primarily the local public, the plan did not receive final approval for 14 years, and then only in a watered down version. But even this prolonged controversy involving the General Management Plan paled by comparison with one generated by an announced new commercial venture near the park. Both literally and figuratively, a proposed 300 foot observation tower would loom large among the problems the park would soon face.

Ottenstein tower - opened July 29, 1974, demolished - July 3, 2000
Photo by Rick Dugan
Hagerstown(MD) Herald

"heritage important enough to save"

In 1968, unknown to either the public or the NPS, a group of local businessmen had developed plans to construct a 300-foot observation tower next to the battlefield. Joining the group in February 1970 was developer Thomas Ottenstein of Silver Spring, Maryland who quickly assumed control. One of his first actions was to lease a 110' x 100' piece of ground at 777 Baltimore Street (near the Jenny Wade house), on which he intended to build the tower, and in July, Gettysburg officials granted a building permit for the construction.

When word of the project began to leak out opponents immediately began to organize, but it was not until September, after an article concerning the tower appeared in the *Gettysburg Times*, that the general public became aware of Ottenstein's intentions. Although some citizens and local officials viewed the project favorably because of what they saw as a new source of tax revenue, negative reaction from others was vehement. NPS director George Herzog called it an "environmental insult."(1) That, for the tower's bitter opponents, was putting it mildly. Until the announcement of the Ottenstein venture towers on the battlefield, none of them more than 70 feet tall, had been viewed with equanimity, a benign presence that gave visitors a better vantage point from which to see and understand the battle area. The first such structure was a 60-foot wooden tower erected, in 1878 on East Cemetery Hill, by George Arnold of Gettysburg. The fact that he intended to make money from his tower seemed to cause no concern. In fact, an article in the *Gettysburg Compiler* stated, "George Arnold has the whole movement in charge and it is to his untiring energy that the public will be indebted for this long needed feature on the battlefield."(2) As tower longevity goes this one was rather brief. It was sold – for $20 – in 1895, dismantled, and replaced by an iron tower further along Cemetery Ridge in Zeigler's Grove. This tower was one of five constructed under the direction of the Battlefield Commission. But if Mr. Arnold's tower was well received Mr. Ottenstein's certainly was not. Once word got of his intentions got out reaction was swift and furious.

One of the arguments by proponents of the tower was that it would enable visitors to see every part of the battlefield while opponents argued that the reverse would also be true. It would be impossible to get out of sight of the tower no matter where the visitor happened to be on the field. Frank

Masland of Carlisle, a member of Pennsylvania governor Milton Shapp's administration, which opposed the tower, commented, " 'It has been said that we will probably be judged not by the monuments we build but by the monuments we have destroyed. The people of Gettysburg must soon decide whether or not they believe their heritage is important enough to save.' "(3)

The Gettysburg Civil War Round Table conducted an open discussion on the tower while the Gettysburg Borough Council told angry citizens that the borough was powerless to stop the tower and blamed lack of zoning which the council said it had tried to initiate " 'several years ago but nobody was ready for it. Nobody wanted a limit on what to do with their property.' "(4) Meanwhile plans for the tower went on. The site had been shifted to a parcel of land, purchased by Ottenstein, in Colt Park directly behind the Home Sweet Home Motel on the left flank of Pickett's 1863 battle line. The land was transferred to Ottenstein in March 1971 and work began on the foundation in May of that year. This action set in motion a new round of attempts to stop the project based on legal, environmental, and historical grounds. None worked and the people of Colt Park were faced with the possibility of visitors staring into their back yards from a 300-foot high observation tower next door to their homes.

By July opposition was still increasing. Local citizens had filed a lawsuit against the tower, in the primary elections voters had approved a Pennsylvania constitutional amendment that could be used against the tower's construction, the U.S. Secretary of the Interior and the Pennsylvania General Assembly had registered their opposition, and Pennsylvania Governor Milton Shapp vowed to prevent the tower from becoming a reality. While all this was going on Ottenstein and NPS officials had negotiated a second change in the tower location to a new site east of the Taneytown Road. But the change failed to pacify opponents and rumors of political pressure began to surface. As reported in the *Washington Post* of December 19, 1973, "The Pennsylvania Attorney General's office charged yesterday that federal approval of a controversial tourist observation tower overlooking the Gettysburg battlefield was granted on the basis of 'improper, coercive and illegal political influence.' " All other efforts to stop the tower having failed, the state had filed a civil suit in U.S. District Court listing a "five count complaint against Interior Secretary Rogers C.B.Morton, National Park Service Director Ronald H. Walker, and Thomas Ottenstein."(5)

According to the same article, the suit noted that on July 14, 1971 Secretary Morton had written Pennsylvania Governor Shapp that the tower, " '...may well constitute the most damaging single intrusion ever visited upon a comparable site of American history.' "(6) Yet three weeks later Morton gave the go-ahead for the tower, granting the right-of-way through NPS land that was necessary for construction to proceed.

The *Washington Post* article then continued, "The key to the reversal, according to the state's suit, was an Interior Department aide named J.C.Herbert Bryant who was employed by Nathaniel Reed, Assistant Secretary of the Interior Department of Fish, Wildlife and Parks."(7) In the suit, the state charged, " 'Bryant exercised absolute and independent control of the project.' "(8) The state further declared that the decision to " 'terminate opposition to the tower…is believed to be the result of improper, coercive and illegal political influence generated against defendants Morton and the National Park Service in a manner and by such means as are not yet fully known.' "(9) The article went on to state that some sources indicated "the possibility that a Maryland state official may have been connected with the tower project."(10) Others noted that Ottenstein was from Maryland as was then vice president Spirow Agnew.

In his agreement with the NPS to change the tower location, Ottenstein transferred ownership of the Colt Park land to the NPS and, in addition, agreed to donate five percent of the tower's "taxable income", a donation which he estimated could run as high "as $200,000 per year,"(11) to a non-profit foundation established for charitable or historic preservation. But the National Park Foundation never saw the first penny of the "estimated" $200,000 per year. In exchange for the land and promised donations the NPS agreed to provide a 22 foot right-of-way from the Taneytown Road, over park lands, to the tower site. Amid much criticism NPS officials declared that their action did not indicate approval of the tower but simply " 'made the best of a bad situation'."(12)

Bitterly opposed to the tower from the beginning, the state had filed suit in Adams County Court to block construction, but that suit was lost as were all appeals up to and including the Pennsylvania Supreme Court. Throughout 1971, '72 and '73, while documents were written, charges of illegal political pressures were made, lawsuits were filed, protests raised, and government intervention was sought, Mr. Ottenstein continued to build his tower. One case was still pending when the tower opened for business on July 29, 1974.

Five days earlier, Mrs. Marion Smith of Fairborn, Ohio, having seen the tower, declared that she would have the remains of her husband, Air Force Colonel N.T. Smith, removed from the National Cemetery and buried elsewhere. According to Mrs. Smith her husband, although eligible to be buried in Arlington National Cemetery, had said, " 'I want to be buried at Gettysburg where it's peaceful and quiet.' "(13) It is quite likely that he did not anticipate either the tower itself or the music being broadcast over loudspeakers by the tower operators.

Although aware of the opposition, the Adams county commissioners,

Cumberland township supervisors, borough officials and a number of local citizens offered no objections, their eyes cast on the tax revenue it was presumed the tower would generate. County commissioner Harry Biesecker, a strong proponent of the tower, "…showed the court a petition he said was signed by 2,500 local taxpayers who favored the tower" stated an article in the *Gettysburg Times.* (14)

Preservationists, historians, and private citizens from all walks of life called the tower a monstrosity and, in the intervening years, it continued to be a source of controversy, even more so when, in the mid-1990's loudspeakers were installed over which music was played each day the tower was open. Marches, Civil War songs, country music, etc. could be heard as far away as the High Water Mark. A contemplative visit to the National Cemetery or adjacent Evergreen Cemetery was impossible. Visitors and park officials complained but to no avail. The only concession made by the owner was to lower the volume a bit and turn the music off during funerals.

In 1970 the Adams county commissioners, led by Harry Biesecker, had already begun expressing concern over the amount of land being sought for addition to the national park including the Rose Garden Motel on the Emmitsburg Road. In a letter to the two U.S. senators from Pennsylvania and U.S. Representative William Goodling the commissioners stated, " 'In this day and age, when every taxing agency is looking for additional ways to bring in needed taxes to operate their municipalities it doesn't make sense to have the federal government acquire valuable real estate which is then removed from the tax rolls forever.' " The letter went on to complain, " 'Where are our children going to build their homes when there is no more private land in Adams County?' " (According to the Pennsylvania Geologic Survey, Adams county covers almost 546 square miles.) The letter then added plaintively, " 'Are we headed for another Williamsburg?' "(15)

Ironically seven months later an article in the *Gettysburg Times* referred to maps which indicated that the park should purchase " 'a block- wide strip northward on Steinwehr Avenue about as far as the Prince of Peace Museum (now the Emporium)' "(16) The plan was described by the borough manager as " 'an excellent beginning' " for discussion although he admitted that, while Cumberland township would doubtless benefit, " 'I don't know how the plan contemplates making up the tax loss in Gettysburg.' "(17)

In February 1972 the town council, at the request of a group of local citizens, asked the state to purchase six residential properties on Steinwehr Avenue and turn them over to the National Park Service in order to protect the boundaries of the National Cemetery from commercial development. One citizen said he " 'loathed the idea of any encroachment on the annex with hot dog and pizza stands, etc.' "(18) The American Legion expressed the same

Evening News article by saying, " 'We are not exploiting anything. We didn't ask for the Civil War.' " His attitude about the visual clutter of the commercialization near the park stated in the same article, " 'Aesthetics to me is a bunch of nonsense.' "(26)

In early 1973 one of those "vulgar exploitations" so roundly condemned by Mr. Sharkey, was slated for removal when the Park Service purchased Stuckey's store along the Emmitsburg Road.thus removing " 'the last distraction from Longstreet's assault.' "(27)

By the mid-'70's "plan" was becoming a buzz word in Gettysburg. There was a plan for a Route 30 by-pass, a Master Plan for the national park, and a McHarg Plan for Gettysburg borough, Cumberland township and the park, all subject to public review. Ultimately only the NPS Master Plan, in a much watered-down form, became reality, and even that was not until 1982.

In one bit of public housekeeping the park agreed to erect a community service bulletin board near the interim Visitor Center where churches and service organizations could place their individual signs. In exchange these groups agreed to remove their signs from the plethora of advertisements lining the highways into the town and which only served to confuse the visitors. The bulletin board remains in place today providing a useful reference for those interested in the groups represented there.

Meanwhile the park land acquisition efforts continued. A request to the county commissioners that 55 acres of county land, near Barlow's Knoll, be donated to the battlefield met with this emphatic reply from Commissioner Harry Biesecker, " 'No way!' "(28) In a February 1974 interview for the *Harrisburg Sunday News* he had continued his attack on the park for eroding the county tax base. Ignoring the history of park land purchases he had also charged earlier that the park always paid more for property than would be paid by private enterprise. " 'We want to know where it's going to stop. Does the Park Service have to own every foot of land that a Union or Confederate soldier stepped on? …if the park continues to purchase property without paying an assessment to local government it may become impossible for local government to operate.' "(29)

In March, in the same paper, Biesecker exploded at finding that the NPS hoped to place 7400 acres of the county on the National Register of Historic Places. Calling the state and federal officials " 'a bunch of sneaks' " (30) because they had not contacted the county commissioners, he refused to accept the explanation that such action would not affect the county tax base and again demanded that the park pay borough, township and school district taxes.

Later in 1974 the park purchased Fantasyland for $1,382,650 but little objection was raised about the sale since the park agreed to grant a lease to

Stuckey's Pecan Shoppe, souvenir stand and gas station at the intersection of Emmittsburg & Millerstown Roads   GNMP

the former owners to keep the amusement park open for another 10 years, " 'or until the National Park Service completes its plan to restore the Taneytown Road to its 1863 appearance.' "(31) This rather fanciful idea required the purchase of other properties along the road and restoration of the road itself to a dirt surface. Other properties along the road were indeed acquired by the NPS but the state-owned highway retained its asphalt surface and the plan itself faded into oblivion.

However the state was involved in another action that also directly affected the park when it filed papers to acquire the Crouse junkyard, on the Baltimore Pike across from the park entrance, through right of eminent domain. Although pertaining only to the junk and not the land itself, this action effectively ended the use of the land as a junkyard and removed one of the most often stated visitor objections to the environment surrounding the battlefield.

As 1974 moved on discussions were increasing about the location of a new park visitor center. The National Museum purchase was viewed by the park as a stop gap measure until a facility suitable for, and capable of, handling the ever increasing number of tourists could be constructed elsewhere. Several sites had been considered both on, and adjacent to, park land but the anticipated construction of a highway by-pass north of the town led the park administration to select the Butterfield farm, a 96 acre parcel of ground on the Carlisle Road (Pa.34), as the best alternative. Situating a visitor center here would provide easy access from the by-pass and enable the park to establish a chronologically correct tour route of the battlefield by beginning with the first day's battle.

Once the preferred location became public knowledge there was an outcry of protest from many quarters. The "tower turmoil" now became the "farm fight", with the park again at the vortex of the whirlwind. Local merchants raised the specter of a devastated business district if the visitor center was moved, while the county Planning Commission suggested two alternatives, both outside of Gettysburg west of town, one of which the Park Service would have to buy. At the same time the county commissioners, led by Harry Biesecker, raised furious objection at the prospect of the park buying any more land and again brought up the tax issue. In addition a homeowners association objected strenuously to one of the sites suggested by the Planning Commission on the grounds of traffic congestion and increased noise.

The November 14, 1974 *Gettysburg Times* reported, "The commissioners held that the Butterfield property is prime development land for either industry or home building."(32) At their December meeting the commissioners adopted a resolution which said in part, "…that the county of Adams institute suit to enjoin this unnecessary acquisition which would be detrimen-

Crouse junkyard on the Baltimore Pike   GNMP

tal to the best interests of the taxpayers of Adams County."(33) In their suit, brought in Middle District Court in Harrisburg, the commissioners claimed that the purchase of the farm for a visitor center "poses potential threat of serious and irreparable environmental damage to the area including adverse effects on the ecological systems, water and air pollution and health and life systems."(34) This from the same people who, a few weeks earlier had been touting the property as "prime development" land. A spokesman for the commissioners said that the suit "seeks only to prevent the National Park from buying the farm and in no way will affect any future sale of the farm to anyone else."(35)

Meanwhile the public remained split on the issue. The *Gettysburg Times* of January 6, 1975 reported on two editorials which demonstrated the diversity of opinion. The *Philadelphia Inquirer* had editorialized, " '...it occurs to us that most people go to Gettysburg not to visit a visitor center, but to view and commune with America's most celebrated battlefield.' " Reported in the same article was the *Chambersburg Public Opinion*'s observation that the commissioners' suit and the overt reason for bringing it raised some questions, " '...or at least that is the surface idea of the suit.There may be a number of festering sores underlying the action, and even some political undertones plus a measure of political greed…. The park can't leave the area but it can be hurt by too hasty decisions or too emotional reactions by either side. The Park Service must beware of the appearance of land grabbing. Public officials in the area must be jealous of letting policies or greed damage the national treasure they so fortunately have in their midst.' " (36) At the same time Representative Goodling was quoted as saying "Personally, I am opposed to the acquisition of additional land (by the NPS) in Gettysburg… ."(37)

In testimony at the ensuing trial the county planner said that the purchase of the farm would have a negative effect on businesses in the Baltimore Pike/Steinwehr Avenue area of the borough if a visitor center were to be built as anticipated. However the regional director of the National Park Service stated that, "It is possible that a visitor center will never be built on the Butterfield farm."(38) but that the NPS wanted to purchase it as an historic area abutting other park land, and acknowledged that the construction of a visitor center was contingent upon completion of a U.S.30 by-pass. On February 1, 1975, three days before the offer to the Butterfields was due to expire, the court ruled in favor of the National Park Service, which 90 minutes later signed an agreement to purchase, for $500,000, a farm which the owners had bought 26 years earlier for $13,000. The case was settled but neither the by-pass nor the visitor center on the Butterfield farm has ever been built.

During the time the suit was being tried in court the county commissioners had passed a resolution that offered the Park Service the opportunity to buy, or exchange for land of equal value, 25 acres of county land near Barlow's Knoll, if the park agreed to forego purchase of the Butterfield farm. Harry Biesecker claimed the objective was to "open the Barlow's Knoll area of the park to tourists."(39) This after having offered for sale to any buyer, all county land around Barlow's Knoll, to be used for any purpose. The NPS replied that while the suit was pending, "We're not agreeable to negotiation with the county on that basis."(40)

The Chamber of Commerce too had its say regarding the possible construction of a visitor center on the Butterfield farm. In the July issue of its' magazine *"C of C Briefs"*, the committee assigned to study the park plan wrote, " '…if the Visitor Center is moved to the Butterfield farm, Steinwehr Avenue will quickly become a commercial ghetto. It will rot and die leaving behind the entrails of bankruptcy and unwanted buildings to deface Gettysburg for decades to come.' " Given the commercially crowded condition of Steinwehr Avenue and the massive local resistance to zoning it was ironic that the statement went on, " 'On the other hand without suitable and severe zoning in the townships the Biglerville Road will quickly become a quagmire of cheap, crowded together, 'Coney Island' like junk food shops, over cluttered with motels, gas stations and 'tourist trap' attractions.' "(41)

In an interview with the local paper Harry Biesecker agreed. saying " 'there's only 60 to 70 lots left to build on in the borough.' " He then went on to echo the Chamber of Commerce, " 'the move of the visitors center will result in complete disaster for the borough...the businesses will follow and what we'll have is a bunch of trees on empty lots.' "(42)

While the county commissioners were attempting to forestall the Butterfield farm purchase by offering to sell or exchange county land with the Park Service, Representative Goodling, who had already been asked to intercede in that matter, was again contacted. This time it was by the Gettysburg Travel Council in an attempt to prevent the park from removing the "Dutch Beefhaus" a restaurant on Steinwehr Avenue which the NPS had purchased. The council envisioned the facility, adjacent to the Cyclorama entrance, as a mini-visitor center and sought to keep the building in place but the park, anxious to restore as much land as possible in the area, was not deterred.

Although purchase of the 96 acre Butterfield farm in the spring of 1975 caused an uproar among local residents, the park's acquisition of the 152 acre Winebrenner farm, southwest of the Peace Light Memorial, in the fall of that same year drew scarcely a murmur. Perhaps this was because several groups had proposed it, rather than the Butterfield farm, as a suitable location for a new visitor center although no mention was ever made by the NPS of this possibility

It was at this same time that the park was also negotiating with a number of willing sellers for another 182 acres within the park boundaries. Among them was the owner of the Peace Light Inn, a restaurant/motel at the intersection of the Mummasburg Road and Reynolds Avenue, just a stone's throw from the Peace Light Memorial and adjacent to the Winebrenner farm. Negotiations were also underway with four of the five landowners to the west of the Inn along the Mummasburg Road. And once again the name Rosensteel appeared in NPS transactions when 22 acres on Big Round Top were purchased from the estate of Margaret Rosensteel.

However it was the county land near Barlow's Knoll, and the Butterfield farm, on which most of the attention was focused. A month after the court decision permitting the Park Service to purchase the Butterfield farm the county commissioners had agreed to permit NPS appraisal of the land in the Barlow's Knoll area for possible purchase or exchange. By the end of the year the NPS had developed a plan to exchange 46 acres of "surplus" and widely scattered parcels of park land for 61 acres of county land near Barlow's Knoll. Later that plan was revised to trade 50 acres of government land for 29 acres of county land. But in July 1976 the offer was rejected. Commissioner Biesecker was quoted in the July 23 *Gettysburg Times* as saying that " 'at one time' " the county was interested, but " '...they (NPS) have been dilly-dallying around to just about the point of no return.' " He went on to say that the commissioners saw many problems with the transfers " 'such as the county getting involved in the real estate business.' "(43) It was not until 2000 that the park actually secured protection of a section of undeveloped county land north of Howard Avenue. In 1999 the Friends of the National Parks at Gettysburg had purchased the Foust property just to the north of the county land in question and placed an historic easement on it before it was resold. This action preserved a crucial portion of the first day's battle ground.

By early 1977 the revision of the 1969 Master Plan (General Management Plan) for the park was released to the public and, as before, objections flew thick and fast. Major elements of the plan included creating a chronologically correct tour route, closing the National Cemetery to vehicles, eliminating several park roads including Crawford, Warren and Sickles Avenues, the conversion of United States Avenue to its historic appearance as a farm lane, and of course the potential construction of a new visitor center on the Butterfield farm. Although at an Adams County Planning Commission meeting Harry Biesecker and others voiced their objections, one commission member, according to the *Gettysburg Times*, pointed out that " 'Gettysburg was first to take advantage of the Park Service boundaries when they worked in their favor.' ", and added that the community " 'could not expect the Park Service to reconstruct its boundaries to serve the best interests of the borough.' " (44)

The issues raised in the Master Plan that elicited the greatest public response were 1) the tour route, 2) the visitor center relocation, and 3) closing the National Cemetery to vehicles. Although there was a substantial body of local support for the park plan the most vociferous opponents were also from the borough and surrounding areas. By contrast responses received from beyond Adams County were overwhelmingly positive on these three issues.

The slow, tedious job of land acquisition and battlefield restoration continued. A house on 1.5 acres at the corner of the Mummasburg Road and the park avenue leading from the Peace Light was purchased and the house sold for removal, a practice the park was following with increasing frequency. Since the houses were usually relocated to sites nearby they remained on the tax rolls. This practice was also applied to motels that had separate "cabin" units. A number of these units, now being used as private residences, can be found throughout the county. A second house in the same location near the Peace Light was also later purchased and removed.

The Park Service was also taking steps to protect the National Cemetery Annex from being surrounded by commercial development. Six houses on Steinwehr Avenue were in the process of being purchased, action that had been requested four years earlier by the American Legion and borough council. By August 1976 four of the six houses had become NPS property, the others followed suit not long after. Once purchased, they were either sold and removed or razed if no buyer could be found. About 20 years later the Cemetery Annex itself would become the site of a major contribution to the park by the Fraternal Order of Freemasons of Pennsylvania. The park was also able to purchase the Battlefield Motel situated near the center of Pickett's historic march route on the Emmitsburg Road. It was razed, as was an apartment building located on a portion of the first day's battlefield on the old Harrisburg Road north of town.

During the energy crisis of 1973 the Peace Light flame had been extinguished as an energy saving measure, but under a special permit the flame was allowed to burn during the 1976 battle anniversary. However, when this was done, testing revealed leaks in the 38- year old underground gas line leading to the monument, casting serious doubts whether the flame could ever be reignited once it was extinguished on July 4. But continued inquiries from visitors about the lack of a flame led some local residents to consider the possibility of an alternative type of light, which would be effective but also less costly to operate and would eliminate the need for repair of the aging gas line. In November 1977 a committee of the Chamber of Commerce succeeded in securing approval for an electric "flame" to replace the original gas one. An octagonal, 5 foot high bronze lantern was the chosen design and in May 1978 the Peace Light glowed again although, as history later showed, this would not be the final change to the "eternal flame."

In July 1977, unable to reach a satisfactory agreement with the owners of the Suburban Motel on the Old Harrisburg Road north of the town, the Park Service initiated condemnation proceedings to secure the motel and the 16 acres of land, adjacent to Barlow's Knoll, on which it stood. In 1976 the owners had received a Cumberland township permit to construct a commercial campground on the land, an action the government found to be a "threatened and adverse" use of land bordering property listed on the National Registry. The owners then offered to drop their camp ground plans in exchange for permission to build a restaurant and add motel units, but this too was rejected by the NPS and the case went to court in Harrisburg, Pennsylvania. It was not until May 1978 that a jury reached a decision to award the owners $360,000 for the property. They had asked $400,000 and had rejected a park offer of $300,000. Before all the buildings could be removed a fire of suspicious origin, the third one in a 24-hour period, destroyed one of the houses on the property, a structure that the sellers had planned to move to another location. By September the debris had been cleaned up, the remaining buildings removed and the land restored to its original appearance.

Thomas Ottenstein again made news when, in the fall of 1979, the tower builder offered to donate funds for replanting the famous Peach

Dedication of the electric replacement Peace Light - 1978   GNMP

Orchard. In 1977 the trees then present were found to be diseased and the only remedy was to remove them, treat the soil and replant new trees. However, as reported in the March 28, 1979 issue of the *Gettysburg Times*, park Superintendent John Earnst protested a letter sent by Ottenstein to at least 110 local establishments asking each "to support John Earnst" by contributing $50.00 to the effort. Not only was Earnst completely unaware of the letter, he had believed that Ottenstein would make the donation himself. In the article Earnst was quoted as saying, "Ottenstein took advantage of my name to encourage my friends in the community to make contributions that were not necessary. ...and he didn't even have the courtesy of sending me a copy of the letter. I have no idea why he would ask for twice as much money as is needed to restore the orchard. I was gullible and unsuspecting enough to feel that he really wanted to do something for us personally, that he wanted to make a personal contribution." Earnst also noted a brochure advertising the tower which stated that a portion of the admission fee was given to the National Park Foundation. "We have never received anything from him", said Earnst.(45) Somehow the estimated $200,000 potential contribution never went beyond zero.

In February the park had been made aware of an archeological treasure when local historian William Frassanito discovered a Matthew Brady photograph of Devil's Den in the Army War College files in Carlisle, Pa. Taken just after the battle, the photograph clearly shows the Devil's Den ridge, known as Houck's Ridge, as open pasture. It is even possible to discern several cows in the photograph. This ended speculation by some historians that Houck's Ridge was wooded at the time of the battle. "There is no doubt that the photo shows the ridge as it appeared in 1863", said park historian Kathy Georg Harrison.(46) Although the ridge was cleared periodically until 1895 this was not the case after the War Department took over responsibility for the battlefield. Harrison explained that. "What were felt to be pretty trees were saved and pin oaks were planted for decorative purposes."(47) Today the ridge is again open land, as is the west face of Little Round Top. But even the clearing of Little Round Top, in 1980 was not achieved without local controversy.

Peace Light Inn (hidden by sign). Motel units are at left. Peace Light monument can be seen in distance. GNMP

The park was anxious to provide visitors with a look into the past, to show them what life was like for those living on the battlefield when war struck. To this end the Granite (Slyder) farm was opened to the public as an 1863-style working farm, in the spring of 1978. Settling there in 1849 John and Catherine Slyder and their three children had worked to make the raw land into a home and became, for the most part, self-sufficient. They were succeeding until July 1863 when fighting between Union and Confederate troops raged across their land on both July 2nd and 3rd. When hostilities ceased the house and barn both were used as hospitals filled with wounded. So devastated was the farm that the Slyders moved to Ohio at the end of the war, abandoning all hope of reestablishing their home here. Now the park sought to recreate the historical scene. A park employee, using period equipment and a team of Percheron horses, conducted farm operations as they had been done before the battle. As popular as the effort was with the visitors, lack of funds forced the park to cease this living history operation in 1983. The farm now serves as a private residence for park personnel.

Thomas Ottenstein again made news in 1979 when he appealed a Dauphin County Court ruling that the tower operator had to pay a local amusement tax. According to the *Gettysburg Times of January 9, 1979* "Their basic contention…is that the tower, which overlooks the battlefield, is an educational facility and exempt from a seven percent tax on admission. Overview Partnership Limited stopped paying the tax in July, 1976…and hasn't paid it since."(48) The appeal, and a subsequent appeal to Commonwealth Court, were both rejected. The tax had to be paid, retroactively.

Fires seemed to dog the Park Service motel purchases. Before fire destroyed the home on the Suburban Motel property a far larger blaze had destroyed the Peace Light Inn. The Inn, built in 1941, consisted of a restaurant with family living quarters above, a number of small cottage-style motel units, and two houses. It had been purchased by the Park Service in 1976 for $630,000 but under the terms of the sales agreement the seller was permitted to operate the restaurant for another five years. During this time the motel units were slated to provide housing for the park's summer Youth Conservation Corps and Young Adult Conservation Corps programs.

The night of the fire members of the family, who still occupied the upstairs of the Inn, smelled smoke about 3 a.m. and fled the building with only the clothes on their backs. Although notified almost immediately, by the time firemen could reach the scene the structure was engulfed in flames and a total loss. However, unlike the Suburban Motel fire this one was not suspicious but was traced to a gas leak in the basement of the building. Following an agreement with the Park Service concerning $223,000 in insurance money the owners opened a new restaurant on U.S. 30 east of town while the Park

Service sold the two remaining houses and the motel units, all of which escaped damage. The fire debris and the buildings were removed and the area restored to open land.

As 1979 closed so did the Texaco gasoline station which had been operating next to the park entrance on Steinwehr Avenue. Purchased by the park in May 1979, it was scheduled to be closed and removed almost immediately. However, because of the gasoline shortage that year, the Chamber of Commerce asked the park to permit the organization to operate the station on weekends during the coming summer months as a convenience to visitors and to preserve for the community the gasoline allotment assigned to the station. This arrangement was agreeable to the park and the station remained open not, the Chamber emphasized, to make a profit – all profits would be turned over to the park – but simply to provide a needed service to visitors. The station was closed at the end of August and the park was presented with a check for $5,788. Once closed the park moved quickly to raze the building and restore the land.

The decade of the '70's had brought mixed results for the national park. There were some major achievements, most notably the successful purchase of the Butterfield farm, the Winebrenner farm and the Peace Light Inn. However there were some dispiriting defeats as well, primarily the unsuccessful effort to prevent the Ottenstein tower from becoming a reality and the public's continued rejection of the revised Master Plan. Park officials may have been inclined to view the passing of the decade with a sense of relief but this was doomed to be short-lived.

Lee-Meade Inn on Emmittsburg Road - looking east Little Round Top on left, Big Round Top on right -   GNMP

"a rugged grandeur that is perennial"

1980 opened on a reasonably quiet note for the park. The land acquisition plan was released to the public and Superintendent Earnst expressed the hope that there would be no further need for boundary expansion. The 51 tracts within the federally designated park boundaries comprised about 250 acres and would, he said, be purchased only from willing sellers. Those owners not choosing to sell their land would be expected to use it in ways compatible with the park and, except in extreme cases, condemnation was not a contemplated action.

Claiming that removal of the parcels listed in the plan would have an adverse effect on the local tax rolls, the county commissioners announced that they would seek Congressional legislation to prevent any further land acquisition by the park. However, a few days later, the commissioners altered their stance, choosing instead to seek an increase in federal "in lieu of" payments, funds the federal government paid to each taxing body "in lieu of" the taxes the property would otherwise generate. During the first five years after a property was purchased by the government these payments equaled the full tax receipts but at the end of this time they dropped precipitously. Superintendent Earnst pointed out that the schools were already receiving the admission tax from park venues and commercial interests related to the battlefield. But Commissioner Robert Klunk, in a puzzling bit of logic, rebutted that by saying the tourist businesses which paid the amusement tax employed people who had school age children who in turn utilized the tax revenues.

Questioned about whether park expansion could be justified Earnst noted that all of the properties scheduled to be acquired were on state highways or park avenues. " '...and could be put to any use because there are no controls in Cumberland Township.' "(1) In meetings he attended Earnst continued to stress that zoning which protected land adjacent to the battlefield was the ultimate solution since the land would remain on the tax rolls while at the same time preserving the historic integrity of the park. It was a forlorn plea falling on deaf ears.

Not until February 1982 did the Cumberland township supervisors instruct their planning committee to begin work on an historic district, while at the same time Straban township officials ran into a chorus of protest at their meeting on the subject. Two months later 350 township residents presented the Straban supervisors with a petition in opposition to establishing an historic district in the township. All this despite the assurance that federal funding for a new sewer system would be lost if the supervisors failed to take just such action. "Historic district" was simply a designation given to an area where structures and/or land of historic importance predominated. In such areas alteration of the existing historic scene or further development was carefully regulated but the properties remained in private hands and on the tax rolls.

Earnst was not alone in seeing zoning as the solution to unwanted growth, both within the park and within Cumberland Township. Local citizens too, although still few in number, were beginning to express similar opinions. As reported in the *Gettysburg Times*, the Cumberland Township supervisors, at their March 1980 meeting, heard from local residents who supported the concept of zoning. Mrs. Charles Appler said, " 'Gettysburg is growing. There are people coming in. There had better be some planning for the future.' "(2) Her husband was a bit more outspoken, " 'I may be unpopular in Adams County for wanting zoning but by God, I still want it!' "(3) To this County Commissioner Wayne Cluck replied that if the supervisors were to support the idea they would " 'get a lot of flak' "(4) at the necessary public meetings.

One individual especially qualified to take note of the changes occurring within the area was David Eisenhower, grandson of the late President. " 'It's not a wilderness anymore.' " he said in 1982 referring to the continuing development. " 'It was really a stowaway place when he (the president) found it.' "(5)

But pleas for zoning went unheeded. At their August meeting the Cumberland Township supervisors, by a vote of 2 to 1, refused to begin work on a zoning plan. Supervisor William Bowling, one of the dissenters, said he was opposed to zoning because he believed that the township residents " 'have to deal with enough rules and regulations.' "(6) Representative Goodling meanwhile was quite frank in his opinion of additional land acquisition by the park. " 'I see no need to remember any more about the Civil War than we already remember.' "(7)

While the townships were struggling with zoning and historic districts the park was struggling with budget cutbacks that slowed restoration and stopped further land purchases. In the spring of 1981 budget cuts had forced the closing of the living history program at the Slyder farm and only a grant from Eastern National Parks Association enabled the park to reopen the program in the summer of 1982.

As for land acquisition, the park had not purchased any land since late in 1979 and this raised concerns, not only within the park but among some community organizations as well. Early in 1981 Robert Weiland of the Retail

Merchants Association was quoted as saying, " 'With this freeze in land acquisition to my knowledge there is no way to prevent land developers from coming in. We need some sort of historic district or zoning to protect that land.' "(8) But Cumberland Township rejected both ideas, although Straban Township did take some rather hesitant steps to consider an historic district. In both townships the requirement that federal funding for a regional sewer system was contingent upon establishing historic districts eventually forced the issue.

By the end of March 1982 the park was embroiled in yet another controversy which, while it had nothing to do with land acquisition, had everything to do with the park's care of land it already owned. Matthew Brady photographs taken on the battlefield shortly after the fighting ended show unequivocally that both Little Round Top and Houck's Ridge were open pasture land at the time of the battle. Since then periodic efforts had been made, especially on Little Round Top, to keep the area free of brush and trees. But the efforts were sporadic and over time, nature being what it is, much of the west slope of Little Round Top had become covered with redbud trees and other shrubs, making it a favorite spot for local residents to visit when the blossoms appeared in the spring. So they made their voices heard when the park undertook to remove the growth and once again restore Little Round Top to its historic appearance.

Calls to the Department of the Interior, to the park, to Representative Goodling (again), letters to the editor and demands for a Congressional investigation, indicated the fury unleashed by the park action. Letters to the editor abounded. "Congratulations to the local resident…and others who are raising their voices against the Park Service's destruction of Little Round Top. …I find this wanton destruction appalling"(9) raged one citizen. Another wrote, "The battle was a terrible wound…let nature's beauty help soothe and heal that wound. Historians can study from maps and documents."(10) Then there was the resident who wrote, "…it seems simple minded to claim that tourists could not imagine a bare hillside if the guides are instructed to tell them it was once that way."(11) No mention was made of the thousands who do not hire guides. Another local resident said, "The National Park Service is guilty of undemocratic procedure in failing to hold public meetings for an exchange of ideas prior to beginning their massive desecration of the battlefield."(12) This particular writer formed the "Committee on National Parks to Prevent Tree Cutting at Gettysburg Battlefield", and Representative Goodling initiated a congressional investigation.

But there were some who took an entirely different view. Historian and local resident William Frassanito wrote to the paper, "Though definitely non-historical and, in my opinion downright ugly fifty weeks out of the year, this 20th century jungle was inadvertently quite pretty for a week or two at blossom time each spring. So quite naturally local grumblings have begun in earnest. In fact it seems that virtually every project the National Park Service undertakes in its mission to preserve, protect and restore this unique national shrine meets with a negative and often cynical response from the local populace. ...My hat goes off to these dedicated National Park Service professionals...and I thank them for providing me, as well as countless Americans...a unique chance of a life time to experience Devil's Den the way it was in 1863."(13)

Those who sought to prevent the removal of the trees and shrubs demanded that if the intent was to restore the battlefield to 1863 then the monuments and roads should be removed, park houses used by rangers should have the electricity, phones and indoor plumbing taken out and the inhabitants should ride to work in horse drawn buggies on dirt roads. This argument resurfaces periodically whenever some individual or group objects to some phase of the efforts to restore the battlefield.

Dr. Robert Bloom, Professor of History at Gettysburg College, another who looked favorably on the restoration project wrote, "Every community needs a whipping boy. For our town the National Park Service serves the purpose." Noting that there were residents who felt that they, not the Park Service, should decide what was done on the battlefield, he went on, "Maybe that would not be bad. (The) battlefield would soon be carved up to afford building sites and be swallowed up by commercial establishments. We would then be spared the inconveniences wrought by thousands of visitors invading our community, ...the bucolic charm which distinguishes other Adams County communities could then descend on Gettysburg and we all could rusticate together." Referring to the "Trees" committee he said, "Apparently all its members desire is to let nature take its course and allow the scrub growth to flourish untended on the battlefield. They have as yet raised no objection to having the grass mowed."(14)

Perhaps the most succinct support of the park came from Robert Fidler who ended his letter of approval by saying, "...the attraction of these rocks is not an ephemeral prettiness for a few weeks, but a rugged grandeur that is perennial."(15)

The representative of the Congressional sub-committee investigating the matter reported, " 'There is no legal basis for any action... . The Gettysburg National Park was established as a historical facility. ...the cutting is within the Park Service's mandate to protect the historical integrity of the park. The Congress did not set up the park to preserve natural values, it was established to preserve historical values.' "(16) And there, except for continued local grumblings, the matter ended.

If cutting trees and shrubs caused negative reactions to the park, NOT cutting brush and weeds had the same result. Cumberland Township had passed a weed ordinance – but no zoning – in the fall of 1980 which required that weeds over 10 inches tall, near public roads, had to be kept mowed. In the opinion of the township supervisors the park ran afoul of the ordinance when it refused to cut the weeds on a small lot adjoining Larson's Motel on U.S. 30 at the west edge of the borough. The supervisors said the weeds on the lot had to be cut. The park said 300 tree seedlings had been planted there and cutting the weeds would mean cutting the tiny trees so the weeds would stay. The motel owner said he hadn't complained about the weeds, while the township supervisors complained that other landowners were adopting the attitude, " 'Why should we do it (cutting) and the park doesn't do it?' "(17) One supervisor even questioned the existence of the seedlings. But the park held firm, federal law took precedence over the local ordinance, and the weeds – and trees, survived.

While all this was going on, the farming scene on the battlefield was undergoing a steady transformation. The large modern equipment required removing historic fences to create larger fields while contour plowing and erosion controls had a significant impact on the appearance of the battlefield, especially those fields over which Pickett's men had charged. Park official Hal Greenlee defended all this by saying that the land was being put back into production with major benefits to the local economy. Despite the major changes in appearance he insisted, " 'Our goal is to restore, maintain and interpret the battlefield as it was in 1863'."(18),even though the 1863 appearance was being eliminated by modern farming practices.

In other areas of the battlefield monuments continued to suffer from senseless activities. In 1980 vandals had pulled over the statue of General Pleasanton at the Pennsylvania monument doing $12,000 in damage and it was not until August of 1981 that the repaired statue was returned to its rightful place. Nor was vandalism the only source of damage to park resources. Periodically speeding drivers would lose control of their vehicle and cause major damage to whatever obstacle happened to be in its path. Monuments, cannon, even bridge abutments suffered in these collisions.

But on a more pleasant note, after 16 years of struggle, the Tennessee Monument Commission, which had been seeking to raise the needed funds for a state memorial, announced success. Ground breaking would take place in October and the dedication of this, the last Confederate state monument to be erected on the battlefield, was scheduled for July 3, 1982.

In June 1982 another draft of the proposed General Management Plan, which had first seen the light of day twelve years earlier, was released in what the local paper termed, a "scaled down" version of the original plan. " 'It's a pretty sanitized plan.' "(19) said Superintendent Earnst, and contained

Gen. Wells bronze tablet. Figures broken by vandals, later the tablet was stolen - since recovered GNMP

Cannon damaged by reckless driving on park avenue GNMP

only a few of the controversial proposals of the earlier versions. Gone was a proposal to move the park visitor center, and rather than close the National Cemetery to vehicles, a one-way traffic system was proposed. However non-historic avenues such as Warren, Crawford and Sickles, continued to be slated for removal and the park still had the intention of altering the tour route so that visitors would view the battlefield sites in the proper chronological sequence. Even this watered down plan evoked public outcry. The elimina-tion of park avenues and the construction of a new by-pass road around Devil's Den was a particularly contentious issue. One member of the local Audubon Society even voiced concern over the effect the proposed new road would have on the parks' vulture population since it would run through their nesting areas. Meanwhile no objections were raised when both the Peace Light Inn motel units and the Round Top Museum were removed.

Opinions on the General Management Plan from outside the area were mixed although generally supportive of the park. The proposed road changes involving Devil's Den caused the most alarm. There was much less objection to changing the National Cemetery traffic patterns. Expressing the attitude of many, one Minnesotan wrote of the cemetery, " 'It should not be open to vehicle traffic no matter who is inconvenienced. It should be a place of quiet meditation.' "(20)

Walter Powell, president of the Licensed Battlefield Guides Associa-tion protested the elimination of some roads and changes in the tour route. " 'We represent a large percentage of the people who tour the battlefield. We take some 200,000 people (out of over one million) around the battlefield each year so we are in a unique position to know what is needed. … Reversing the tour route and eliminating some of the roads on the battlefield will impose a hardship on businesses that conduct tours over the battlefield.' "(21) Because they are not employed by the Park Service the battlefield guides are considered independent business people.

Although faced with continuing protests, the General Management Plan (GMP) received final approval in December 1982 and by May 1983 the upper drive in the National Cemetery was closed to vehicles and a one-way traffic pattern established for the lower drive.

Work on implementation of the GMP continued to move ahead. In 1986, after additional public meetings to discuss three alternative plans for the Devil's Den area, a fourth alternative was developed and adopted by the park. As with the other alternatives, this proposal aroused the ire of a substantial number of citizens. In responding to the outpouring of criticism Superintend-ent Earnst wrote to the *Gettysburg Times,* " 'I believe we have been extremely careful and sensitive in considering all aspects of this important issue and that this process has resulted in a sound decision.' " Furthermore the park administration, despite vigorous opposition from members of its own staff, had obviously dug in its heels when Earnst also declared, " 'Our intention is to proceed as soon as possible…with projected construction to take place beginning in fiscal 1990.' "(22)

The "decision" included removing Warren Avenue, which would become a foot path, removing Crawford Avenue entirely, and removing Sickles Avenue through Devil's Den itself. The rational was that Crawford Avenue was an intrusion on the historic appearance of the Valley of Death, and Devil's Den would be better appreciated if it were not a "windshield" experience. Parking areas were to be constructed near the Wheatfield for those wishing to hike to Devil's Den on foot.

But resistance continued to grow. By the summer of 1988 a Devil's Den Access Committee had met with National Park Service Director William Penn Mott, to explain their opposition, and petitions to rescind the decision, with over 11,500 signatures, were presented to Representative Goodling in the hope that he would be able to prevent funding for the project. Lack of consideration for the needs of the handicapped, the elderly, and children, along with the construction of a new road and placement of additional parking lots on ground which had seen heavy fighting, were among the reasons cited for the opposition. However Mott voiced support for his people in the field. " 'I'm disappointed' ", was the reaction of Phil Cole, spokesman for the Devil's Den Access Committee. He expressed the committee's intention to seek support from a national constituency and vowed, " 'The Park Service doesn't realize that this problem won't go away.' "(23) But go away it did, in 1989, although for a totally unexpected reason.

While the GMP was undergoing still further public scrutiny one major restoration project undertaken by the park in the early 1980's involved the farmhouse on the Rose farm. According to park historian Kathy Harrison, the 220 acre farm had been acquired by the park in "bits and pieces" over the years, (Mr. Little's letter in 1937 had expressed his concern over the fragmentation of the farm) and it was not until 1979 that the farmhouse itself became official park property.

The farm had been the scene of terrible fighting on July 2, 1863 that left hundreds of dead and wounded in the fields surrounding the house. One estimate had it that 1300 Confederates were buried near the house although Harrison said a more reasonable figure would be 500. Later all the bodies which could be found were moved to other burial sites. Once the park took possession the house was refurbished with electricity, water, heat and modern plumbing installed, and it is now used as a park residence. The barn, which also served as a hospital after the fighting, had been permitted, by a succession of owners, to deteriorate badly. A severe storm in 1934 had blown off the roof, which was never replaced, and another storm in 1985 blew in the stone gabled south wall. After this steps were taken to stabilize the structure but only the foundation remains in place today. Restoration was scheduled for the "future" but in this case the future has yet to arrive.

Although there have been monuments on the battlefield since the 1870's the many post-battle hospitals in the area had gone unrecognized until 1983 when Historic Gettysburg-Adams County placed its first marker on park land at the intersection of Buford Avenue and the Mummasburg Road. Using information researched and provided by park historians and funding from the Hospital Association of Pennsylvania, the group hoped to mark 28 Union and 35 Confederate hospital sites in the Gettysburg area. Union hospital markers had white lettering on a blue background while Confederate hospital markers had white lettering on a gray background. Unfortunately weathering over time has reduced many of the markers to barely legible letters on a uniformly gray surface.

Towers again became a controversial topic in the spring of 1983 when the Gettysburg Municipal Authority received a permit from the borough to construct an 80 foot tower on property it owned on Cemetery Hill just east of the Holiday Inn. The growing community needed the additional water supply according to the Municipal Authority and the two existing towers lacked the necessary capacity. Despite objections raised by the park, and rejecting as too costly the park recommendation that a lower tower with pumping system be installed or that the tower be built elsewhere, the Authority went ahead with construction.

Concerns about commercialization detracting from the ambiance of the battlefield had been a long-standing issue. But in the spring of 1987 that ambiance was enhanced a bit when the Park Service announced it would raze a building that for years had been advertised as Confederate General Longstreet's headquarters. Located on West Confederate Avenue near what is now known as the Eisenhower tower, the property had been purchased by the park in 1970. Park historian Kathy Harrison recalled, " 'Across the road was a refreshment stand, a dance pavilion, and a group of guest cabins, a whole touristy little area. The structure was probably moved to its present location in the 1930's and a sign put on it that it was Longstreet's headquarters.' "(24) Apparently this was done as a ploy to lure tourists to the other attractions nearby. Harrison went on to state that there was no evidence that Longstreet ever used any building as his headquarters but instead utilized a tent as did most of the Confederate commanders. It was her belief that the "headquarters" had been part of a blacksmith shop which an 1890's photograph shows stood just a few yards from the building in question. Although a part of it was considered to be about 100 years old other portions were made up of materi-

Concession stand at intersection of West Confederate Ave. and Millerstown Rd.

GNMP

als from the 1920's, '30's, '40's and '50's.

The "headquarters" may have been razed and disposed of but two other park buildings experienced a different and more unique fate. In 1982 Mike and Jacinto Miller had purchased from the park, the Rosensteel home and museum on Little Round Top, intending to use the materials in the construction of a new home near Arendtsville, a small town about 8 miles west of Gettysburg. They paid $301, " '...which was about $200 too much' " said Mike, and were given 30 days to remove the buildings. The *Gettysburg Times* article about the couple also reported that, "With the help of numerous friends, even more relatives, suggestions and guidance from the Park Service, encouragement from countless tourists, and a 30-day extension, the buildings came down..."(25) The couple moved into their new-old house in the fall of 1984.

Despite the fact that the Peace Light had been re-lighted using an electric lamp rather than gas, the lantern had never received complete acceptance. So in 1987 a Gettysburg Peace Commission initiated an effort to restore the gas flame to the monument in 1988, the 50th anniversary of its dedication and the 125th anniversary of the battle. The idea received a cool reception from NPS Director Mott who told the commission, " 'Our concern is with the cost of operating the gas flame if it is restored.' "(26), and there was merit to his argument. The sodium vapor lamp then in use cost the park about $200 per year to operate while the cost of operating a gas flame was estimated to be between $13,000 and $19,000 per year. Complicating matters further was the deteriorated condition of the gas line leading to the monument.

Acknowledging the cost differential but still seeking to restore the flame, the committee began to explore other avenues of financing, an effort spearheaded by local state Representative Kenneth Cole. Finally an offer by Columbia Gas Company to absorb the cost of replacing the worn out gas line and to provide the gas directly from the well head rather than through a middleman, provided a breakthrough. This, plus the offer of three York, Pa. firms – Hamilton Construction, Stewart March and Co. and Modern Landfill – to subsidize the cost of the gas, assured that the project would be successful.

Near the end of the decade the 125th anniversary of the Battle of Gettysburg was the occasion for several additions to the park. Not only was the Peace Light restored to its original form but statues and paintings played an important part in the observation.

Five Union generals from Pennsylvania had fought in the battle at Gettysburg and in the early 1900's the state decided that each should be honored with a statue on the battlefield. Statues of generals Alexander Hayes, John Geary, and Andrew Humphries were placed on the battlefield in short order. But in 1913 the project was stopped for lack of funds, and the statues of generals Samuel Crawford and John Gibbons were never erected. This omission was rectified in the 1988 thanks to Jacob Sheads, a retired history professor living in Gettysburg, who noticed mention of the project in some of his reading. Sheads contacted fellow historians and others who took up the cause and began efforts to raise the necessary funds. They were assisted by the state of Pennsylvania which, 75 years late, provided $125,000 for completion of the abandoned plan. Thus during the 125th anniversary observance of the battle the statue of General Gibbons was placed on Hancock Avenue near where he led his troops and General Crawford's statue was placed on Crawford Avenue at the base of Little Round Top where he had commanded his men in action.

While statues were being placed on the battlefield paint was being applied to park owned buildings. But not just any paint, it was paint of the authentic color for each building. Park historic landscape architect Reed Engle had spent five years of research determining the actual colors originally used to paint the historic buildings and said, " 'After working with 6000 or so samples, it's getting to the point where I can finally quickly recognize what I'm looking at.' "(27) Thanks to Engle's efforts, which involved the use of old photographs, historical documents and microscopic analysis of 1" x 2" wood samples, 40 buildings had been repainted the correct color by 1989. Not only white but also tan, brown, even chartreuse buildings dotted the battlefield as the tastes of the 1863 owners began to come alive. In fact, according to Engle, zinc white, the color heretofore most used by the park, did not even exist in the 19th century. " 'We discovered through our research that what we call whitewash was actually grayish in color because whitewash was mixed with lamp black or kerosene.' " (28) The white houses with colored trim were not historically correct either but were of a style common in the 1920's. The colors now being used, said park historian Robert Prosperi, " 'are as close as possible' " to the colors " 'the soldiers...would have seen during the battle.' "(29)

There was other painting going on in the park as well. Until 1988 the Philippoteaux cyclorama painting, done in 1884, was the only mural on the battlefield depicting the fighting in 1863. However on July 1, 1988, 125 years after a brigade of the 154th New York regiment waged a desperate battle to stave off the advancing Confederates near what is now Coster Avenue, a mural honoring their bravery was dedicated. Neither circular in form nor inside a building, the mural had been painted on the side of the Coldsmith Company warehouse facing the Avenue. Artist Mark Dunkleman had spent 11 years researching material for a book which he had co-authored on the 154th New York, and while doing so had made the sketches from which the mural evolved. These sketches were based on eyewitness accounts of the fighting in which Coster's 274 man brigade suffered 200 casualties in some of the bloodiest fighting of the three day battle. Dunkleman believed that the 80 foot long mural was an appropriate way to honor their heroism. It took the artist and his friend, billboard artist John Burjman, only five weeks to complete the painting. Dunkleman said historians who saw the sketches agreed that they were " 'about as accurate as we can make it, given the information we have.' "(30) The mural remains there today, seldom visited by any except those accompanied by a battlefield guide and even those numbers are small. Of the land on which the 154th New York struggled to protect their retreating comrades only this tiny strip remains, the rest has been lost to development.

In May 1985 a little noticed action by the Adams County commissioners had set in motion a series of events that would have far reaching implications for the park. Tax exempt status was granted on a 31 acre parcel of ground known as the Taney farm, which had been purchased by the Gettysburg Battlefield Association for $50,000. The land, which had been on the market for some time with no interested buyers, was tucked away near the eastern face of Culp's Hill. It had seen heavy fighting and was considered by the park as historically significant even though it was situated outside the existing park boundary. Inaccessible except by a limited use park avenue, and part of it in flood plain, the property, not far from Spangler's Spring, was for all intents and purposes unusable for development. But its purchase, and efforts by the GBPA to transfer it to the park, brought on what the *Philadelphia Inquirer* on June 17, 1986 called, "A nasty, unseemly little skirmish…over what appears to be an innocent attempt to donate 31 acres to Gettysburg National Military Park. That dust-up is scheduled to come to a vote today, when the pro-preservation troops of Representative Peter H. Kostmayer, the Bucks county Democrat who sits on the Interior Committee, faces off against the enough-already forces of York county Republican U.S. Representative Bill Goodling. Mr. Goodling is prickly as a nettle that (1) Mr. Kostmayer is meddling in his hallowed district by offering a bill to accept the land, and (2) the national park is about to take another bite of land and make it 'difficult for real estate people, for builders… .' Park historians have testified to its significance and on that there seems little dispute. Mr. Goodling is arguing, instead for good old-fashioned development, a rather shaky argument since the tract is already in the hands of a non-profit battlefield preservation group that is seeking to donate it free of charge. In fact the congressman's objection to the acquisition – although he might have a point on Mr. Kosymayer's backhanding of protocol – seems the very epitome of narrow-minded provincialism."(31)

The vote in the House of Representatives, which required a 2/3 majority to pass, lost by 10 votes and the Taney farm, on which the annual taxes were $431, remained a bone of contention until later in the summer. At that time a second vote was taken which required only a simple majority. Ironically this passed by a vote of 408 to 1, but with strings attached. Goodling had demanded a freeze on further additions to the park until a committee, which was to include local elected officials, could complete a study on the future size of the park. It was his claim that 95 percent of the local populace was opposed to further park expansion. " '...we want to make sure that everything we do is very, very significant, not in the eyes of the dreamers (preservationists) who sometimes don't live in the real world, but by the general population.' "(32)

The *Harrisuburg Patriot News* took a somewhat different approach. "There would be little point to the commercial interests that local officials and Goodling seem to favor if it were not for the existence of the park and the remarkable history it preserves. In the long run, the better and more attractive the park and surrounding area, the more visitors it is likely to inject into the community. The biggest threat to the battlefield and to Gettysburg is the ongoing possibility that commercialization will overwhelm and destroy the park's appeal."(33)

So when Congress approved the Taney farm gift it was with the understanding that steps would be taken to establish, once and for all, the boundaries of Gettysburg National Military Park. At the time existing park boundaries encompassed 3,865 acres of which the park owned 3,622. The other 243 acres remained in private hands as in-holdings. The boundary study began in 1987 when a series of public meetings were held to explain what land the NPS felt was necessary to preserve the historical integrity of the battlefield, and to receive public comments on the matter. " 'The goal of this planning process' " said a representative of the NPS Planning Division, " 'is to set a park boundary for the future, preserving historic and cultural resources needed to interpret the battlefield.' "(34) A diminished tax base, restrictions on economic growth, and development restrictions on land bordering the park, were the primary concerns of citizens who attended the meetings. However Gettysburg businessman Andrew Larson commented, " 'We all have to keep in mind that we're looking down the road for who knows how many generations. We have to decide what we want to leave them for the next 100 years. By then national parks maybe the only worthwhile land we have left. We really shouldn't concern ourselves with what we want today. This might be our last chance to do things right.' "(35)

In October 1988, the date set by Congress, the report was submitted recommending the addition of 1900 acres to the existing battlefield. However only 250 acres were designated as essential for outright purchase. The remaining 1650 acres could be protected in several ways including the purchase of historic easements on property that would effectively preserve the land while leaving it on the local tax rolls. Included among the parcels of land listed for protection in some manner was land on Herr's Ridge, Barlow's Knoll, East Cavalry Field, South Cavalry Field, the 20th Maine monument area, Pitzer's

Woods, the Spangler farm, additional land on Culp's Hill, and the Ottenstein tower. Even if fully implemented the boundaries would include only about 5800 acres of the more than 15,000 acres of battle ground which General Sickles had included on his map just after the war. Also included for protection was some Gettysburg College land that would become the center of another firestorm in the early 1990's.

Prior to introducing the boundary bill in Congress Representative Goodling stated bluntly, " 'If people want to purchase land they think should be part of the park it will have to be within those boundaries. I don't want to hear any more about someone finding some land where some Civil War soldier fought and thinking it should be part of the park.' "(36) Sylvester Brown, owner of the 228 acre farm directly behind the Virginia monument, summed up the feelings of most of the affected landowners when he told the *Lancaster News* of January 29,1989, " 'I know most of my farm falls inside the (new) boundary. If they compensate us enough I don't think we'd mind so much.' "(37) The owner of a car dealership at the intersection of Hunt Avenue and the Baltimore Pike added. " 'I'm concerned that we get fair treatment.' "(38)

Meanwhile in January 1989 the administration of the park changed hands. John Earnst took an NPS position in Oregon and Daniel Kuehn, an historian by training, assumed the superintendent's duties at Gettysburg. He promised to make a quick decision on the controversial Devil's Den issue and gave hope to its opponents by saying he was " 'philosophically opposed to it' " adding " 'The plan is not written in stone.' "(39) Phil Cole's reaction after meeting with the new superintendent was, " 'His attitude is super.' "(40)

In February Kuehn announced his decision. The roads would not be removed. " 'Anyone wishing to visit Devil's Den by car may do so…' " he said. " '…the original plan adds impact elsewhere so I came to believe it was like cutting off our nose to spite our face to take out those roads.' " (41) Thanks to Superintendent Kuehn, Devil's Den today remains as it was before the whole controversy erupted. However the area was taken off the new official tour route in an effort to reduce tourist impact on this surprisingly fragile area.

Kuehn's tenure at Gettysburg was short, only one year, since he made the decision to retire in 1990. However his brief stay at the park produced some significant changes. The controversial Devil's Den plan was scuttled, the National Cemetery, also at his direction, was completely closed to vehicles, and plans were drawn up for a new park administration center although funding was never received. One final change did occur on the battlefield prior to Superintendent Kuehn's retirement when park personnel and friends cleared three acres of the Slaughter Pen near Devil's Den, returning it to its 1863 appearance and, in the process revealing a landscape long hidden by brush and weeds. It was a project Kuehn had wanted to undertake since his arrival and was, his staff believed, a fitting farewell gift.

And so the park entered the decade of the '90's hopeful that the boundary issue had been laid to rest and that controversy would, for a while at least, become a thing of the past. But that was wishful thinking.

Texaco station just north of the Cyclorama entrance on Steinwehr Ave. - 1969 GNMP

"the park belongs to the whole nation"

As 1990 opened the park "boundary bill" was winding its legislative way through Congress, the concept of a "memorial landscape" was being introduced on the battlefield, and the auto tour route did an about face in the interest of understanding and accuracy. " 'In the old route, the first thing visitors saw was the last thing that happened' ",(1) Jim Roach, chief of interpretation at the park, said of the change, which had been implemented by Superintendent Daniel Kuehn during his tenure at the park.

The idea of a "memorial landscape" arrived with historic landscape architect Reed Engle who told the *York Sunday News* in January that destruction of both buildings and countryside during the battle also destroyed the evidence needed to accurately restore the 1863 scene. " 'We can't ever take it back to 1863' " Engle said.(2) But he believed that restoring the battlefield to its 1890's appearance, based on more accurate records available from that time, was entirely feasible. It would be the landscape the veterans saw when they returned and would differ little, except in detail, from the 1863 landscape.

However when restoration began with the construction of a 5½foot fence along the Emmitsburg Road to replace the historically inaccurate 4½ foot fence that had been erected there earlier, controversy erupted again. Arguments were raised that the fence interfered with the view of the Pickett's charge area for visitors traveling the Emmitsburg Road in cars. Yet as Engle pointed out, " 'Fencing is critical to Pickett's charge...' " adding, " 'There were a lot of fences in that area during the battle.... The field was not a wide open expanse like it is today.' " He also noted that " 'Those fences were very sturdy. It was not very easy to knock them down so the soldiers...had to climb over them.' "(3) And indeed in some battle action accounts written afterward the fences were mentioned as major obstacles to the Confederate advance. Comparing the 5½ foot height of the original fences to the existing 4½ foot height Engle said, " 'That's a major difference militarily. It (Emmitsburg Road) was a sunken road with two fences that were extremely difficult to get over. They (Confederates) were sitting ducks.' "(4) But sitting ducks or not the voices of criticism grew even louder. The battlefield guides were particularly strident in their opposition, preferring to maintain the battlefield in its then current condition. To their way of thinking nothing, not even in the interest of historical accuracy, should interfere with the view. The guides, and others, were even more displeased when the park, rather than keeping the grass mowed over the entire battlefield, allowed it to grow untouched in some areas in order to approximate more closely the historic scene. This incurred the anger of those who preferred a manicured look for the park. William Little, a guide, complained, " 'No part of the battlefield is like it was. The grass could be cut back everywhere... .' "(5) But Superintendent Jose Cisneros, while announcing some modifications in the mowing program, was quoted as saying, " 'A battlefield is a battlefield. We don't want to give the impression these guys were playing in a football field.' "(6)

By the time the grass cutting issue was dying down, both literally and figuratively, the legislative process had run its course and President George Bush signed the Gettysburg National Military Park boundary bill on August 17, 1990. With a stroke of his pen he added 2050 acres to the park, added another 5250 acres as an historic district around the park, and created a civilian Advisory Commission as a local consulting agency to work with the park administration.

Complaints were few about the acreage added to the park since the committee which recommended the additions included a number of local citizens. The historic district raised a few more objections but it was flexible enough to satisfy most borough residents. However the Advisory Commission was immediately labeled a "farce". William Frassanito, a local historian was outspoken in his opinion. " 'The whole advisory commission system is a farce. It's nearly always a bunch of blue-ribbon VIP's with no desire or power to make a real difference.' "(7) GBPA president Walter Powell said, " 'I don't see them as an active group.' "(8) On the other hand Representative Goodling, who had pressed for just such a citizens commission in the boundary bill legislation, expressed confidence that it would be a viable group. " 'It will create communication, help eliminate problems before they fester.' "(9) Future events would prove all three wrong to some degree.

Once the boundary bill became law the park was the immediate recipient of an additional 266 acres, donated to the park by the Mellon Foundation and the Conservation Fund, which significantly enlarged that portion of the battlefield known as East Cavalry Field. This acreage had been chosen by the two groups as essential for the preservation of an area still lightly visited but critically important to the fortunes of the Union army on July 3, 1863. Following this donation two years later, in 1992, the American Farmland Trust purchased an easement on another 100 acres to ensure its preservation historically, a method which has since then been used to preserve other farms in the area. Under terms of the easements owners agree not to alter the historic appearance of the land in any way but they retain ownership of the property which remains on the tax rolls. Any future purchasers of the property are bound by the same restrictions.

By the end of 1990 the Friends of the National Parks at Gettysburg, a new support group founded in 1988, had begun an ongoing campaign to bury all of the utility lines along roads in the park. After a lengthy struggle to get agreement among all parties involved, documents were signed on July 16, 1994 which allowed the work to begin. The initial success is evident along the Emmitsburg Road, along the Mummasburg Road from the borough limits to beyond the Peace Light memorial, and the outlook is bright that the intrusive wires and poles will be removed from all park roads in the near future.

In the case of the Friends utility line initiative reaction was almost universally favorable. But illustrative of the fact that few park actions are without detractors was a letter to the *Gettysburg Times* of February 25, 1991 referring to the Peace Light and the Gulf War asking, "Why is the Peace Light still burning?" Believing that the Peace Light should burn only during times of peace the writers went on, "Does the park think this is a time of peace? We think the park service has its head buried in the sand. …Out of respect for those men and women, we think the Peace Light should be turned off."(10)

Those who hoped the boundary legislation would bring to a halt the seemingly endless controversies over land acquisition were in for a rude awakening. In March 1991, the NPS filed condemnation proceedings on 18½ acres, owned by Harold (Red) Yingling, at the intersection of by-pass U.S.15 and the Taneytown Road. The disputed property had been included within the legislated park boundary, and listed for eventual acquisition by the park. All documents were readily available to the public and the boundary had been discussed in public meetings. However that failed to deter Yingling from purchasing the acreage in 1990 for $200,000. He then established Yingling's Auction Service in a large metal building constructed on the property. This initiated legal action by the NPS which had been unable to reach any sort of agreement with the owner as the project was progressing. Yingling's reaction was explosive. "…we have been constantly harassed, threatened, intimidated, photographed and now finally attempted rape of our family through a phony sales agreement the Department of Interior sends us to sign…"(11) In response to this tirade and later threats by Yingling to gather petitions from the entire county in support of his position, George Lower, president of the Friends stated, " 'I think it is unfortunate that Yingling let himself get into this situation.' " Then, responding to Yingling's threats of a petition Lower added, " 'He is welcome to do that, he's got Adams county, but the park belongs to the whole nation.' "(12)

However throughout the year letters to the editor from local residents ran heavily against the park. Writing of the condemnation action taken by the NPS one irate citizen raged, "You talk about communism, if this isn't it I don't know what is."(13) Another wrote, "...if this disgraceful act can be committed against the Yinglings then none of us are safe."(14) In another letter Yingling replied to the executive director of the Friends, who had written in support of the park, "Mrs. Greenlee, this is the real world out there where people have to work nights and weekends to make a living, and pay taxes to pay your family (her husband was a park employee) and the arrogant bureaucratic system." Yingling concluded his letter by saying "...we are tired of being squeezed, lied to and intimidated with the arrogance of these people and we're not going to take it anymore. The Yinglings know where conspiracy lies."(15)

When asked about his position Representative Goodling told the *Gettysburg Times* " 'I can't side with the Park on this issue but the preliminary study in 1988 included this (Yingling) property. They would have known.' " He then acknowledged that he had forwarded, to the NPS, over 2000 signatures supporting the Yinglings and added, " 'There again if you had all of these signatures taken over again after presenting all those who signed with a 'chronological chain of events' I really don't know if you would have as many signatures.' "(16)

The "chronological chain of events": August 1988 – the 18½ acres are included in the proposed new boundary bill; 1989 – Yingling agrees to buy the land, he then asks for, and receives from Cumberland township, a change in zoning to commercial which immediately raises the value of the land. At this same 1989 meeting then park superintendent Daniel Kuehn opposed the change in zoning and informed the supervisors that the land was included in the new park boundary. Yingling later admitted that at that meeting he had heard Kuehn's statement that the "... 'NPS would, if pressed, condemn commercial properties built within the new boundaries, if the owner declined to sell voluntarily.' " When asked about this statement Yingling replied, " 'That's correct. We heard him say this. Of course, we've heard this, like forever. Like forever.... The people in this area have heard this scuttlebutt for a lot of years anyway.' "(17); January 1990 – the U.S. Senate approves the boundary bill; May 1, 1990 – U.S. House passes the boundary bill; May 9, 1990 – Yingling purchases the property; July 1990 – House and Senate bills go to committee to resolve differences; August 1990 – final bill is approved by Congress and signed by President George Bush on August 17, 1991; Yingling begins construction on the property; February 1992- Yingling refuses NPS offer to buy the land and building at fair market value; October 2, 1992 – NPS files condemnation papers in court; October 24 – 1992 Yingling finishes construction.

But no chronological chain of events was going to pacify opponents of the park and the landowner continued to stoke the fires of controversy, painting it as a classic example of a small business fighting a predatory big government agency. Throughout the last half of 1991 and much of 1992 the Yingling situation remained a virulent local issue. Most letters to the editor continued to support Yingling in his "battle". In his April 6, 1992 letter to the editor Yingling accused those who wrote in support of the park of using "scare tactics...to depress our economic growth and tax base in our area", and of "sanctioning blatant falsehoods."(18)

Such inflammatory rhetoric made it certain that the issue would not be relegated to the back burner. But in September 1992 "sources" began to suggest that the NPS and the Yinglings were about to settle out of court. In November the whole rancorous saga mercifully came to an end when the Yinglings agreed to accept $548,000 for the property along with the right to continue in business for two years while securing a new location. Since then the business has relocated and the land returned to its former appearance.

Harry Biesecker, by now back in private life, took on Representative Goodling, the boundary bill, and 911, all in the same letter to the editor of the *Gettysburg Times.* "What reason does our congressman have for needing someone (co-author Rep. Kostmayer) to draw up the legislation concerning our region?" Of the NPS he said, "The saddest part of the NPS plan is the harassment of buying private property on which private enterprises and 'small businesses' need to rely on." He then continued, "...and now we are looking at yet another $1.8 million for 911...all of this so that each household with a telephone can have a $1.50 surcharge added to the phone bill for the service."(19)

Meanwhile the park and Cumberland Township found themselves at odds over Wheatfield Road. The park had posted "No Commercial Vehicles" signs on the road and the township was quick to object even though pickup trucks and farm vehicles used by local farmers were still permitted. The argument centered about "Whose road is this?" since use of the road as a shortcut had become a way of life for local residents and businesses. " 'It's a matter of economics' " said the owner of a refrigeration business. " 'Who is to say who can make a profit on that road and who can't?' "(20) In August the park agreed to cover the signs until an attorney for the Department of the Interior could determine the extent of Park Service control over the road. Although government documents indicated that the road was most likely under the control of the park a compromise agreement was reached in February 1992 between the park and the township under which the existing signs were removed but truck weights on the road were limited to 13 tons.

But while the park was dealing with the Yinglings as well as complaints about grass cutting, fences, and roads, a far more serious problem was in the formative stage and when full blown it became the most divisive issue the park had yet faced. It pitted, for the first time, historians against the park and created a schism between the park and the Gettysburg Battlefield Preservation

Unfinished railroad cut as seen from Chambersburg Pike 1863   GNMP

Unfinished railroad cut - close up 1863   GNMP

Association which continues to this day.

The roots of the conflict went back to 1987 when representatives of Gettysburg College met with the administration of the park to discuss a proposed exchange of an easement on college owned land for a transfer, to the college, of seven acres of park land at the base of Oak Ridge west of college owned property. This would allow the college to move a portion of the Gettysburg Railroad, which ran through the west edge of the campus, to a less intrusive position, while at the same time protecting from development a significant area of the first day's battle. In a public statement made later the college made its point, " 'By moving the tracks to the base of Oak Ridge, we hope to open the western portion of our campus for further development. *If this acreage had not been made available for safe and convenient use, the only alternative site for new buildings would have been the area verging on the site of the first day's battle on the north side of the borough.' "*(21)(author's italics) This quiet threat was the first step in what proved to be a long, acrimonious debate. The NPS, although faced with the prospect of college buildings on an historic 47 acres of battle ground, was excoriated for agreeing to a land exchange deemed unforgivable by its critics. The difficulty of mitigating the problem was well expressed several years later by Representative Goodling in testimony on May 9, 1994 before a U.S. House sub-committee investigating the matter, " 'I must say to the committee that representing my constituents in this area is certainly not always easy.' "(22)

There were two parcels of land involved in the exchange. The larger 47 acre portion owned by the college, was situated on the north side of the Mummasburg Road, bordered by Howard Avenue on the west and the Carlisle (Biglerville) Road on the north. A section of this land had already been disturbed when the college, in the process of creating additional playing fields, had filled and leveled the ground, effectively eliminating the original topography. The second parcel was a seven acre plot owned by the National Park Service, situated at the foot of Oak Ridge south of the Mummasburg Road and directly west of property already owned by the college.

The college proposed granting the NPS a development easement on its 47 acres in exchange for title to the seven acres of NPS land at the base of Oak Ridge which the college desired. At the time the tracks of the Gettysburg Railroad, a lightly used remnant of the old Harrisburg – Gettysburg Railroad, crossed the college property between the main campus and the stadium, athletic fields, and maintenance facilities to the west. Once the exchange was finalized the college intended to lease the railroad a right-of-way at the western edge of the seven acres which would permit the removal of the tracks from their existing location to a position at the base of Oak Ridge.

The exchange was approved by the NPS in the spring of 1990 and took effect once the boundary bill became law in August of that same year. Although the proposed transaction was discussed in public meetings on the park boundary matter, little was heard from the local community until work on the new railroad bed was begun just after Christmas 1990. When historians and other residents discovered the extent to which the northeast portion of the famous railroad cut had been altered their anger knew no bounds. At a meeting of the Gettysburg Community Relations Committee in January 1991, Andrew Larson, owner of the motel on Oak Ridge just across the cut from where the work was underway, declared, "You wouldn't believe what they're tearing up back there...they're destroying the whole landscape!' "(23)

The area in question is the eastern end of the famous railroad cut which parallels the Chambersburg Pike. In the cut itself the Confederates suffered significant losses during the early stages of the first day's battle.

Other citizens expressed frustration that, while aware of the general plan, they had remained in the dark about the details. Local historian William Frassanito fumed, " 'As far as we know nobody, nobody, not the (Pa.) Historical and Museum Commission, not the (local) planning commission, not even the park's own historian, were ever apprised about anything that would have anything to do with the railroad cut. ...It was obviously a deal made in secret.' "(24) Another GBPA member, Walter Powell, chimed in, " 'Even though it is not visible from the main tour route, it is no less an adverse impact than if they had removed 5 acres of Devil's Den.' "(25) The next month at a Gettysburg borough council meeting Frassanito again spoke up, " 'It defies logic that they did as careful a job as they say they have. A fast one was pulled here.' "(26), and thus a conspiracy theme began to take root.

Meanwhile other local residents were also expressing their dismay. One wrote, "The best outcome, in my view, would be to find legal means to force replacement of the moved earth."(27) but another writer noted that the section removed from Oak Ridge was primarily "diabase lava" and "red sandstone"(28) making reconstruction of the damaged portion of the ridge virtually impossible.

Battlefield guide Elwood Christ also took issue with the re-contouring done by the college on the 47 acres involved in the exchange. "...the college's project resulted in the obliteration of ground contours and the destruction of an unknown amount of archeological remains." Then, referring to the railroad cut he added, " Like the Howard Avenue debacle the college seems to be more interested in preserving athletic fields...than in the preservation of Seminary(Oak) Ridge and its historic artifacts."(29)

In essence what took place was the removal of about three acres of Oak Ridge adjacent to, and including, the railroad cut in order to accommodate a new rail connection with the CSX rail line which ran through the cut itself.

Modern day railroad cut before excavation   *GNMP - Frassanito photo*

Excavation of railroad cut/Oak Ridge - 1991   *GNMP - Frassanito photo*

The college defended itself by repeatedly stating, " 'The record clearly shows that Gettysburg College proceeded in a proper manner. We followed all applicable procedures...' "(30) But that only added fuel to the fire. Even though an archeologist, hired by the college, had found no significant artifacts in the area involved that too failed to quell the uproar. Nor did it help when the college stated, " 'The land swap was discussed openly during the hearings for the boundary study. And there was even an article in the newspapers about the plan to move the railroad.' " Then, in a statement that seemed not unlike passing the buck the college added, " 'Of course the railroad work is being done by the owner of the railroad.' "(31)

In May, Andrew McElwaine, a former aide to U.S. Senator John Heinz (R Pa.) was quoted as saying, " 'They (the college) assured us that there would be no damage to historically significant areas. When we saw what was done, we were horrified. It makes us feel pretty bad. Our trust in the college was apparently misplaced.' "(32) All the while the college continued to insist that the portion of the railroad cut in question was "less historically significant" than the 47 acres on which an easement had been granted to the park.

There was even disagreement among Park Service officials. Joe Miller, Associate Director for Management and Operations of the NPS mid-Atlantic Region was quoted in the March 24 *York Sunday News* as saying, " 'If we had all the information we needed I assure you it (the land exchange) would not have happened.' "(33) But Mid-Atlantic Regional Director James Coleman was quoted in the same article. " 'Nobody withheld any information. If we had paid a little better attention the Service would have reevaluated its agreement with the college.' "(34) And both the college and some park officials said the NPS should have been aware of the extent of the excavating that would be done. Oddly little attention was paid to the threat of constructing buildings on those 47 acres where so much heavy fighting took place on July 1, 1863.

An article in the July 22 *Hanover Evening Sun* reported that GBPA "...printed 2000 copies of a 14 page booklet outlining the destruction of that part of Seminary (Oak) Ridge", charging that the NPS "has betrayed a national trust and, in partnership with Gettysburg College, may have violated federal laws." According to the article the booklet was sent to "Civil War groups and publications across the U.S., to key Congressional leaders and to the National media..." One GBPA member was quoted as saying that " 'the organization would not rest until those responsible for the incident...were looking at the world through striped sunlight.' "(35)

So Representative Goodling found himself in the middle of another fight about the battlefield. This time he supported the park, saying, " 'They had meeting, after meeting, after meeting that was open to everybody. Everything was discussed. Now I read about how everybody is upset over all this.' "(36)

In another interview he was quoted as saying, " 'The people who are upset about this had their chance to complain before the legislation was passed.' "(37)

In July 1991 that is where the matter stood. The college had indicated a willingness to build on part of the Union 11th Corps battle line of July 1, 1863 unless it could secure NPS land on its western border; the NPS approved of the land exchange without being aware of the details involved in moving the railroad; a substantial portion of the east end of the famed railroad cut had been destroyed; little attention was paid by those doing the complaining to the potential use of the 47 acres; and the uproar continued.

In October 1991 the GBPA filed a lawsuit against Gettysburg College, the Gettysburg Railroad, U.S. Secretary of the Interior Manuel Lujan, former NPS mid-Atlantic Regional Director James Coleman, and the National Park Service, charging the violation of several federal laws in the land exchange between the college and the park. In a November interview with the *Gettysburg Times* William Frassanito of the GBPA welcomed having the matter resolved in the courts and charged, " 'This was a deal made by bureaucrats behind closed doors, there was political influence, we suspect very strong political influence.' "(38) and he pointed a finger at Representative Goodling. Goodling's reply, " 'I don't want to disappoint the gentleman but I don't think I've given two thoughts to the railroad issue in two months.' "(39)

The lawsuit sought return of the seven acres to the NPS and restoration of the land to its original state which, by several estimates, would cost at least $12 million dollars. Meanwhile charges and countercharges flew between the GBPA and the college with the latter indicating a counter- suit was being considered, and saying that the GBPA lawsuit was unfounded, false, and malicious. To this GBPA member Mark Nesbitt was quoted as saying that the association did not feel threatened, and indeed would welcome such a lawsuit, " '...because then everything would be out in the open and people under oath have to tell the truth.' "(40).

An exceedingly detailed account of what had transpired between the NPS and Gettysburg College was published in the March/April issue of the *Civil War Times Illustrated*. Written by Martin Sipkoff, it revealed as much information as Sipkoff was able to obtain.

As before, college president Gordon Haaland said, " '... the college completed all the procedures required for such a land exchange...' ."(41) However, Sipkoff wrote, "...park historian Kathy Harrison, the person most responsible for judging the land trade's impact on the park's historical and topographical integrity and the one individual most likely to strenuously object to excavation, was not informed excavation was planned. It was Harrison's impression, and the impression of several park personnel, including former park superintendent Dan Kuehn, that the school would move the railroad to the base of Seminary (Oak) Ridge, a move that would have left the ridge virtually intact."(42)   He went on to say that communication between the regional office of the NPS and the park "was poor, an organizational flaw that contributed to the controversy."(43)

Sipkoff also reported that "College business manager VanArsdale, in a lengthy discussion while walking along the eastern base of the ridge on August 6, 1987, told senior park historian Harrison and park planner J. Fred Eubanks, that the college planned to move the railroad tracks to the base of the ridge. Asked about the impact of the project to the tree line along the top of the ridge – a section that was completely excavated four years later- VanArsdale told the two officials no damage to the top of the ridge was planned. 'When we discussed the plan, there was never a problem in my mind as to what was to occur.' said Eubanks, who is now retired. 'If there had been any discussion of altering the land forms, there would have been serious problems with the land trade. I mean big time problems.' This was the only discussion Harrison was to have with VanArsdale about the movement of the railroad tracks. That walk along the base of the ridge formed her understanding of what was to occur there, an understanding she had until excavation began more than three years later."(44)

The article went on, "Over the next two years, during negotiations with the NPS over the land deal, bulldozers flattened much of the land where the school was offering to give up easement rights. The school's plan was to turn most of the 46 acres into athletic fields. This flattening of the land angered park officials, including Harrison and then park superintendent Kuehn. They were upset that the topographical features of the land were being changed – land they were to receive as part of the Seminary(Oak) Ridge exchange. 'I don't like it but what can we do?' said Kuehn."(45)

According to the Sipkoff article, in early 1989 a local surveying firm drew up a map which showed without a doubt, that in order to install the railroad spur as desired to connect with the CSX tracks, three acres of Oak Ridge would have to be excavated. But no one was certain whether the map was ever sent to the regional NPS office. It obviously never reached local park officials. The college would say only that, " 'The college cooperated fully with NPS and supplied all information we were asked to supply.' "(46) As for the park being aware of the map Sipkoff wrote, "That map is apparently the only document definitively portraying the need for excavation in order for the railroad spur to be constructed. According to a notation on a copy of the map now in the Gettysburg park library, it was received by Harrison from park assistant superintendent Bob Davidson on February 7, 1991, weeks after the excavation began and nearly two years after Gettysburg College received it."(47)

Sipkoff also reported on Superintendent Kuehn's comments on the college position that the excavated site was " 'historically insignificant'" and quoted Kuehn as saying, " 'In any case the topographical destruction of that section is unconscionable. The park historian would never have signed off on that land trade if she had known about the excavation. That would have gone against everything she has fought for in the past.' "(48) Sipkoff reported that Kuehn retired from the Park Service in November 1989 disgusted with the growing "indifference at the highest levels of the Department of Interior over preservation and protection of public land. He said that up until just before he retired he kept asking VanArsdale for details of the proposed land trade, details that were not forthcoming. 'I never dreamed, never dreamed, that the excavation would occur.' Kuehn said. 'None of us did. It is beyond anything I could have imagined.' "(49)

Given the college action in leveling the playing fields before granting the park an easement, and the events involving the railroad cut, the often published statement by the college that "we value our historic heritage"(50) has a strange ring to it.

On July 2, 1992, the federal court in Harrisburg, Pa. dismissed the GBPA case, ruling that the land exchange followed federal procedures. A bitterly disappointed GBPA declared it would appeal and William Frassanito, in a *Gettysburg Times* interview, termed Judge Sylvia Rambo's ruling " '...incredibly sloppy. We think she just wanted to get rid of this thing, we think she saw it as a nuisance.' "(51) The GBPA appealed the case to the Third U.S. District Court of Appeals which, in February 1991, upheld Judge Rambo's ruling to dismiss all charges against the college, the NPS, and the railroad.

Amid all the acrimony over the railroad cut/land exchange there was one significant bright spot for the park. Plans had been approved for the Grand Lodge of Free and Accepted Masons of Pennsylvania to erect a memorial to the 18,000 Free Masons who fought on both sides during the Civil War. Created by sculptor Ron Tunison, the two bronze figures atop a granite base depict an actual event which took place on July 3, 1863 during Pickett's charge.

Confederate General Lewis Armisted and Union General Winfield S. Hancock had been friends, members of the Masons and fellow officers in the U.S. Army but when the Civil War began the two men took opposing sides. As the Confederates reached the Union line on that fateful day both Armisted and Hancock were wounded within a few yards of each other. Hancock was taken from the field by his men while several Masonic brothers in the Union ranks responded to Armisted's Masonic signal of distress. As he was being carried off Armisted by chance encountered Captain Henry Bigham who had himself been slightly wounded. The captain was an aide to the wounded Hancock and also a Mason. After learning of Bigham's connection to Hancock, General Armisted asked the officer to relay a message of regret to his old friend and entrusted his personal effects to Bigham. Hancock survived his wounds but Armisted died two days later on a nearby farm. The two friends never saw each other at Gettysburg.

Since all of the principles in this incident were Masons the Pennsylvania Grand Lodge believed it only fitting to honor them as representative of all Masons in both armies. The "Friend to Friend" bronze memorial shows Armisted in the arms of Captain Bigham and is surrounded by a semi-circle of granite panels on which are inscribed the names of every state to have had men fighting at Gettysburg. In addition to establishing a $25,000 endowment fund for the care and upkeep of the monument the Masons also donated $500,000 for improving the National Cemetery Annex where the memorial is situated. The funds thus donated allowed the park to establish a new parking area with handicapped access, install paved walks, landscape the grounds, install appropriate fencing, and create a lighted plaza with a flag pole at its center. Today, thanks to the generosity of the Masons, the annex is, as NPS Deputy Director Rowland Bowers said at the dedication ceremony in August 1993, " '...a perfect compliment to the historic setting of the National Cemetery.' "(52)

But even the best laid plans can, and in this case did, go awry. Not until later in the summer did a visitor call attention to what some termed a "monumental" mistake. A resident of Mississippi discovered that there was no granite panel representing that state although Mississippi soldiers fought at Gettysburg. It had been inadvertently omitted and a panel bearing the name of Kentucky, which had no troops in the battle, was included. The error was apparently not noticed immediately because there were 29 panels, the proper number. Correcting the mistake not only meant removing the Kentucky panel but moving five others in order to insert the Mississippi panel in its proper location. Everyone was baffled by the mistake. Several groups, both within the Masonic organization and the NPS, including historians, had to approve the plans yet the error went unnoticed. But Pennsylvania Grand Master George Hohenschild said simply, " 'We're the ones who messed up.' "(53), and park historian Kathy Harrison mused, " 'We were all there, but I guess everybody was looking at the monument and not the wall.' "(54)

When it comes to mistakes on monuments however the Pennsylvania monument is second to none. Harrison pointed out that this monument, which honors the 35,000 Pennsylvania men who fought in the battle, underwent " '945 changes in the four years after it was erected in 1910. 230 names were misspelled, 214 added, 496 removed.' " In this latter case research revealed that those men had either not been at Gettysburg or had died before the battle or, Harrison added, " 'Others were removed because their tent mates thought they acted like a coward and didn't want them on there.' "(55)

While the Masonic mixup was being corrected another monument project was under way. Maryland had 3600 men in combat at Gettysburg, 2400 Union soldiers and 1200 in the Confederate ranks. But not all units had markers or memorials on the battlefield. Therefore the Maryland state memorial was designed to honor those who fought on both sides. Aided by a $75,000 matching grant from the state legislature, using a 40 ton block of granite donated by Arundel Quarry, and with donations of transportation and masonry work, funds were raised and the memorial became a reality. Located just east of the Cyclorama building, it was dedicated in October 1994, much to the satisfaction of the citizens who had put their time, effort and money into the undertaking.

Despite the addition of these monuments there had been, for some time, a growing concern among park staff about the proliferation of monuments on the battlefield. While a number of regiments still lacked markers the monuments being erected honored individuals or states and were not directly related to the battle action itself. Position markers were always acceptable but, " 'The ones we're concerned about here are monuments to generals, various groups, left-handed swordsmen, whatever.' "(56) park historian Harrison told the *Hanover Evening Sun*. The battlefield already contained at least 1320 monuments of various sizes and descriptions, including one to the Soldiers and Sailors of the Confederate Army, placed directly on the battle line of Law's (Confederate) Brigade. " 'It could have been better located.' "(57) said Harrison. Although the Maryland monument had already been approved, as was a statue of Confederate General James Longstreet, the park was reluctant to approve any more. Since then only the Delaware state monument has been approved and located near the Maryland monument. The Longstreet statue was placed in the woods near the present park amphitheater on West Confederate Avenue close to the approximate location of his headquarters.

Even though a "hold" was placed on further monumentation upkeep of those already in existence remained a significant problem. The park had adopted a policy of requiring an upkeep endowment for each new monument but most of the park's monuments were erected long before any such policy was in place and upkeep for those depends on private donations and government funding. Harrison pointed out that the Park Service spent $50,000 on monument upkeep at Gettysburg in 1992 and still was falling behind in the needed work. Sometimes, she said, even upkeep was not enough and repairs were too costly for the park budget. " 'In 1976 we took down the 4th Ohio monument that was developing cracks and bulges.' "(58), making it unsafe in high winds.

Safety also became an issue elsewhere on the battlefield when mountain bikers demanded the right to use the horse trails. Although the trails were limited to horses and hikers that use alone had grown to over 25,000 people per year. But the bikers rejected the argument that safety would be compromised by mountain bikes. " 'These are recreational, not historic trails. It is simply not fair to close them to one large group of users while keeping them open for other, smaller groups.' "(59) wrote local resident and president of the League of American Wheelmen, Robert Nordvall. Despite the fact that the park Advisory Commission recommended that trail use not be expanded to include mountain bikes Nordvall said he had discovered a loophole in federal law that permitted exceptions. " 'I intend to keep pursuing this until it's resolved.' "(60) he declared, hinting at a possible lawsuit. However the trails remain closed to mountain bikes.

In the summer of 1993 a draft of the park's Land Protection Plan was released to the public and meetings were held so that local residents could review and comment on it. The plan described in detail each parcel of land within the new park boundary, what type of protection the park would seek, and how high a priority the park placed on each parcel. All landowners were contacted and understandings sought on what they were willing to do. Park Superintendent Cisneros observed that most landowners were in agreement with park plans. Others, as expected, did not want to sell anything or at most just an easement. He added that while the park would like to act quickly on the high priority parcels, in order to remove or prevent any modern development, any action taken would depend on federal funding being available and upon willing sellers.

As anticipated the Land Protection Plan had its critics. One African-American resident of Granite Schoolhouse Road claimed that NPS efforts to purchase homes in that area " '...are essentially racist' " because the homes purchased over the years "...belonged to black people."(61) A resident of West Confederate Avenue said he didn't " 'want the park service telling him what he could or could not do with his property.' " When he asked what would be done if he put an in-ground swimming pool in his back yard one park official replied, probably nothing, but " '... not in the front yard.' "(62)

Another issue, never anticipated by the originators of the national park, had begun to surface some months earlier. It boiled down to "What are the proper uses of the park?" As a large, open, quiet area, free of high speed traffic the park had begun to attract all manner of activities having no connection to the Civil War. Road races, fund raisers, walk-a-thons, mass bicycle rides, frisbee playing and sun bathing were becoming more and more prevalent and the park Advisory Commission expressed concern. " 'The concern is what is proper on the battlefield, which is a memorial to those who fought and died here.' "(63) said park superintendent Jose Cisneros. Kent Brown, Civil

War author and also a commission member added, " 'I think the consensus of the commission is that the protection of the field as a memorial is of first importance. You would no more want to do these activities here than in your family cemetery.' "(64)

By the fall of 1993 another controversy was slowly but surely maturing. Despite the mantra "growth is being stifled by the park", repeated at virtually every public meeting involved in land protection by the park, growth was indeed taking place, in some areas quite rapidly. Developers had done what was to be expected, they simply leapfrogged the park and began to build on open land beyond it. By this time Adams county, because of its proximity to Baltimore and Washington, was becoming an area of rapid growth, and having taxes lower than in nearby Maryland added to its attractiveness. All of this had an impact on park roads as residents began to use them as commuter routes in the absence of any new or upgraded county roads.

At the same time that more and more commuters were using park roads visitation was on the increase and the combination was overloading avenues never intended to handle large volumes of traffic. Visitors pulling off next to trees and monuments were causing damage and commuters ignoring speed limits were creating safety problems on rapidly deteriorating park avenues.

Federal money was appropriated for repair work but it came with restrictions attached. To be approved for two-way traffic roads needed to be 22 feet wide. However park avenues, many built before 1900, were only 18 feet wide. To widen them would mean cutting down countless trees, many historic in their own right, and moving a number of monuments from the historic locations where the veterans had placed them. Unwilling to do this, and therefore unable to widen the avenues, the park had only two viable options: 1) create one-way traffic patterns on the most heavily traveled avenues with parking on one side and moving traffic on the other, or 2) let the avenues continue to deteriorate, patch them as maintenance funds became available in the park budget, and hope for no serious accidents.

As with almost all park plans, when the possibility of one-way roads was made public – especially West Confederate and Reynolds Avenues, favorite commuter routes for those with jobs in Baltimore and Washington, - there was a public outcry. Adams County Planning Commission members and the county Director of Planning were quick to point out that any such changes would change traffic patterns in the surrounding townships and increase traffic within the borough of Gettysburg. At one public meeting on the roads, county commissioner Harry Stokes told park officials, " 'We share our roads with you and would like for you to share your roads with us.' "(65) In April the county and borough officials met with the NPS regional director in an effort to retain two way traffic patterns on park avenues, and managed to secure a delay on the decision until a more complete traffic study could be done.

The results of a week long survey, done in May 1994, a heavy tourist month, indicated that " '...there would be no significant impact on the major alternate routes around the park.' "(66) But a group called the Gettysburg Open Road Committee disagreed vehemently. Committee chairman Paul Smith declared, in the July issue of the *Civil War News* that, " 'The concealed intent of the National Park Service is to generate revenues. ...Everyone visiting the battlefield will be forced to ride a bus and pay for the privilege. It would be as compulsory as federally mandated busing for public schools. ...We are asking for an exemption of entrance and parking fees.' "(67) Why this statement was made is puzzling since neither entrance nor parking fees ever existed in the park and none were suggested in the road proposal.

By now the park had a new superintendent, Dr. John Latschar, also an historian by training, who was able to mollify local officials by offering park funds for studies to assist in mitigating any problems caused by the change in park traffic patterns. " 'This is something we think we can live with.' "(68) Borough Manager Charles Sterner told the *Hanover Evening Sun* in December.

When construction began park avenues were closed in a specific sequence in order for the work to be done, and as each avenue was finished it was reopened as one-way if that was included in the traffic plan. West Confederate Avenue was the first to be so designated, with others following suit as work was completed. Not until the summer of 2000 was the overall project finished and the entire one-way plan put into effect. Because of the time involved local residents were able to adjust gradually to the new patterns and, Mr. Smith not withstanding, cars still freely travel all battlefield roads, albeit on some avenues in one direction only. Bus rides remain a commercial venture and no parking or entrance fees to the battlefield exist.

In July of the same year the park began rehabilitation of a double log barn which had stood on the Slyder farm at the foot of Big Round Top since before the Civil War. Years of neglect had taken their toll but many of the beams and some of the siding was salvageable. Park personnel, as was park practice, used the traditional tools and methods of the 1800's and were able to restore the historic structure in about three months. Park historian Harrison told the *Gettysburg Times* " 'When you touch the logs on that barn you know they feel the same today as they did to the farmer who built this barn, and to the wounded soldiers who were lying in there suffering after the battle.' "(69)

But while one-way roads were being considered and historic barns rebuilt the railroad cut controversy continued.

Despite having lost its legal battle against Gettysburg College and the

National Park Service the GBPA relentlessly pursued political avenues as a way of seeking retribution. William Frassanito told the *Civil War News* in January 1994, " 'The only thing that will satisfy the GBPA is that a full blown hearing occur and that they lead to a Justice Department investigation and indictments.' " Then he added, " 'I don't have very high hopes that a congressional subcommittee hearing, even if it reveals the truth, will lead to anything.' "(70)

Another report in the same issue noted that. "Gettysburg College is working to halt erosion at the cut. Excavation was hardly completed before it became apparent that park property was eroding down the vertical face of the 25 foot high cut. A wall of gabions (broken stone enclosed in wire baskets) intended to buttress a portion of the cut was beginning to slump and was clearly inadequate....William Walker, spokesman for the college said the college, 'acknowledged we were responsible' for the erosion. Total cost to the college to halt it is $250,000 he said."(71)

Finally, on May 9, 1994 GBPA got its wish when Representative Mike Synar (D Okla) held a hearing on the NPS/ Gettysburg College land exchange. Appearing before the U.S House subcommittee on Environment, Energy, and Natural Resources, were members of the college administration and faculty, officials of the NPS, Representative Goodling, GBPA members Frassanito and Powell, and several independent historians among others.

In his statement Dr. Gordon Haaland, president of the college repeated a familiar theme, " 'Had the exchange not taken place Gettysburg College would have had no alternative other than to look to the 46 acre tract that clearly figured in the battle, as a site for future college development.' "(72) In his written statement for the committee Haaland said, " 'This was prime development property, and it would have been possible for Gettysburg College to sell the long frontage along the Biglerville Road and other parcels for a substantial amount of money.' "(73) He did say however that the college preferred not to take either step.

But perhaps the most remarkable statement came from NPS Director Roger Kennedy, who told the subcommittee, "Whether or not there are archeological artifacts under the surface, it is what happened on the surface that matters. It is the experience of death and loss because that is what war is about... . ...Furthermore it seems to me that it is useless for the Director of the National Park Service to come before you and assert that this was not a mistake. I don't think it is a betrayal of my colleagues for me, as a new person, relatively new to the service, to assert that it was not a mistake. It's consequences are very sad.... And I think it is beyond debate that the procedures and processes then in place were indeed inadequate... ."(74) In his formal written statement to the subcommittee Director Kennedy also added that the NPS "has learned from this experience. It is in the process of making changes to ensure that safeguards not in place in the past will be there to govern future exchanges."(75)

After the hearing former Representative Kostmayer told the *York Sunday News*, " 'I think the law was broken. If not the letter of the law then certainly the intent of the law, and I'm the guy who wrote the law.' "(76) The *Harrisburg Patriot News* reported Representative Michael Andrews (D Texas) as saying, " 'Congress must take a stronger role if the kind of historic vandalism that occurred at Gettysburg is not to be repeated.' "(77) His statement had a familiar ring to it since construction of the electric trolley in 1898, which also caused significant alteration of the battlefield landscape was called "vandalism" by its many opponents.

In the days after the hearing college president Haaland said the exchange, " 'was in the public interest.' "(78); Walter Powell of the GBPA said, " 'We feel completely vindicated.' "(79); and Representative Goodling said, " 'There were no back room deals or coverup.' "(80)

That is where the issue remains. The erosion was controlled; the railroad continues to operate; the 47 acres-despite its altered topography-remains open land except for tennis courts, there were no indictments, no one is looking at the world through "striped sunshine", and the railroad cut issue is raised at nearly every public meeting involving any disagreement with park actions, as evidence (in the eyes of the protestors) of NPS ineptitude in planning and the management of park resources.

But as traumatic as the NPS/college land exchange issue had been it only served as a prelude to what transpired when, in 1995 the park began the development of a new General Management Plan and raised the possibility of a new visitor center to be built under a public / private arrangement. In view of the events which followed it would be more than somewhat accurate to quote the phrase, "You ain't seen nothin' yet!"

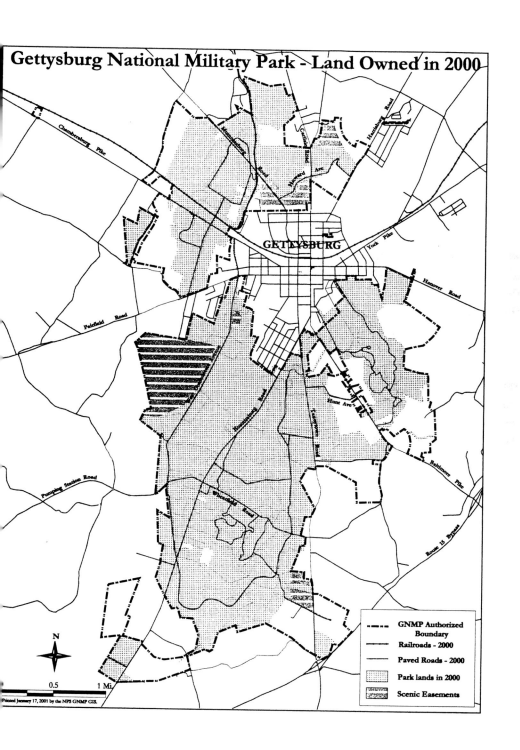

Gettysburg National Military Park - Land Owned in 2000

N

0.5   1 Mi.

Printed January 17, 2001 by the NPS GNMP GIS.

Legend	
– · · – · · –	GNMP Authorized Boundary
—+—+—	Railroads - 2000
——	Paved Roads - 2000
(shaded)	Park lands in 2000
(pattern)	Scenic Easements

Chapter 8

"the preservation of our heritage"

Land preservation, the tower, the railroad cut, and the prospect of a new museum, all were part of the 1995 menu for the park.

In January the first land protection project by the Friends of the National Parks at Gettysburg was successfully completed when the group purchased the development rights to a 26 acre parcel of farmland on East Cavalry Field. Combined with a farmland preservation easement purchased by Adams county, 135 acres of the cavalry battleground was thus preserved, and this was only the beginning for the Friends. In July 1995 the organization purchased outright 6 acres of the 20th Maine position on Little Round Top which had remained in private hands. At the ceremony transferring title to the land, Michael Weikert, whose family had owned the land since the 1700's, said, " 'This is the preservation of our heritage.' "(1) The land was the location of Company B of the 20th Maine position and has on it a granite marker identifying it as such. Overlooked and seldom visited because of brush and trees, the Friends opened up the site so that visitors are now able to form a clearer picture of the position from which Company B played such a crucial role in repulsing the Confederate charge on the entire 20th Maine line on July 2, 1863. The Friends actions came at a particularly propitious time for the park since Congressional budget cuts had virtually wiped out any land acquisition funds the park had hoped to obtain.

An unexpected plus for the battlefield was the discovery of two of the cannon used by Hall's Maine Battery which fought a desperate battle along the Chambersburg Pike on July 1, 1863. Friends member Jerry Coates, a student of Civil War weapons, had discovered the location of the cannon during research at the National Archives. One was already on the battlefield although with a different battery, the other cannon was at Fort Union National Monument in New Mexico. Both newly found guns were eventually returned to the position they had held in the early hours of the first day's battle. Prior to this the whereabouts of only three of the hundreds of cannon that were fought at Gettysburg had been known. One is at the park, one is at the Providence, Rhode Island state house, the third is in a private collection. Those guns had been identified by the inscriptions on the muzzle of each gun, and on the battlefield today any iron (black) cannon tube with inscriptions are authentic Civil War artillery pieces as are all of the bronze cannon tubes. The iron tubes with no inscription on the muzzles are replicas.

Another member of the Friends, Charles Smithgall, undertook responsibility for a much needed project to repair the steadily deteriorating cannon carriages on the battlefield. The cast iron carriages, that replaced the original wooden ones, were first made in the 1890's by Gilbert's Foundry, which is still standing at the junction of North Franklin Street and Railroad Lane in Gettysburg. Civil War veteran Calvin Gilbert also cast the iron avenue and house markers as well as the iron fence surrounding the Copse of Trees. With time however, many of the iron carriages had developed cracks and the layers of paint used to make them appear authentic were constantly peeling. Smithgall had noticed a number of broken carriages stored in a park building and planned, by combining the useable parts, to restore at his own expense, 12 to 14 of them and return them to various sites on the battlefield.

Nor did the Friends activities end with land acquisition and cannon carriage repairs. In August the first phase of the undergrounding of utility lines began on the Emmitsburg Road. Poles were removed and overhead lines placed in conduits below the land surface. This phase of the project, one of the earliest Friends initiatives, was completed in 2000. Work is now continuing along other roads and within the next few years the entire battlefield should be free of all intrusive wires and poles.

But while the park was gratefully acknowledging the Friends efforts another matter, with less pleasant results, continued to haunt park administrators. The railroad cut controversy just would not go away. In November 1994 the park Advisory Commission had declared its support for a partial restoration of the railroad cut on Oak Ridge that would remove the new railroad spur for which the excavation had been made, would remove the gabion walls erected by the college for erosion control, and would partially restore Oak Ridge to a more gentle, less erosion prone slope. The Friends and others acquiesced in this choice which, it was estimated, would cost about $2 million. However this alternative did not meet with universal approval. In fact the GBPA adamantly opposed anything less than full restoration of the area. On the other hand a call-in survey done by the *Gettysburg Times* showed that the majority of respondents opposed spending any federal money for restoration on the railroad cut. One caller asked, " 'Why should we taxpayers pay for their (NPS) mistake? Nobody cares but them.' "(2)

In late January 1995 NPS Director Roger Kennedy approved the plan but even at that time Representative Goodling had already voiced his opposition to any restoration, saying in reference to the report he would receive, " 'We'll read it and then file it.' "(3), indicating that he would not bring it up in the U.S. House of Representatives for funding. Faced with this obstacle, and with the choice of spending available funds for this project or for a sewer system for the entire park, Director Kennedy altered his stance and selected what amounted to a cosmetic solution which disappointed many and further infuriated the GBPA. The college would landscape the area, repaint the engine shed roof a less visible color, and increase maintenance activities to clean up construction debris still in place. " 'The course of action desired by some - ridge reconstruction - requires funding that simply is not available,' " said Kennedy.(4) Under the accepted agreement the college would pay all of the costs involved.

Representative Goodling was quoted in the local paper as saying, " 'As I said, the issue is dead. You might as well let it die and give it a proper burial. And then we'll get on with the business of taking care of the park….' "(5) But the GBPA refused to let it die. Instead the group announced its intention to publish an extensive account of the result of the land exchange. " 'We have a substantial body of material' ", said Walter Powell, in an interview for the September issue of the *Civil War News*. " 'Individuals who have good reason to hide will be fully exposed.' "(6)

And then there was the tower – an issue that seemed to appear annually along with the dandelions. Private efforts to raise funds to purchase the tower were cancelled when it became evident that they would conflict with another potential project – the construction of a new museum. This latter was a park endorsed endeavor which would involve a public/private partnership and require a substantial fund raising effort. James Holochek of Baltimore had been involved with the creation of the Maryland memorial and following that proposed to create a foundation which would purchase and remove the tower. Obviously disappointed by the cancellation, he told the *Philadelphia Inquirer* in February, " 'I sort of feel I've been taken advantage of.' "(7) According to the paper, "The park's new superintendent, John A. Latschar, decided that a new museum was higher on his list, and 'the two projects came into conflict over potential funds because they're so similar' park spokeswoman Katie Lawhon said."(8) This "demotion" of the tower project came despite the NPS having been directed by Congress in 1989 to find a way to acquire and dismantle the tower, without of course, providing any funding.

In the meantime tower owner Ottenstein set about to place a carnival at the base of the structure. NPS reaction was expressed by Superintendent Latschar who said that if the carnival was a ploy to get the Park Service to buy the tower it was useless. " ' I'm not going to call his bluff and I've got no money. No matter what he does the Park Service is not going to buy the tower.' "(9) Upon the arrival of the carnival one local resident, with family members buried in Evergreen Cemetery adjacent to the tower, wrote angrily to the local paper, "I am vehemently opposed to such a business venture! …It is impossible to visit the cemeteries and spend a few quiet moments in prayer and reflection with a dearly departed loved one in such an environment. The carnival/country music blasting from The Tower loudspeakers makes prayer and reflection impossible... ."(10) A week after it arrived the carnival left, but the loudspeakers remained in place and active. Soon after the departure of the carnival Ottenstein said he was considering decorating the tower as a huge orange pumpkin for Halloween. Asked about the 5% after taxes he had promised to pay the National Park Foundation, which had never received a cent, he replied, " 'A lot of builders in the country have, in a taxable sense, depreciation and amortization and development costs such that they don't pay taxes.' "(11) So much for the $200,000 he had originally estimated, when he was seeking to build the tower, would go annually to the Foundation. Referring to the agreement he signed in 1971 he said, " 'I really was having my constitutional rights taken away. I didn't realize that I was dealing with federal government bureaucrats who are whores.' "(12) And the loudspeakers played on.

But while the railroad cut and the tower were providing their annual annoyance a new and entirely different issue was developing which would eventually engulf the park in the most bitter controversy it had ever faced. This despite the fact that the beginning was a benign, even pleasant event which initially promised great things for the park. In March 1995 an announcement was made that the park, the Friends and local developer Robert Monahan were considering a possible partnership under which Monahan would construct a museum and Imax theater on the site of the former Fantasyland, which at that time was being used as a maintenance storage area. In exchange for a multi-decade lease on the theater Monahan agreed to raise $10 million dollars to construct a 50,000 square foot cyclorama gallery and museum adjoining a 30,000 foot square theater which Monahan would construct using his own funding. In addition the existing Cyclorama building would be razed and the land restored to its 1863 appearance. In one of the alternatives proposed for the plan, parking for the buildings was to be situated in Guinn Woods just south of Fantasyland, an historic and pristine part of a 150 acre farm which had been owned by the William Guinn family from 1776 to 1876.

Under the agreement the Friends group would act as a third party intermediary between the NPS and Monahan, and would also assist in raising the needed $10 million dollars for the museum. It was acknowledged that poor storage facilities had put the park artifacts at risk and exhibition space was entirely inadequate in the 74 year old Visitor Center. In fact Congress had authorized a new museum for the park in 1989 but again, had never appropriated the money for its construction. Therefore Monahan's proposal fell on receptive ears.

But at a public meeting following the announcement a number of objections were raised. Residents of the area near the proposed building site raised concerns about noise, trash, and especially increased traffic on the narrow, winding Taneytown Road. At the April public meeting of the park Advisory Commission Eric Uberman, owner of the Wax Museum on Steinwehr Avenue, cast aspersions on the manner in which the agreement with Monahan had been reached asking, " 'Is this to avoid the safeguards that Congress has put in place relating to private businesses within the national parks?' "(13) Monahan replied, " 'Mr. Uberman I resent that there is any sense of impropriety in this project. I am offended by that. And I'm just almost at a loss for words.' "(14) At the end of the meeting the Advisory Commission, by a majority vote, recommended that the public comment period be extended another 30 days to allow for further consideration of the proposal. With the acquiescence of both Monahan and the Friends, Superintendent Latschar reluctantly agreed to the extension. However by early May the Friends Board of Directors began having second thoughts about taking on a task of such magnitude and in mid-May the announcement was made that, in agreement with the Monahan Group, the Friends were withdrawing from the project.

At the next public meeting on the subject in late May, Eric Uberman, who in April had locked horns with Monahan, now turned his sights on Superintendent Latschar, demanding that full and complete details of the agreement with the Monahan Group be made public. Dr. Latschar refused saying that if an agreement was finally reached then the details would become available to the public. By September the question had become moot because of a significant alteration of plans. In a change of heart Monahan stated that he would build his Imax theater elsewhere without NPS involvement and the Park Service put the museum proposal on hold until a "systematic examination" of all options could be made.

That examination began in November 1995 when the first public meeting was held by the park in an effort to get greater public involvement in a revised museum project. Based upon public input an entirely new plan was developed. It was announced that a "Request for Proposals" would be drawn up and released nationwide in a search for partners in a museum, or museum/visitor center project.

A committee of park personnel and community representatives working together developed a formal "Request for Proposals"(RFP) which was released in December 1996. In the RFP it was specifically stated that "No specific site for the complex has been proposed or selected."(15) However an "area of consideration", located in Adams county, was designated within which any proposed site had to be located. The RFP also stated flatly, "NPS will consider a credible proposal to donate the Visitor Center/Museum facilities as superior to proposals which call for development of Related Facilities."(16) In short what was hoped was that some philanthropic group or individual would build and donate the complex to the NPS. With reference to Related Facilities the RFP was quite clear; "Related Facilities are to complement and enhance the activities of NPS. All related facilities must be appropriate, historically accurate, and relevant."(17) Unfortunately no proposals were submitted which provided for an unencumbered donation to the park, all involved "Related Facilities."

The RPF also listed 10 criteria on which each proposal would be evaluated and included the specific statement, "Further necessary environmental and planning procedures may result in recommended changes to the selected proposal."(18) This indeed proved to be the case. The RFP also made it clear that all activities and services were to be subject to NPS approval and "NPS approval over all aspects of the Complex's design and construction" was the final requirement.(19)

When the May 1997 deadline for the return of proposals was reached and no proposals for the donation of the complex were forthcoming attention turned to the six proposals formally submitted, all of which included Related Facilities. Among the proposals submitted was one from Robert Monahan, but to the surprise of some no proposal was received from Eric Uberman, who had made such a fuss when the first Monahan proposal was made known to the public, and who had led the chorus demanding a national search for a partner.

Two of the six proposals submitted did not meet all of the specific requirements stated in the RFP and were disqualified. The remaining four underwent further careful scrutiny before a final selection was recommended to the director of the NPS Robert Stanton. No member of the Gettysburg National Military Park staff was permitted on the selection committee with the exception of park planner Deborah Darden who had taken the lead in drafting the RFP. However her role was strictly in an informational capacity, she had no vote on the proposals themselves. Nor were any representatives of the local community invited to participate although the committee did receive advice from several professional designers and financial experts. The selection committee itself consisted entirely of NPS administrators from various sections of the country and the entire group was held to the strictest standards of secrecy during its deliberations. Even Superintendent Latschar was given no information until the evaluations were completed and the recommendation readied for new NPS Director Stanton.

But park activities did not come to a standstill during this time. While the RFP was being written park speed limits, an "Adopt-a-Position" program, and reduction of the park deer herd all required attention.

To the annoyance of those who lived on the Emmitsburg Road the

Pennsylvania Department of Transportation, at the park's request, lowered the speed limits on that section of the road between Wheatfield Road and the borough limits by 5 miles per hour. Local residents objected vociferously at a park Advisory Commission meeting, one saying, " 'I think it's a burden that has been placed on the residents.' "(20) Another voiced his displeasure by saying, " 'It just doesn't make any sense. In my mind it's just a speed trap for the local people.' "(21) Superintendent Latschar countered their criticism by stating that the speed limits were lowered in the interest of visitor safety. Acknowledging that the residents were correct in pointing out that no tourists or other pedestrians had been injured or killed on that road in the past five years he declared, " 'But I'll be damned if I'm going to wait until they are.' "(22)

Another matter which required considerable attention and was not finally resolved until the dismissal of the final court case in 2000, was the size of the park deer herd. Overbrowsing of historic woodlots, as well as crop damage, particularly in corn and alfalfa, was a growing concern. Since the early 1990's the park had been considering ways to reduce the herd within the park boundaries. Following a series of public meetings and the publishing of an Environmental Impact Statement, a decision was made to reduce the herd by initiating a "ranger only" shooting period of several months in the fall and winter. The goal was to lower the deer population from an estimated 325 per forested square mile of the park to the Pennsylvania recommended 20-25 per forested square mile. Some residents near the park who continually lost shrubs and plants to the deer praised the program. Others, who regularly fed the deer or simply enjoyed their presence, abhorred it, and animal rights groups went to court to stop the process. The NPS successfully defended itself against numerous lawsuits and appeals which ended with the dismissal of the final appeal in the spring of 2000. In the meantime the herd had been reduced to the desired number and only maintenance action is anticipated in the future.

While care of crop fields and woodlots is a relatively recent issue, care of the entire battlefield has been a problem since the early days of the park and further additions of land and monuments had only made matters worse. To cope with the almost impossible task of "housekeeping" on the battlefield the park initiated an "Adopt-a-Position" program open to any individual or group willing to commit themselves to the care of a specific portion of the battlefield for at least two years. The response was much greater than anticipated. Civil War Round Tables, re-enactor groups, descendants of men who fought at Gettysburg, history buffs and interested members of the general public responded willingly. Currently over 360 positions are being cared for in one way or another. Groups not affiliated with a specific monument help by clearing brush, painting buildings or fences, picking up trash, cutting weeds, anything that will enhance the care and appearance of the park. Park Watch, another group of over 125 volunteers, patrols the park providing park rangers with additional eyes and ears, alert for signs of trouble. Although they serve in an observation capacity only vandalism and other illegal activities, while not eliminated, have been reduced.

But no illegal activity had been involved when, in early 1996, a keen eyed visitor walking along the railroad cut noticed embedded in the side of the cut some bones which had become exposed through erosion. Although not unheard of, it was the first time in 50 years that such a discovery had been made on the battlefield. The bones were determined to be those of a male between the ages of 20 and 40, but initially it could not be said with certainty that they were those of a Civil War soldier. The *Harrisburg Patriot News* editorialized in May, "Contrary to perceptions, we do not know everything about the Civil War, we do not know everything about the Battle of Gettysburg, including where the bodies are buried. ...Though more than a half century has passed since the last confirmed discovery of a battle victim's remains, it is likely that some still rest there today."(23) When the excavation was completed later in the summer the bones were sent to the Smithsonian Institution for further analysis. About 2/3 of the skeletal remains were recovered but beyond that only a shirt button and a piece of leather shoe sole were found, not enough to provide further identification. However the agreement was that these were indeed the bones of a soldier killed in battle and as such they were given a proper military burial in the National Cemetery.

In an article in the *Civil War News* of May 1996 supervisory ranger Scott Hartwig said the discovery did not surprise him. "...He said his 'hunch' is that the bones are that of a Confederate. Union remains were more completely rounded up, but the Confederates, particularly in individual graves, might vanish without a trace." Park historian Kathy Harrison was quoted in the same article. " 'As many as 1200 to 1500 Union and Confederate bodies were unaccounted for.' " And she added, " '...this is a cemetery. A lot of old veterans referred to the ground here as a cemetery, because their comrades were still buried here. They knew that better than we do.' "(24)

Meanwhile in early October 1997 all four proposals for the museum/visitor center were sent to Washington along with the selection committee's comments and recommendations. The final decision however rested with Director Stanton. Unfortunately, as so often happens, the name of the preferred bidder was leaked and on October 15, 1997 the newspaper *USA Today* reported that the proposal of Robert Kinsley, a developer from York, Pa., had received the committee's recommendation. In response NPS Chief of Public Affairs David Barna insisted that "'no choice had been made officially.'"(25) The NPS position was that no decision was official until the appropriate documents had been signed. This had the effect of leaving Super-intendent Latschar twisting in the wind under a barrage of angry attacks from some of the probable losing bidders and others. He was constantly having to repeat the NPS position while simultaneously defending the Park Service and himself against charges of collusion and conspiracy in the selection process because the official announcement was not forthcoming. Rumors abounded and everyone opposed to the concept of a public-private partnership for the museum/visitor center had ample time to sharpen their axes. It was hinted that the delay was caused in part by time having to be spent convincing skep-tical congressmen that the park was not "selling it's soul to the devil" in per-mitting commercial activities within the proposed complex.

Somehow overlooked in all of the controversy was the simple fact that the park already had commercial ventures in place on the battlefield. Eastern National Parks Association managed, and charged admission to, the Cyclo-rama painting and the Electric Map, and operated a bookstore in each of the two buildings in which they were housed. Although non-profit in nature the operation was without a doubt a commercial enterprise. A business which was strictly for profit that operated on the battlefield was the Battlefield Tour Cen-ter fleet of buses which carried tourists over a programmed tour of the battle-field. This same firm provided shuttle bus service to the Eisenhower Farm – for a fee. The Licensed Battlefield Guides, each one considered an independ-ent contractor, conducted their business from a desk in the Visitor Center lobby and were provided with a special guide waiting room in the Visitor Cen-ter as well. Although charged a yearly license fee by the Park Service the guides retained the fees they charged to visitors for their services. All of these enter-prises still exist on the battlefield today.

The Kinsley proposal included an Imax theater-which would show Civil War films, a gift shop, craft store, bookstore, the Cyclorama painting, the electric map, a restaurant, and facilities for the Licensed Battlefield Guides and other tour groups to schedule tours. There would also be a center to provide information about other points of interest both within the town and beyond. The facility was, not, as some opponents, including Eric Uberman, continued to call it, a "mall".

But before the selection of a partner had even been announced oppo-nents were already denouncing the entire project. Political consultant and Civil War buff Jerry Russell who had never attended a meeting on the plan, raged, "This is not only a rape of the battlefield, it's a bailout for the @#$%^&* tower!"(26) Walter Powell of the GBPA stated flatly, " '…we haven't seen any evidence that the park is competent enough to deal with developers.' "(27) If there had been any hope that things would quiet down once the formal announcement was made it quickly vanished.

Although many railed about "commercialization" of the battlefield and demanded that Congress provide funds for the building, there were a few more reasoned voices. Senator Slade Gorton (R Wash) in an interview with the *Gettysburg Times* said of the successful Kinsley proposal, " 'I certainly approve of it in its general form at this point. ... What I like...is the fact that you will have your visitor center in a place where no portion of the battle took place. It'll be able to restore areas where the battle did take place to what they looked like on the first of July, 1863.' "(28) His statement regarding restoration of "areas where the battle did take place" referred to a key section of the Kinsley proposal which was the removal of both the current Visitor Center and the Cyclorama building and the restoration of that part of the field.

Gorton also noted the concerns of having for profit businesses within the park and demands that the project be federally funded to avoid such a situation by saying, " 'Well bluntly that's not going to happen. There's not a sufficient amount of money to do that.' "(29)

Representative Goodling later expressed his opinion in a letter to a constituent in July 1998. "I support the idea of public-private partnerships as a way of preserving our national treasures, provided that the resulting partnerships are done in tasteful ways which do not compromise the integrity of our parks and all they represent. ...The existing visitors center is entirely inadequate and restoring some of the most sacred ground on the battlefield should be another long term goal."(30)

Restoration of the ground on which the Visitor Center and Cyclorama buildings are now located would be possible due to the location chosen by Robert Kinsley for the new building. Located on Hunt Avenue it is a few hundred yards south of where the tower then stood and about 500 yards east of the Fantasyland location selected by Mr. Monahan in his initial proposal. But even this caused an uproar.

One resident cited the presumed presence of bog turtles, an endangered species, as an argument against the Kinsley location although research later showed that the animals in question were "box" turtles, found in relative abundance throughout the county. Others declared that this land too was pristine, sacrosanct ground, scene of important battle action and should not be disturbed. In an effort to settle this matter the park Advisory Commission invited a panel of noted historians who were experts on the battle, to visit the park, analyze the procedures used to develop the General Management Plan (which was also under consideration), and express their opinions on whether the site selected by Kinsley was the scene of actual fighting.

After the visit retired Brigadier General Harold Nelson, a noted military expert on Gettysburg and other Civil War battles, wrote to the Commission, "I know of no evidence of battle action or battle activity that NPS historians have missed in their evaluation of the LeVan and Fantasyland sites." Referring to action that involved Culp's Hill he added, "If the Visitor Center is placed on the LeVan site, all of this can be easily interpreted without disturbing any significant terrain, thus increasing visitor understanding of the artillery action along the Baltimore Pike."(31) Another outstanding historian, Dr. Gary Gallagher, wrote, "There simply was not significant action of any kind on either the LeVan or Fantasyland tract."(32) Despite this and testimony of other historians the opposition continued to insist that the LeVan site was of equal importance with the battle action areas slated to be restored. (The name "LeVan site" stems from the name of the owner of the land then under consideration. It is a 45 acre tract situated at the southeast corner of Hunt Avenue and the Baltimore Pike, and was purchased by Kinsley in 1999. In 1998 he had purchased a 2 acre plot of land on the southwest corner of the same intersection with the intention of removing the RV sales center which stood there and restoring the land to its historical appearance. (This project has since been completed.)

However the verbal battle abated not a bit and voices of the opposition became more and more strident as the weeks passed. Robert Monahan, who had publicly expressed confidence that his proposal would be selected, filed a protest with the Secretary of the Interior Bruce Babbitt demanding a full Congressional investigation into the selection process. In October 1997, reacting to the *USA Today* report, he had told the *Hanover Sun* " 'I was shocked that they would choose a plan that would put this center on hallowed ground within the permanent boundaries of the park.' "(33) This ignored the fact that his original proposal would have placed a museum and commercially operated Imax theater less than 500 yards from the proposed Kinsley site, and even closer to the main area of battle action on July 3, 1863.

At about the same time that Monahan was bemoaning the prospect of a proposal other than his own being selected, Civil War Wax Museum owner Eric Uberman admitted at a public meeting that he had accepted $1,160.54 from another local businessman to help defray expenses incurred in the effort to prevent Monahan's original proposal from going forward. " 'I present you with the check,' " he said, offering copies of the document to the reporters present.(34)

Nor was the museum/visitor center proposal the only item on the park agenda at this time. In January 1997 the first steps were taken to develop a new General Management Plan (GMP) to replace the one which had been followed since 1982. Between January and August of that same year the park conducted nine public workshops in addition to mailing a newsletter to the 2500 names on the park mailing list, seeking as much public input as possible before completing the management plan alternatives required by the GMP process. Eventually one of the proposed alternatives would be selected as the operative guidelines under which the park would be managed for the next 15 to 20 years.

Because the museum/visitor center project and the proposed GMP were so closely interrelated the decision was made to combine the two into one larger entity. In October 1997 the first of a series of additional public meetings was held with the two projects now considered under a single "umbrella". More public meetings were scheduled over the ensuing eight months but these, while giving the public an opportunity to offer suggestions, also served to increase the volume of opposition. By early 1998 erstwhile foes Uberman and Monahan had joined forces to bring down the Kinsley proposal, the GMP, and as events would show, Superintendent Latschar as well.

However there were some significant voices in support of the park, among them the *Harrisburg Patriot News* which editorialized, "Somebody had to offer a way out of the battlefield's downward spiral in the absence of Congress providing the necessary resources. That somebody is Latschar and everyone who cares about Gettysburg would do well to lend him their support in this vital effort of preservation and visitor enhancement."(35)

George Will wrote in the *Washington Post* "There is again conflict here(Gettysburg), this time swirling around a proposed use of private money to replace the current visitor center with one better able to preserve artifacts and attract and educate visitors. There are ringing denunciations of alleged plans for 'selling off' American history and for building a 'mall' on hallowed ground."

He went on, "Such overheated rhetoric is partly local merchants' commercialism gussied up as patriotism and partly reflects a presumption of philistinism in the National Park Service. ...The new Center...would be built on ground that during the battle was a staging area, where no clash of arms occurred. ...Local merchants resent that there will be food services and relevant shops at the new center, as there are at, for example, Washington's National Gallery. ...Latschar aspires to build an 'interpretive museum' that, using interactive media and other teaching devices, will explain why the war came and why men walked through fields of fire. ...Confusion is common about, as well as in, combat. One visitor here – a senior military officer no less – said he had also visited Antietam and Chickamauga, and wasn't it interesting that so many battles had occurred on Park Service land? Another visitor expressed skepticism about a guide's description of the fierce fighting because there are no bullet marks on the monuments."

Will concluded by saying, "Given that the vast majority of Americans have never heard a shot fired in anger, the imaginative presentation of military history in a new facility here is vital, lest rising generations have no sense of the sacrifices of which they are the beneficiaries."(36)

Other supportive comments were also heard. One visitor had written in the February 24, 1998 *Gettysburg Times* "If I want to get to your business I will. ...If you market it they will come."(37) Dr. Richard Rollins, a noted historian who was another of the six invited by the park Advisory Commission to analyze the development of the General Management Plan and the proposed museum/visitor center location, told the local paper, " 'It is very, very impressive. It should have been done a long time ago.' "(38) In addition the results of a survey sent to all members of the Friends group showed that of the questionnaires returned 2,658 favored the plan while 332 opposed it.(39)

In the fall other nationally known historians also analyzed the proposed GMP and had this reaction, " 'Our team of historians enthusiastically endorses the proposals in this draft general management plan.' " wrote Dr. Nina Silber of Boston University. Dr. Eric Foner of Columbia University, and Pulitzer Prize winner Dr. James McPherson of Princeton University concurred. The statement went on to say that "without question" the park needed a new visitor center and museum.(40)

Meantime opponents of the GMP were deaf to all such commentary. In February 1998, losing bidder Monahan had announced that he was considering a court challenge to the NPS selection of Mr. Kinsley's proposal. " '...I personally feel the public is being compromised by this charade.' " he said.(41)

On February 24, 1998 both sides had an opportunity to express their views at a Senate sub-committee hearing in Washington. GBPA president Walter Powell asked the Senate to stop the General Management Plan and museum/visitor center proposal. "Frankly" he said, "it extends to the broader and more troubling issue of whether we can really trust the actions and pronouncements of the current administration of the Gettysburg National Military Park to be in the best interests of the American public and the resource."(42) This of course, was a direct slap at Superintendent Latschar. But other statements made at the same hearing were of a decidedly different nature. Senator Dale Bumpers (D Ark) remarked, "Mr. Chairman, I know you visited the battlefield yesterday. I was up there last month. I think everyone who has been there agrees that the present archival storage and preservation facilities are inadequate. Looking at the Cyclorama painting there is no doubt that it needs to be restored. And I think it makes sense to move the existing visitor center and administrative facilities to a less prominent part of the battlefield."(43)

In his statement Senator Rick Santorum (R Pa.), a steadfast supporter of the park, declared, "While holding a special place in the hearts of many, the

Gettysburg National Military Park has always suffered from having too many personal superintendents. …what interest or concern are they pursuing? Who do they represent and what is their association with the town, it's people, or even the Park itself.? …Those that seek to delay the construction of a new visitor center serve no one, least of which is the park itself and its hundreds of thousands of visitors."(44)

In a March 1998 public meeting Robert Kinsley told the audience, " 'We have taken into consideration your concerns about the main facilities. We are listening to your concerns about the site.' "(45) Indeed, in the ensuing months the scope of the building was reduced considerably although the site, supported by historians, remained the same. After a number of public meetings and continued negotiations with the NPS, the craft shop and gift shop were eliminated, the Imax theater was changed to a normal screen theater, and the restaurant modified from a table service facility to one serving only light snacks. But even these extensive modifications failed to appease the critics. Walter Powell's reaction to the reduction was, " 'The issue here is not scaling back, that's a smoke screen. The bottom line is private development within the park.' "(46)

At a borough council meeting, also in March, Emmett Patterson, owner of McDonald's on Steinwehr Avenue, stated flatly, " 'I want to see my business protected… .' "(47), and Robert Monahan said of the plan, " 'It's a mess.' "(48) It was an attitude shared by many of the Steinwehr Avenue business owners. At the same meeting a complaint was voiced by council members and county officials that they had not been informed of what was transpiring even though both bodies had members on the park Advisory Commission and all public meetings had been announced before hand in the local paper. In fact since 1995, when the first Monahan proposal was unveiled the Advisory Commission had held eleven meetings at which representatives of both governing bodies had been present when the museum/visitor center and the new GMP had been discussed.

However by now it seemed clear that only a total rewriting of the GMP to suit their own purposes, coupled with abandonment of the Kinsley proposal entirely, would satisfy Monahan, Uberman, Powell and their cohorts. On the other hand on May 3, 1998 the *York (Pa) Sunday News* editorialized, "The arguments have become stale, the public hearings pointless. The small group of naysayers keep saying nay over and over, refusing to compromise…"(49)

But nothing changed, the opposition continued unabated. Finally, on February 23, 1999, one puzzled writer, referring to the many public meetings held by the NPS, wrote to the *Gettysburg Times,* "Why were those people now so outspoken about the GMP not in attendance when the series of meetings started? …How can these people think that the National Park Service or the

Gettysburg Military Park owes the town of Gettysburg anything? The GNMP has zero responsibility in its mission, to care for the town and the businesses in it. GNMP is charged with taking care of the resources and artifacts at the park."(50)

However not all letter writers regarded the park with such equanimity. One letter to the editor of the *Gettysburg Times* declared, "The new facility is not being built to enhance the experiences of the visitor as to the battle of Gettysburg, it's being built to get profits. Profits that will be taken away from the businesses in Gettysburg. …The power people are at play and there isn't anything that can stop it. There is too much money involved and too many reputations and careers are on the line, private, professional and political."(51) The actual Kinsley proposal envisioned raising about $25 million dollars through a non-profit foundation and financing the remainder of the costs through commercial loans which would be repaid with profits from the restaurant, shops, electric map, Cyclorama program, and theater. Once the loans were cleared the building and the land upon which it was built would be turned over to the NPS as a gift. Despite the reduction in facilities the financing plan remained the same. But still the opposition persisted and cries for government funding of the project continued.

Again congressmen stated what by now had become the obvious. In April Representative Ralph Regula (R Ohio) was quoted in the *Washington Post* as saying, " 'First come the 'must do' priorities – we've got to keep the National Parks open. Next is 'need to do' – clearing the backlog of maintenance at the parks. And then there's 'nice to do' – build a visitors center or acquire a piece of land. With the (budget) caps 'nice to dos' are gone, and maintenance may have to wait.' "(52)

Even this, and Representative Goodling's forthright statement that Congress would appropriate no money for this type of project, failed to convince some opponents of the plan. They insisted that the park should ask Congress for the funds to construct the new museum/visitor center. An angry letter writer attacked Superintendent Latschar in the *Gettysburg Times*, "Two questions for Superintendent Latschar. Did you make a very early deal with Kinsley to build the new center, so that talk of competition was a fraud? Did you let the present visitor center go to rack and ruin to strengthen your argument that it ought to be torn down?"(53) This despite the fact that published figures showed the park having spent $703,000 between 1993 and 1998 on upkeep and improvement of the current Visitor Center and enhanced care of the museum artifacts.

Nor was this the only negative letter about the superintendent, who was regularly the target of verbal attacks by the public. In June one writer declared, "…it is more difficult to explain the rational for Dr. Latschar's record of bad planning, worse communication, and general mismanagment. ...All this has been done with a level of arrogance seldom matched in the public service field... ."(54)

By now it had become evident that Superintendent Latschar would continue to come under further relentless attacks by opponents of the GMP and museum/visitor center proposal. In October 1998 the NPS, and John Latschar in particular, had to endure in silence, two public hearings of over two hours each, at which members of the public could present arguments pro and con on both matters. Because these were public hearings and not simply public meetings NPS personnel were not permitted to make statements or answer questions, a fact that infuriated many of the more than 200 in attendance each day. These sessions proved to be by far the most acrimonious of all the public gatherings held on the GMP and the museum/visitor center proposal.

The first hearing began with a favorable comment from Thomas Wolf who said, "I am in favor of the new visitor center and the museum in expanded quarters. The Kinsley plan may require some minor adjustment, but I support it and certainly the concept behind it. Unfortunately a small, vociferous group of local businesspeople and a few politicians have opposed the plan...for mostly selfish and shortsighted reasons mainly because they fear a possible short-term effect on their tourist related businesses. ...I urge, I beg this small group of mainly businesspeople to abandon their parochial and selfish view and to support this nationally beneficial concept of an expanded visitor center and museum..."(55) Gerald Bennett stated, "...the proposed partnership to build a new and expanded visitor center at the LeVan site with a modest and necessary level of commercial venture is most appropriate in light of the balance of positive benefits to park visitor and local community."(56)

But others were less accepting. John Fenstermacher, lawyer for Angela Rosensteel Eckert in her lawsuit against the park stated, "Tonight we get one more chance to attempt to counter the one-sided propaganda that the National Park Service has spread... . Because some Congressman or politically connected individual liked the Kinsley group it got chosen... . I find it incredulous that Gettysburg National Military Park could not get funding for repairs, restoration or construction when we have a $70 billion dollar surplus. ...The trashing of our National Park at Gettysburg by its administrator, the National Park Service, must stop."(57)

Countering that attack was Margaret Blough who said, "The issue is not whether or not there is a budget surplus. ...Senator Santorum and Congressman Goodling in the recent *Gettysburg Times* article...have made it clear that there could be a $70 TRILLION surplus, but Congress has no intention of funding this visitor center."(58)

Still the attack continued. Eric Uberman declared, "Misinformation, confusion, the play on words, semantics if you will, delays, information released only through the Freedom of Information Act requests, are all the hallmark of the General Management Plan and are in and of themselves reason enough that this plan not be accepted. We ask why the National Park Service in Washington trusts the original commercial partner Kinsley and the Gettysburg National Military Park after the scandalous arrangement they originally tried to foist on the public here. Can the National Park Service in Washington, D.C. trust the Gettysburg National Military Park to protect the national interest of Gettysburg after its disgraceful performance thus far?"(59)

Robert Monahan, one of the losing bidders, attacked even more directly, "I feel that…because of the things that I am aware of that many of you are not and eventually you will find out, but I believe that the Superintendent here has not discharged his duties responsibly. I think this administration has lied, misrepresented, and misinformed the American public and the people of this community, and I think that the Superintendent of the National Military Park at Gettysburg should be removed!"(60)

His comments were followed soon after by Elsie Fox who declared, "I am very concerned with the rudeness that has been displayed by the Superintendent to all of us at these meetings. You have just looked at me Dr. Latschar. That's the first time I have seen you make eye contact with anyone this evening."(61)

It was in this vein that comments continued to be made and this same atmosphere pervaded both evenings of the public hearings. When they were over the community was divided as never before and at least one borough official and many citizens expressed both shock at the virulence of the attacks and embarrassment for the town of Gettysburg.

In February 1999 the opponents of the park succeeded in arranging a hearing before a U.S. House of Representatives sub-committee chaired by Representative James Hansen (R Utah). The same complaints were heard and the same anti-park arguments were presented. A member of the NPS administrative staff in Washington presented the Park Service position and the situation remained unchanged.

Perhaps one of the most amazing articles in opposition to the GMP and the Kinsley proposal was published in the August 1999 issue of the *Civil War News* when Pete Jorgenson wrote, "You may never drive through the Gettysburg battlefield again. The issue isn't about whether or not a new museum should be built… . The issue is about who is going to benefit financially. …Will it be the local businessmen already in place along Steinwehr Avenue or will the financial center of Gettysburg tourist traffic be shifted to an isolated commercial development well within park boundaries? There, with the tourists captive to their privately run parking lots, a privileged group of politically well connected individuals will establish 'non-profit' shops and restaurants designed to pay big salaries and benefits to their hand picked administrators and developers. …This, the prime tourist attraction at Gettysburg, will be well cordoned off. Only paying bus passengers will have access. …Greed and political reality demand that your opportunity to spend money in the park be carefully regulated. …That big steel structure looming over the battlefield will probably get a minor name change. It will be called the Gettysburg National Park Service Security Tower where rangers with binoculars and telescopes will spot people trying to 'sneak' onto public lands without paying parking and tour fees. …Supporters of the 'big brother' approach to control the flow of tourist dollars emanating from the Gettysburg battlefield include Sen. Rick Santorum (R Pa.) in league with Superintendent John Latschar and Borough president John Eline along with a host of non-public figures who will financially benefit from this on-going, three year saga of a 'public-private' partnership… the people with connections who'll use publicly generated funds and a privately managed park facility to line their pockets with fees, salaries and concessions… . Those really pushing this project seek control of the tourist dollars flowing into Gettysburg. The museum and new visitor center is nothing but a sideshow to distract public focus from the real issue."(62)

For outbursts such as this there was simply no answer. Nothing the NPS, John Latschar, Robert Kinsley, Representatives Goodling and Regula, Senators Santorum and Bumpers, the Advisory Commission, the Friends, noted historians or any private citizen might say could hope to alter such an attitude.

Meanwhile in May the GBPA, through its lawyer John Fenstermacher, had threatened a lawsuit if the organization was not given the same right to raise funds on the battlefield as was presently granted to the Friends of the National Parks at Gettysburg. Anthony Conte, regional solicitor for the Department of the Interior quickly replied that GBPA did not have National Park Service partner status and had "no basis to demand that it be allowed to conduct fund raising activities within Gettysburg NMP."(63)

While all of this was going on yet another controversy appeared on the horizon, generated again by the General Management Plan.

As part of the GMP the Cyclorama painting was to be removed from its present location to be repaired and rehung in the new visitor center complex. The present Cyclorama building would then be razed and the land restored to its 1863 appearance. For years a thorn in the side of many historians who considered the building a modern intrusion on an historic Civil War battlefield, they greeted the prospect of its removal with unrestrained delight. But as with everything else associated with the GMP this too brought a chorus of protests. This time most voices raised were not from local businessmen but from architects, some of whom viewed the structure, designed by Richard Neutra, as a shining example of his expertise in modern architecture. For this reason they, along with members of the Neutra family, demanded that the building be retained and placed on the National Register of Historic Buildings. Although the NPS and the Pennsylvania Historical and Museum Commission had approved removal of the building and felt that retaining it would be inappropriate, the Keeper of the National Register in Washington, D.C. decided that the structure could in fact be given such a designation. In her decision she wrote, "…the Cyclorama building is a rare example of Neutra's institutional design on the east coast and one of his very few Federal commissions. While not currently analyzed in detail in publications it is one of a very few of his works often mentioned or illustrated."(64)

But the matter did not end there. Following receipt of additional information from the NPS the President's Advisory Council on Historic Preservation convened a meeting in the building itself in April 1999, during which the differing points of view were heard. Architects from the park itself, as well as from other NPS venues, explained the impossibility of renovating the poured-in-place concrete structure so that the endangered Cyclorama painting could be exhibited in a properly controlled environment and hung in the correct manner, something impossible to do at present because of the configuration of the building itself. Others spoke of the inappropriateness of the building in its present setting. On the other side of the coin officials of several architectural organizations spoke in favor of retaining the building, as did a group of local citizens led by Eric Uberman.

Some weeks later the Advisory Council released its report. Referring to the decision of the Council the report stated, "That basic choice will be dictated by establishing priorities among competing historic resources, and these priorities will in turn result from weighing, at the highest policy or philosophical level, the historic values represented by each resource."

The report continued, "With rare exceptions, the millions of people who have visited the GNMP since 1962 have come to see the battlefield and not Neutra's architecture. Neutra has a secure place in the pantheon of American architectural history. There are other Neutra buildings, there is only one Gettysburg Battlefield. The proper treatment of the Building would be considered under quite different criteria of course, were it on some other site without superior historical competition.. The continued existence of the building is consequently pre-empted by another controlling historic preservation objective. In such circumstances it is not necessary to enter upon any examination of whether the building can be adapted to another use or can feasibly be altered to accommodate the Cyclorama painting or whether the Painting can be accommodated without any such alteration. For the purpose of the unpleasant choice posed by its unfortunate siting it should be assumed that the building is completely functional in all these aspects. The result is the same. The building must yield."(65)

But rather than end the controversy the report was rejected out of hand by those who wished to see the building remain. The Neutra group continued its efforts in Washington to prevent removal of the building, while at the same time over 200 identical letters were received by the park stating that, "IT AIN'T OVER 'TILL IT'S OVER! ... Touch this National icon at your PERIL! ...YOU DO NOT HAVE A CLEAR ROAD TO DESTRUCTION as far as we are concerned. We recommend a full-blown congressional and media investigation into the questionable basis for the flawed GMP under which you are claiming to proceed at this time. Consider this a CALL TO ARMS of the world of preservationists who care about this battlefield and this building, and who do not want to see its history re-written for your shallow purposes despite all the pious rhetoric of 'ethnic cleansing' that is being mouthed as the reason for destroying this one monument out of many that dot this historic ground now. If necessary, we will descend upon you by the hundreds and block the bulldozers from their work when the time comes."(66) (Capitalization is in the original document.)

Despite such hysterical outbursts, and through all of the acrimonious controversy that surrounded the General Management Plan, the museum/visitor center project and the fate of the Cyclorama and old Visitor Center buildings, a few calm voices were sometimes heard. Gerald Bennett expressed his feelings at an Advisory Commission meeting in 1998 when he said, "Our tourist market is being impacted even now as we debate the visitor center issue, by a combination of change elements which none of us singularly or collectively can control. Our only opportunity is to manage the forces of change to our benefit. Left to drift unfettered these forces will most certainly bring about a serious depression in our visitation beginning in the immediate future and accelerating as we move through the first decade of the 21st century. Such a calamity will depress the sales volume of our merchants, and our local economy in general, to a far lower level than commercial operations at a new visitor center. ...The time when Gettysburg could sit back and expect tourist visitation to grow in relation to the increase in the national population is gone. ...The existing visitor center is woefully inadequate as a modern, relevant visitor attraction. We must have a facility whose museum presents a coordinated history of the Civil War, its role in our nation's evolution, an understanding of how our lives today are effected. ...Blocking the creation of the cornerstone for a relevant area attraction just does not make any long term economic sense. Retaining the status quo will not cut it."(67)

In a different, yet similar vein, a local resident wrote to John Latschar,

"I am writing to let you know that I think you are doing an excellent job at a nearly impossible task. You clearly are trying to do the best by everyone and everything. ...I wouldn't be surprised at any time to read in the local paper – shall I even mention how badly you are treated by a biased local press – that you have decided you don't need this and are moving on. Please know that there are people here who realize what a difficult task you have and what a good job you are doing. Unfortunately we rarely come to the hearings because we have no complaints or arguments to voice, and the press has no interest in what we think. ...I'm not signing my name because I hope you will see me in many people with whom you come into contact. Sincerely, an Adams county resident."(68)

On April 22, 1999 a strong voice of support was heard in Gettysburg when Secretary of the Interior Bruce Babbitt observed Earth Day at the park. Referring to the GMP he said, " 'It's been a long, iterative process in which we have heard again and again from all the different parties. We have discussed this thing endlessly. It is now time for decision.' " Acknowledging that the Park Service decision " 'will not be received unanimously, it is important we do the best we can to restore the landscape and appearance of that battlefield as it was in 1863.' " He went on, "'We're going to get these buildings off this sacred ground.' "(69) Then addressing the issue of the tower the Secretary declared, " 'Let's turn to that tower. It is not worthy of our heritage. On my watch as Secretary of the Interior we are going to deal decisively with this issue. It will be effaced from the landscape it desecrates.' " And he added that if successful negotiations with the tower owner were not possible, " 'I will go to Congress and use eminent domain power as a way of meeting these responsibilities.' "(70)

The opponents of the GMP then attempted to have a bill introduced in Congress that would, among other things, prohibit relocation of the visitor center, prohibit the removal of the Cyclorama building, and finally, "the Secretary (of the Interior) shall carry out the construction projects (reconstruct the Visitor Center, renovate the Cyclorama building) in consultation with the non-profit organization known as the National Trust for Historic Gettysburg."(71), (which at that time had yet to receive a charter.) If passed the bill would have effectively eliminated NPS authority over the Gettysburg National Military Park.

However, having asked Representative Goodling's office for assistance in drawing up the bill (a courtesy provided all constituents), the group released the text of their proposed bill to the press before Representative Goodling had a chance to review and discuss it. This breach of courtesy resulted in a stinging article by the Congressman, who wrote in October 1999, "The Civil War continues in Gettysburg and it appears the Congressman is to take the blame and be the 'fall guy'. I was willing to accept the role until it became 'nasty' and included my family. Referring to the released contents of the "bill" he said, "To my surprise before I even had a chance to review it, it had been sent to local, national and perhaps even international press. The press calls, faxes and e-mails began shortly thereafter." He went on to mention questions he had been asked about his wife having secured a job with Mr. Kinsley (she did not), his purported co-ownership of horses with Kinsley (he did not), and to top it all off, "I discovered the small minds were even smaller than I thought when another reporter asked me whether I owned any Black Angus(cattle) with Mr. Kinsley." (he did not) Representative Goodling went on, "I hope that when all the skirmishes are fought and the pettiness ends, that a new visitor center will still be a possibility."(72)

Finally, on November 23, 1999, after more than four years, as long as it took to fight the Civil War, after seemingly endless meetings, controversy and attacks on virtually everyone associated with, or supportive of, the General Management Plan, Marie Rust, NPS Regional Director of the Northeast Region of the National Park Service, was given the go-ahead by NPS Director Stanton to sign the Record of Decision. With her signature the new GMP became the official guideline for the operation of Gettysburg National Military Park.

Yet the signing of the document did not signal the end of controversy. Opponents vowed to continue the fight. The Cyclorama was still a "hot button" issue, and the park girded itself for more contentious battles ahead related to the implementation of the new GMP.

Nor was the first of the anticipated battles long in appearing. Seven months after the signing of the GMP final resolution of the tower issue came into sight. On June 3, 2000 the Federal District Court in Harrisburg, Pa. approved a government "taking" of the tower through eminent domain and granted NPS possession as of June 15th. The NPS deposited $3 million with the court with the final price to be determined by the court at a later date. Controlled Demolition Inc. of Phoenix, Maryland agreed to demolish the structure without cost to the government in exchange for the salvage rights and permission to use the filming of the tower's demolition in advertising material.

There was the expected uproar from those segments of the community which wanted the tower retained but there was also widespread enthusiasm from those who had, ever since its construction, regarded the tower as an unwanted, unsightly intrusion upon the battlefield.

Bitterly opposed to removal of the tower was engineer Joel Rosenblatt who had designed it. In comments to the *Gettysburg Times* on June 21, 2000, he called its demolition " 'criminal vandalism' ", adding " 'This thing is more than just another tower. It is unusual engineering and design and it's worth saving. It deserves attention for itself.' "(73), which is precisely the complaint voiced to the *Washington Post* by Indiana history teacher Sally Butler the day the tower came down. Referring to the Pickett's charge area of the battlefield she said, " 'It (the tower) ruins the effect because even though you want to focus on the trees where the soldiers focused (during the charge) you can't without that thing staring at you.' "(74)

In an outspoken editorial in *USA Today* on July 3 the tower was called, "The ugliest commercial structure ever to intrude on the sanctity of a national park. …For 26 years the privately owned tower loomed over Gettysburg like the discarded leg of some monstrous insect. Horrible to look at and impossible to ignore, it ruined great swaths of the park's horizon and shattered the visual serenity that helps visitors connect with that somber place."(75)

However some local residents were less than forgiving of the NPS action. John Longanecker, after watching the tower come down, expressed his feelings thus, " 'This is the most undemocratic, unpatriotic act ever committed on these consecrated grounds. Truly this is an act of psychopathic pure nihilism.' "(76) Others had a different viewpoint. Mark Baker of Baltimore, who had driven up to watch the event said, " 'From a historic preservation standpoint that marker is an eyesore.' "(77) Reenactor Henry Szczyko from New Jersey, who had been coming to Gettysburg for years and planned to have his picture taken in front of the statue of Union General Meade said of the tower, " 'Finally that thing won't be there to muck it up. I'm ready to see it gone.' "(78), while 72 year old Ray Butara of Waynesboro, Pa. offered this observation, " 'That thing doesn't belong' "(79) His son Bob added, " '(If) you want to see the site you don't go up 300 feet in a tower. You walk these fields. You see these creeks, trees and stone walls up close. You see the human element.' "(80) To the claim that the tower was a "classroom in the sky", Barbara Finfrock, president of the Friends replied, " 'They were getting an overview but not a realistic view. The realistic view is the soldier's view from the ground.' "(81)

As usual Superintendent Latschar came in for a substantial share of the criticism but before the tower came down one resident of the town offered this support in the *Gettysburg Times,* "It still hurts me real bad that the National Tower still stands to this day! I will most certainly be glad to see it come down at last! Superintendent Latschar is accomplishing much here at Gettysburg and these things are things that Gettysburg has needed for a long time. I am very thankful he is here and I wish people could realize all the good he has done and continues to do."(82) But other writers disagreed as another letter from Gettysburg indicated, "…The Tower helps increase the popularity of Gettysburg and I am angry and disappointed that it will be destroyed. One man should not have all the say."(83) In fact some letters demanded public meetings and a vote on the matter.

Representative Goodling, as expected, was asked by opponents of the NPS plan to intervene and prevent the demolition. However he declined, noting in an article in the *Gettysburg Times* on June 27, 2000 that " '...a boundary study for the battlefield was authorized in 1988 and the tower site was among those listed for inclusion in (the) permanent park boundary.' " He also pointed out in the same article that " '(the) plan was reviewed in public meetings and approved by Congress in 1990.' "(84)

Gettysburg Mayor William Troxell offered a balanced view of the situation when he told the *Gettysburg Times* " 'A great percentage of people who live in Gettysburg wanted to see the tower remain. But as a battlefield guide, who takes people across the fields, all of them thought the tower should come down. It's intrusive. So the Park Service is here to serve the population of the country, and I think they did.' "(85)

Indicative of the depth of feeling against the tower was an incident which took place three days before the scheduled demolition. As he walked across Taneytown Road near the tower Superintendent Latschar noticed a woman standing quietly, looking directly at the tower. Seeing an individual in an NPS uniform she approached Dr. Latschar and said, "In all these years I have never permitted myself to look at that tower but now that you are taking it down I think it's alright to look at it just this once."(86)

Demolition was scheduled for 5:03 on July 3, the same date on which, 137 years earlier, Union soldiers had repulsed the desperate charge of Pickett's and Pettigrew's men. Thousands gathered at vantage points all over the area and following the firing of symbolic cannon on Cemetery Ridge, Secretary of the Interior Babbitt pressed the switch igniting the 13.85 pounds of demolition charges. Twelve seconds later, precisely as Controlled Demolition specialists had anticipated, the 307 foot, 2000 ton tower was nothing more than a pile of rubble hidden from view behind a grove of trees. A quiet descended upon the cemeteries. No more would "Goober Peas" disturb the meditation of those who came to these sanctuaries.

In 1863 a tremendous rainstorm had followed the apocalyptic battle, and in 2000, in an eerie reminder of the past, a heavy rain fell moments after the tower disappeared. Afterward Gerald Bennett, who knew well the history of the battle, remarked, "That is as close to ghosts as we will ever get on this battlefield."(87)

For the future it can be said with more than reasonable certainty that there will continue to be controversy surrounding almost all actions taken by administrators of the battlefield. There will always be those who believe their agendas are superior to the one chosen, or who view the battlefield in terms only of financial gain. But with equal certainty it can be said that the new museum/visitor center will be built, the Cyclorama building and the old Visitor Center will be removed, and the part of the battlefield where they now stand will, among other areas, be restored to its 1863 appearance.

There will be some holding views different from the ones enumerated in the General Management Plan, who will express honest disagreement. There will be others who, because of avarice, greed or sheer personal animosity, will vigorously oppose any NPS action not to their liking. But the park, if properly administered, can overcome these obstacles and implement a GMP which will assure that future generations of Americans will be able to visit a battlefield which resembles, as closely as possible, the appearance it had when Union and Confederate soldiers first faced each other across this "holy ground."

Demolition of the tower - July 3, 2000

Photos by Rick Dugan
Hagerstown(MD) Herald

". . . to hold, and preserve, the battlegrounds of Gettysburg . . . as they were at the time of said battle . . . " April 30, 1864   GNMP

Chapter 9

"an exciting venture"

Despite the fact that in 1989 Congress had directed the National Park Service to purchase and remove the Ottenstein tower – without providing the funding to do so – its demolition on July 3 did nothing to quell the voices of dissent over the action. One citizen wrote, "The act of felling the tower at Gettysburg was faulty thinking at best and criminal action at worst." Then, referring to Supt. Latschar's "heartless decision", the writer continued, "His resignation would be far too late. His firing would be appropriate."(1) Another writer declared, "...I can't believe they destroyed that wonderful tower. ...It was one of the most terrible sights I have ever seen. It took selfishness, hatred, lies, deceit ... by a few selfish people with some political pull."(2) Still another citizen expressed outrage, "How can you people sleep at nights? Your hearts must be made of stone. ...If that tower had no place in Gettysburg then the group of you have no place either ... .(3)

But there were some voices raised in defense of the park. "Enough already!" demanded one writer. "The letters to the editor the last three-plus weeks have been vitriolic and full of half-truths and non-truths. I am saddened to know there are so many mean-spirited people in Gettysburg."(4) And an editorial in the *Evening Sun* stated, "...For more than a decade the National Park Service was very clear about its' intention. The Park Service wanted to acquire the tower and get rid of it. ...People had more than 10 years to speak out in defense of the tower. Instead they acted like the feds had pulled a fast one on them."(5)

In November 2001, because the parties involved could not agree on the price to be paid, the NPS and representatives for the tower and land owners presented their appraisals in the U.S. Middle District Court in Harrisburg, Pa. It would be up to the court to decide the value of both the tower and that of the land on which it stood. Government witnesses testified that the tower had been appraised at $2½ million. However an appraiser hired by the tower owners set the value at $11 million although admitting that he had never been up in the tower, had never seen the program offered, and had spent only about five minutes on the property two months after the tower had been demolished. A third appraiser, hired by the landowner who had leased the land, valued the 2½ acres at $2.6 million.

From the very beginning the laws establishing the park had been clear. It was created to "hold, and preserve the battlegrounds of Gettysburg... with the natural and artificial defenses as they were at the time of said battle ..."(6)

In 1896 the U.S. Supreme Court upheld a lower court judge who declared that the battlefield "should be preserved in its original condition ..."(7)

However over the years benign neglect, coupled with the inevitable piecemeal acquisition of battlefield land, had resulted in the haphazard growth of vegetation which eventually obliterated the topography of much of the land. Cannon once aimed at open ground appeared to be firing into dense woods, and the views which allowed commanders and their troops to observe enemy movements, became hidden behind a dense wall of trees and brush.

Therefore in 1999, after four years of preparation, including over thirty public meetings and hundreds of written comments, the park adopted a new general management plan in which it was clearly stated that 576 acres of non-historic woodlands would be removed, 115 acres of historic woodlands currently missing, would be restored, and 160 acres of historic orchards would be replanted on their original sites. When compared with another restoration alternative which would remove 1015 acres of non-historic trees the alternative chosen seemed rather mild. But the outcry it elicited was anything but mild.

Again letters to the editor abounded. "If you really mean to reestablish the battlefield to its original state, first remove all the monuments including the Pennsylvania ... . Once the monuments are removed you will have the right to remove the trees." said one Gettysburg resident.(8) Another wrote, "Removal of trees will be of no benefit to the vast majority of park visitors ... . Even then, a little imagination on the part of the historians could overcome non-historical vegetation."(9) Still another complained, "The plan will desecrate some of the most beautiful areas of the park."(10) But others held a different point of view. One licensed battlefield guide noted that "It is very difficult to explain to a visitor how thousands of soldiers moved and fought across such terrain. We can make the experience of our visitors much more meaningful if we all can see the battlefield more like it was seen by the men who fought here."(11)

In general land and/or structures not included within the park boundary could not be purchased by the NPS. However in September 2000 Congress changed the boundary to include the Wills house in downtown Gettysburg. In 1863 it had been owned by David Wills and was the home in which Abraham Lincoln stayed the night before delivering his famous speech at the dedication of the National Cemetery. It was now owned by the Eisenhower Society which, finding the upkeep too much of a financial burden, sought to sell it to the borough of Gettysburg. Including the building within the national park boundary made it possible for the NPS to provide $100,000 in federal technical assistance which funded a study to determine the structural condition of the building.

For the price of $500,000 the borough completed the purchase of the house, intending to restore it and make it, along with the restored train station, a magnet to draw visitors to the downtown area. But the borough was immediately faced with the formidable task of restoring the interior of the building which had been significantly altered over the years. Only the exterior remained as it had been in 1863. A cost estimate of at least $2 million for the needed work was to prove an insurmountable obstacle for the town and led eventually to the sale of the Wills house to the NPS.

Inclusion of the Wills house in the park boundary was generally well received within the community but the proposed new museum/visitor center project was to face renewed opposition in the coming years.

In July 2000 the NPS and the Gettysburg Battlefield Museum Foundation, headed by Robert Kinsley, had entered into a legal agreement which solidified their public-private partnership and paved the way for the Foundation to begin fund raising efforts for the new building. In December of that year the Foundation named Robert C. Wilburn as its president. Prior to coming to Gettysburg Wilburn had been, over the years, president of Indiana University of Pennsylvania, CEO of Carnegie Institute in Pittsburgh, and president of Colonial Williamsburg. "This is the beginning of an exciting venture." said Wilburn when he was introduced.(12)

When the visitor center site was announced the Civil War Preservation Trust expressed concerns about the potential for commercialization along the Baltimore Pike which was to serve as the main entrance to the new facility. There were 35 private properties, with road frontage, along a one mile stretch of the highway of which 21 were inside the park boundary but only 6 were protected from development. Of the 14 properties outside the boundary again only 6 were protected. As a start toward preserving these lands the Friends of the National Parks at Gettysburg joined with the Trust to buy a .5 acre site which had been the location of two Union artillery batteries. Purchased for $127,000, the site was considered "historically priceless." In another step to reduce the threat of commercialization the Kinsley Family Foundation donated $300,000 to buy and remove a building at the corner of Hunt Avenue and the Baltimore Pike that had at one time been the location of an automobile dealership and most recently of an RV dealership. Once purchased the land was returned to the open space it had been originally.

But not all the activity at the park was centered around trees, monuments and the visitor center. In October 2000 Rehabitat, a group specializing in rehabilitating birds of prey, released three young barn owls in the McPherson barn just off of U.S. 30 west of town. The site was chosen because the park uses no pesticides or rat and mouse poisons, and the broad, open fields of that area are home to meadow vols, a major food of the owls. The release was especially significant since barn owls are considered a species of special concern in Pennsylvania as their habitat – open farmland – is being steadily lost to development. The least shrew, a tiny mouse-like creature was suffering the same fate for the same reason. Needing open space to survive the little mammal had become nearly extinct in most of Pennsylvania by 1990. Therefore wildlife biologists were delighted to find the tiny creatures on the Eisenhower farm, leading the Pennsylvania Biological Survey to designate the farm as an "important mammal area."

In the meantime the controversy over the park plan to restore the historic appearance of the core of the battlefield by removing non-historic woodlands continued unabated. Patrick Naugle, a leader of the opposition to tree cutting, stated at a meeting of the park Advisory Commission, "The monetary and environmental cost of this rehabilitation cannot be justified by the limited benefit to the few individuals who are familiar with the details of troop movements and the impact of terrain. ...This is not about interpretation. This is about the romantic notion of some historians that this land must appear as it did in 1863." He then presented a petition, signed by over 1800 individuals, opposing the park action and claimed that "opposition is significant and growing... .(13) Tom Vossler, a licensed battlefield guide, viewed the situation differently stating that "visitors are interested in a realistic view of the battle. If this were Gettysburg National Forest or Gettysburg State Park, Pat Naugle's comments would be more germane."(14)

Although Naugle was restrained in his comments others lashed out at the park. One wrote, "Why not include removing the various memorials and all of the statuary since they also were not part of the battlefield's appearance in 1863? Any visitor can learn the reasons why commanders made certain decisions during the battle by making a stop at the Visitor Center before venturing out onto the battlefield. Then those visitors should put their imaginations to work ... .(15) Another complained, "What is this about cutting down trees at Gettysburg Park? Who are these people? Have they no shame?"(16) But when questioned about his position on tree removal Rep. Todd Platts, who represented the district encompassing the battlefield, noted the park's legislated mission "to preserve the hallowed nature of that ground...", and said he believed the tree removal to be "a very deliberate, responsible approach to that restoration effort ... .(17)

But there was no let up in what might be called "the battle of the trees". One writer demanded, "...if they are going to remove trees ... then they should tear up the original roads so visitors can have the mud and dust feel of a dirt road. ... How about those monuments and statues? They were not around in 1863."(18) Removal of the monuments was a frequent theme found in letters from those opposed to the park action. It seemed the writers either did not know, or did not care, that the majority of the monuments on the battlefield had been placed there by the veterans themselves during the 1880's and '90's, many in tribute to their fallen comrades.

Toward the end of the year another disgruntled citizen wrote, "...the whole deal is based on a bare faced lie that the battlefield will be restored to its' appearance of 1863. ...Mr. Latschar must really think that the people visiting the park or living in the area are stupid enough to believe these ... incredibly tall tales. .. Is there no one who can check his drive for power and destruction?"(19) However, referring to the removal of the trees in the Codori-Trostle thicket west of the Pennsylvania monument, another writer pointed out, "For the first time in decades visitors can see from the Weikert house on U.S. Avenue all the way to the distant Codori house and barn as the soldiers would have seen in."(20)

Tree removal was only part of the park restoration plan. For years another high priority had been the removal of non-historic buildings and to that end a big step forward was taken when, in 2001, the Ford car dealership property, on the field of the first day's battle, was sold to the NPS for $1,240,000. In a related transaction the dealership itself was sold to a Baltimore car dealer. Under terms of the entire sale the new owner was given four years to relocate the business after which the existing building and parking lot

Ford dealership removed spring 2006   *photo courtesy of Richard Segars*

would be removed and, using detailed maps, old photographs, and written descriptions, the 6.4 acres of land would be restored to its 1863 appearance. "It was the last major development intrusion on the first day battlefield." said Supt. Latschar.(21)

Visitors hold differing views about intrusions on the battlefield and one expressed his opinion in a brief but succinct letter to the editor of the *Civil War News*. "Well it was my brother-in-law's first time with his family to Gettysburg on the weekend of Sept. 24-26. It was really an eye-opener, or should I say eyesore, when we drove past the car dealership on the first day's battlefield. Sad, sad, sad. Keep it up, maybe we can build a shopping mall on the site where Gen. John Reynolds was killed."(22) Doubtless he would be pleased with the purchase and eventual removal of that "eyesore".

Those who come to Gettysburg National Military Park are often descendants of the men who fought here in 1863. Many of these individuals come here seeking information about their ancestors, but for Raymond Herrington of Texas the visit provided more than just information on a sheet of paper. As he looked at the firearms collection in the museum he noticed a Confederate sharpshooter's rifle bearing a small brass plate with the inscription HCP 1862. Knowing that his great-grandfather, Henry Clay Powell, was a Gettysburg veteran he wondered if the HCP who owned the rifle could possibly have been his forebearer. Months of research by the family, park personnel, the National Archives and the Texas Archives confirmed that the 36 pound rifle did indeed belong to Herrington's great-grandfather who had been wounded in the head on July 2, 1863. The 20 year old Powell had served in the 1st Texas Infantry under Gen. John Bell Hood and had to leave his rifle behind in Devil's Den when he was carried from the field. The mystery of the rightful owner was solved and a delighted Herrington, dressed in woolen Confederate gray, was permitted to hold the rifle. As he did he declared, "This is one of the best things that ever happened to me."(23)

Although the park is primarily a destination for visitors various organizations had, for a number of years, utilized the battlefield for fund raising events but an increasing number of these events, coupled with increasing visitation, led park officials to reconsider this practice. The decision was made to restrict use of the battlefield to those organizations having some affiliation with the park. Under these new standards the YWCA, which hosts nearly 600 participants in Elderhostle battlefield study groups each year, was permitted to continue its annual "Spirit of Gettysburg" 5K run. Initially rejected, the SPCA used a bit of imaginative thinking to gain approval. Their request was based on the story of "Sallie", the mascot of the 11th Pennsylvania Infantry who, two days after the battle was found, thin and thirsty, still guarding the dead and injured of her unit. A statue of this faithful dog is part of the 11th Pennsylvania monument. Thus, since the SPCA is an organization dedicated to animals the reasoning went, the group should be granted continued access to the battlefield. Their argument was accepted by the park administration and the "Dog-a-Thon", renamed the "Liberty Walk", continued uninterrupted.

Periodically those who come to the park evidently feel the need for a battlefield souvenir and so remove items, primarily rocks, from the park. But there have been instances when the rocks seem "cursed". One Texas visitor removed two stones, each about 1½ inches in diameter, from near the Virginia monument but within weeks of his return home he was fighting with his mother-in-law and his marriage was on the rocks. Work was not going well. He had even been ordered out of his car at gun point by police on the way to the airport in Philadelphia, the victim of a fouled up stolen car report. After all this he called the chief of protection at the park, related his story, asked if the officer had ever heard stories about battlefield stones being cursed, and promptly mailed them back. When he contacted the ranger again a month after returning the stones he was asked how things were going. He reported that he and his mother-in-law were getting along again and he had received a promotion at work.

Recognizing the strain on the park budget to maintain the more than 1300 monuments on the battlefield, Pennsylvania state representative Harry Readshaw had set about raising funds for the preservation and upkeep of the 146 Pennsylvania monuments that dot the battlefield, excluding from the funding the huge Pennsylvania state monument. In mid-July 2001 he presented the park with a check for $190,000, part of his goal of $450,000. Earlier Readshaw had given the park a check for $45,505, the final payment on a $165,365 project he had undertaken to provide funding to repair those same monuments. And before the year was over there was need for repair funds when vandals sprayed five monuments with an oily substance in what park security speculated was part of some type of religious ritual.

But vandals were not involved in damage to the Company F, 1st U.S. Sharpshooters monument which had been badly damaged by a falling tree in a 1994 storm. The fluted column had been broken in two and a carved granite eagle on the top had been smashed. However stonecarver Tom Vanacore of Bridgeport, Conn. had carved a new eagle out of Danby white marble and the newly repaired monument was rededicated November 19, 2000

Another monument restoration effort was completed during the summer of 2001. For over 50 years the marker indicating the western terminus of the Union line on Cemetery Ridge, held by the 20th Maine Regiment, had been missing. That situation was remedied on July 2 when a 421 pound marker, carved from New England granite, was dedicated. Two descendants of regiment members attended the ceremony at which NPS Chief Historian emeritus Ed Bearss recalled the history of that famed unit saying that the men of the 20th Maine, "...stood and crouched and bled and died here."(24)

More of Readshaw's funding was needed as time went on. The end of 2003 had seen major damage to two battlefield monuments. In October 80 feet of fencing and a century old cast iron cannon carriage marking the position of Battery E, 1st Rhode Island Light Artillery were destroyed when a motorist plowed first into the board fence and then into the cannon carriage. The driver left the scene but was later identified from a license plate found in the rubble. The cost to repair the fence was estimated to be about $300. However the destroyed cannon carriage would cost between $10,800 and $12,900 to replace. At the site rangers acted quickly to remove the debris since souvenir hunters rapidly began taking pieces. The next month severe damage was done to the 74th Pennsylvania Infantry monument when an out of control SUV rolled over and slammed into it. The impact broke the monument into three pieces and separated the two foundation stones. Park officials hoped to recover the $15,000 to $20,000 needed for repairs from the driver's insurance company.

This disastrous trend continued in early 2004 when the driver of a pickup truck lost control and plunged into the 4th Ohio Infantry monument on the Baltimore Pike. Made of a zinc alloy resembling stone the two foot high marker, put in place in 1887, was damaged beyond repair. "The zinc monuments are much more fragile than the stone monuments," said park spokeswoman Katie Lawhon, "and there are fewer of them."(25) She added that weather was not a factor in the accident. Estimates for recasting the marker ran from $5000 to $10,000. Several granite posts, although uprooted in the incident, suffered little damage.

To make matters worse the park continued to experience major cases of vandalism. In January 2005 two bronze swords were broken off monuments and stolen. One was taken from the 8th Pennsylvania Cavalry monument, the other from the statue of Union general Alexander Hayes and park officials expressed concern that the swords had been stolen for resale on the Civil War items black market. The 8th Pennsylvania Cavalry monument dated back to 1890 while the Hayes statue in Zeigler's Grove was dedicated in 1915. There was also the possibility that the swords could suffer the same fate as a four inch thick bronze plaque stolen from the Gen. William Wells monument several years earlier only to turn up in a Baltimore, Md. scrap yard.

Vandals struck again when eight monuments and signs in the Devil's Den area were hit with paint balls. Fortunately the paint used was water soluble and could be removed without the need for expensive clean up work.

Meanwhile, responding to the call from the park for endowment funds to protect and preserve the more than 1300 battlefield monuments, the Booneville, N.Y. Historical Society set out to raise $5000 for the upkeep and preservation of the monument to the 97th New York Volunteer Infantry known as the Conkling Rifles. The monument had been built at a cost of $1500 and was dedicated July 2, 1889. The fund raising effort having been successfully completed the monument was scheduled to be rededicated in the fall of 2005.

In December 2005 the efforts of Pa. Representative Readshaw, to protect and preserve all the Pennsylvania monuments, paid dividends again. Dubbed Readshaw's Raiders, a group formed to assist Readshaw presented the park with a check for $7100 to repair the 155th Pennsylvania Volunteer monument and soon after placed $7000 in a perpetual trust fund to be used for the monument's future care.

Nor were Civil War groups the only ones concerned about the preservation of the battlefield monuments. School children too contributed to the efforts. In June 2005 a group of more than 50 students from Dalmatia Elementary School near Millersburg, Pa. visited the park wearing "We Love History" T-shirts. While at the park they presented Vic Gavin, supervisory exhibits specialist, with a check for $1000 to be put toward the restoration of

Home Sweet Home Motel removed 2002   *photo courtesy of Richard Segars*

the sword stolen from the 90 year old Gen. Alexander Hays monument. The school had been raising money to restore or preserve historical sites for 21 years according to 5th grade teacher Roseanne Carson. Gavin said of the gift, "...this group of students will help us go a long way toward fixing the monument."(26) The total cost to replace the sword was estimated to be $4000..

Most park visitors know that the Union dead are buried in the National Cemetery but they often ask, "Where are the Confederates buried?" For nine years after the battle their remains lay in poorly marked, sometimes unmarked, graves scattered about the battlefield. But in 1872 an effort begun by members of the Southern Ladies Memorial Association, sought to raise funds to return Southern dead to their own soil. By 1875, using information from those familiar with the battle, 3320 Confederates were returned "home" most of them to Hollywood Cemetery in Richmond, Va. Visitors also ask, "Are there still bodies in the fields that have not been found?" and the answer is "Almost certainly yes." In fact there are nearly 1500 Confederate dead unaccounted for creating the possibility that some of them remain in unknown graves on the battlefield. However out of respect for these soldiers no systematic effort has been made to locate any burial sites.

In June 2002 a significant piece of property was added to the park when the Friends purchased the Home Sweet Home motel on Steinwehr Avenue almost directly across from Ziegler's Grove. The group paid $1.2 million for the 40 room motel and its' accompanying 2 story house which had stood, since the early 1940's, directly on what was the right flank of Pickett's famous charge on July 3, 1863. During the fighting that day the 8th Ohio Infantry took up position on the future motel site and with enfilading fire was able to do great damage to the ranks of the onrushing Confederates. Three Congressional Medals of Honor were awarded as a result of this action and the Park Service plans to erect a marker to these men on the same 1.5 acre tract where the monument to the 8th Ohio still stands. Since the park already owned three lots directly behind the motel its removal opened up a hitherto obstructed vista of the land so important to the troops of both armies. Following the completion of the purchase the Friends resold the property to the Park Service for $930,000, the amount the NPS could pay according to a federal government appraisal.

Directly across the street from the motel site another extensive restoration project was underway. In 1863 Abraham Brien, a free black, owned a small farm near Ziegler's Grove. As the Confederates advanced toward the town Brien and his family fled the area, not to return until after the battle was over. On July 2, Union soldiers occupied the farm and on July 3, used the fences as protection against Pickett's advancing men. After the battle, when the Brien family returned home, they found their house riddled with bullets and their crops ruined. As did many farmers over whose land the battle had been fought, Brien filed a claim with the federal government for damages, amounting in his case, to $1,028. He received $15. In April 2002 the Park Service undertook to restore the Brien house to its original appearance at a cost of $103,000. Finding some of the bullet riddled original siding in the attic, workmen were able to replace the rotted walls of the house with the same type of random width boards used in the 1863 structure. Having served as a pattern for restoration the original boards were placed in the museum for safe keeping.

The Friends also helped preserve another important piece of land when they assisted the park in purchasing a 4 acre property on U.S. 30 west of Gettysburg. It was here, not from what is today's national park, that the first shot in the Battle of Gettysburg was fired. When Ephriam Wisher, owner of the farm came out of his house to see what all the excitement was about a round from a Confederate cannon landed at his feet. The shot failed to explode but the elderly Wisher was so shocked that he took to his bed and died a month later. Future plans for the property include a study to determine how much of the present house dates to 1863. In addition a small parking lot is planned so that visitors wishing to see the site, and now must cross busy U.S. 30 to do so, will have a safe approach to the 1st shot marker placed there in 1886 by Lt. Marcellus Jones and other members of the 8th Illinois Cavalry who fired the first shot.

There had been some good news for the Museum Foundation in October 2001 when Congress appropriated $2½ million of the $5 million it had been estimated would be needed to repair the rapidly deteriorating Cyclorama painting. But it was an estimate destined to increase substantially as professional restorers more closely examined the huge canvas. As time went on the conservators, using digital imaging and microscopic examination, found that deterioration of the painting was more serious than first believed. The manner in which it had been hung had placed it close to the building air conditioning units and as a result, "The painting has been acting as an air filter for 40 years", said Supt. Latschar.(27) Furthermore 6 feet of its length and 15 feet of its height had been removed before the NPS acquired it. "It really suffered a lot before the park service got hold of it", said chief conservator David Olin.(28) He noted that 30 technicians would work on cleaning the massive painting. Cleaning surface dirt and grime from the painting inch by inch was not a "bucket and mop" job, he said.(29) "We're working in detail 8 to 9 inches at a time." he explained.(30) Because of this the cost to restore the painting rose to $9 million, $4 million more than had been originally estimated.

While conservators struggled with the Cyclorama painting the

Friends, in cooperation with the Civil War Preservation Trust, the Conservation Fund, the Adams County Agricultural Board, and the Adams County Land Conservancy, won a preservation victory when, at a cost of $92,000, a conservation easement was acquired on a 45 acre parcel of land adjoining the East Cavalry battlefield. The land had been a staging area for Union cavalry and the original farmhouse was still standing. With that acquisition the Friends, often in cooperation with the other groups, had preserved 420 historic acres since the group was formed in 1989.

East Cavalry field had been the scene of a significant cavalry battle on July 3, 1863 but, separated as it is from the core area of the battlefield, it is a less visited section of the park. Nevertheless its preservation is critical to understanding the full history of the battle. In July 1997 Dan Hoffman, owner of the historic Rummel farm, sold an historic easement on the farm to the Friends and the Civil War Preservation Trust, thus preserving one of the most important areas of that battlefield as well as the original barn which was there in 1863. Over the course of 55 years Hoffman had carefully preserved the barn and when interviewed was asked why he went to all the expense of preserving the old barn rather than build a new one. He replied that he was preserving history. "You don't want to replace a historic barn that has cannon holes in the side and bullet holes in the front." he said.(31)

In the early 1900's battle veterans and historians marked the location of Watson's Union 5th Corps artillery battery by stepping off the distance from what they then believed to be the Trostle lane. Instead they had mistakenly used United States Avenue, at that time a dirt road, as their starting point. However in 2002 the park, using modern technology, located the original lane which had become overgrown and indistinguishable from the land around it. That year, as part of their annual volunteer weekend, the Friends restored the 1863 fence lining the rediscovered lane so that walkers on the battlefield might follow the original 1863 path. Nearly 2700 feet of Virginia worm fence, costing $43,000, had been put in place by the end of the day. But while the historic lane had been restored the battery was left in its designated place.

Toward the end of 2003 a large home on the west side of the Emmitsburg Road was razed as part of the park restoration programs. Built in the 1920's it had been owned by Mary Ellen Sargent from whom the park had purchased the property. A life estate had been granted to the former owner who died in the spring of 2003. Along with the house several dilapidated outbuildings, the remnants of a previous motel, were also razed. With the removal of the buildings, trees, and overgrown bushes, the site was seeded and returned to its 1860's farm field condition. Once this action was completed only two non-historic houses remained on that section of the battlefield.

Again the Ottenstein tower made news when U.S. Middle District

Mary Ellen Sargent property removed 2003   *photo courtesy of Richard Segars*

Court Judge Sylvia Rambo handed down her decision on the tower's value. The tower owners were to receive $3.92 million and land owner Hans Enggren was awarded $1.21 million. Asked to comment after hearing of the decision Enggren said, "I think the best comment is no comment."(32) However this was not the end of the controversy as the Park Service appealed the decision to the Third U.S. Court of Appeals in Philadelphia.

The borough of Gettysburg had received some bad news in January when the estimate to restore the Wills house jumped from $5.2 million to $6.2 million, which raised serious concerns among borough officials. Because of the increased cost borough council approached the NPS about selling the building to the federal government. The NPS offer of $550,000 was $75,000 more than the borough's appraisal and with no federal funding in sight for rehabilitation the council felt it had no choice but to sell. "We just can't saddle the taxpayers of the borough with it." said council president Ted Streeter.(33) The deed transferring the Wills house to the NPS was completed March 23, 2004 at which time Gettysburg mayor William Troxel said. "They're going to develop it and we're going to watch in appreciation."(34)

As the year continued the park suffered a $338,000 funding shortfall due to budget cuts and another congressionally mandated, but only partially funded, salary increase for all federal employees. Volunteers helped take up the slack by contributing 44,690 hours of work which Katie Lawhon called, "A margin of excellence"(35) (That phrase was updated in 2006 by Supt. Latschar to "a margin of survival") and the problems continued to grow. With over 1300 monuments, 400 cannons, 148 buildings and more than 26 miles of roads all needing constant attention, in addition to the summer park mowing schedule, lack of qualified personnel to do the work exacerbated a situation which grew worse by the year. In 2003 eight positions remained unfilled when Supt. Latschar instituted a hiring freeze due to lack of funds. By the beginning of 2006 permanent employees at the park had dropped from 90 in 2001 to 77. Seasonal employees, who numbered 28 in 2001 were down to 5, and the maintenance backlog had risen from #36.4 million in 2001 to $49.7 million in 2006.

By 2001 the Museum Foundation had raised its fund raising goal from the original $39 million to $52 million and the goal would reach $95 million by 2002. $10 million of that amount was not for construction but was to be set aside as an endowment for future care and upkeep of the building. As for the objectives set for the museum Bob Wilburn explained, "The real challenge here is to make the museum not an experience in and of itself, but a gateway for going out on the battlefield and into town. You don't want it to be a self-contained story that begins and ends at the visitor center." In response to concerns that cars would eventually be banned from the battlefield Wilburn stated that while bus tours would be encouraged to minimize traffic on the field, "We will not, in any way, advocate eliminating the auto."(36)

When the design of the proposed new visitor center was unveiled there was some concern by members of the public. But architect Jaquelin T. Robertson said the idea was to design "...something that would look like it belongs there naturally and didn't look like a bunch of big boxes left there the night before."(37) Upon seeing it borough president Ted Streeter expressed his pleasure. "I was very surprised with the design, I think it's a very forward looking and compatible design."(38)

In defending the increased cost of the project from $39 million to $95 million Foundation vice-president Susan Helm attributed it to "an additional $10 million in construction costs, plus several millions more for off site road and intersection improvements and more expensive "exhibitry". The facility is larger than originally planned she said, "...in order to provide additional space to accommodate peak crowds."(39)

However members of a congressional oversight committee expressed alarm over the escalating cost estimates for the new building. As a result committee members called a hearing for March 21, 2002 and voiced skepticism that the Museum Foundation could raise such a large sum of money from private donations. "This hearing will be largely about fleshing out the details." said a spokesman for U.S. Rep George Radanovich (R Calif). (40) Eric Uberman, longtime foe of the new visitor center, announced he would attend the hearing, insisting it was important that the Foundation and the NPS be held accountable. "If no one's held accountable they can do whatever it is they want to." he declared.(41)

In a briefing paper the committee declared, "...the public, and particularly the local community's concerns have never been adequately addressed ... . The sub-committee is concerned that it appears that the NPS and the Foundation do not believe they are constrained by the commitments made ... and that there is no limit on the extent of the proposal."(42) However Paul Hoffman from the Department of the Interior attributed the increase in costs to four factors: 1) general inflation; 2) increasing space in the new facility; 3) enhanced exhibits; 4) the cost of fund raising and the proposed $10 million endowment. He assured committee members that the Foundation had identified 52 prospective donors who had the capacity to give $160 million total to the project, adding that "the Museum Foundation may not break ground for construction until it has sufficient funds in hand to complete the work."(43)

In his testimony Foundation president Bob Wilburn explained that, in addition to a larger building and $10 million endowment, the new figures included "$4.4 million for off site improvements such as overflow parking..., the responsibility to raise $1 million for an interpretive film ..., and $5.5 million in building and exhibit fit-out costs that otherwise would have been passed on to visitors."(44)

U.S. Rep. Todd Platts testified, "I fully support the National Park Service's plan to restore the Gettysburg battlefield to its 1863 appearance while building a state-of-the-art museum and visitor center."(45) And U.S. Senator Rick Santorum (R Pa), testifying in support of the Foundation's plan stated, "We are trying to create a showcase of public-private partnerships here." He added, "A lot of plans were being thrown around and there was no shortage of public hearings."(46) Despite all this U.S. Rep. James Hansen (R Utah) said in a written statement, "The public's concerns, particularly the local community's, have never been adequately addressed."(47)

In a letter to the editor one Pennsylvania resident wrote, "Now they're going to allow this monstrosity of the Visitor Center to intrude on the site. Let's hope the cost, which is already spiraling out of control, will kill the monster."(48) And Eric Uberman, still on the attack chimed in, "They're looking to garnish millions and millions of dollars from tourists by establishing a virtual monopoly inside the park. It's unconscionable."(49) Another Steinwehr Avenue merchant expressed his displeasure, "Does the Park Service really care about local business in Gettysburg? My answer is NO! They never have ..."(50) But a visitor from Texas wrote, "...locals must remember that the battlefield is not there for their profit and aggrandizement. ... this is not 'your' battlefield, it is sacred ground owned by all Americans."(51)

While all this was going on the Pennsylvania monument was closed to all visitors while extensive, and badly needed, repairs were being done. Deterioration of the concrete supports under the monument posed a severe threat to the stability of the monument, a supporting ring in the dome was in questionable condition, and weather damage to the skeleton of the structure, plus water damage to concrete behind, and under the stairwell leading to the observation platform, all presented safety hazards. Dedicated September 27, 1910, the monument contains a statue of President Lincoln plus others of prominent Pennsylvania political and military leaders. On its exterior surfaces are bronze plaques bearing the names of the more than 34,000 Pennsylvania soldiers who served in the Gettysburg campaign. Repairs were estimated to cost $1.7 million with $1 million coming from the state of Pennsylvania. The Friends had agreed to raise the remainder of the funds and hoped to rededicate the monument in November 2002. But the extensive repair work needed extended the completion date until the spring of 2003.

Also on the battlefield one of the sights frequently pointed out to visitors is the large hole in the southern brick wall of the Trostle barn on United States Avenue. The farm had been part of the battle line of Union general Daniel Sickles, and as such was the scene of heavy fighting on July 2, 1863. The hole was created by Confederate artillery supporting advancing Southern troops. Direct descendants of AbrahamTrostle, owner of the farm, had taken care of the cannon ball that had damaged their ancestral home until a gathering of the group on the battlefield in 2001. At that time the cannon ball was presented to the park for safe keeping. During the presentation George B. Trostle, a fourth generation keeper of the iron ball, remarked, "It has been passed down from generation to generation."(52)

Again the park tree removal plan came under attack. At a town meeting U.S. Rep. Todd Platts replied to a question about "the stupidity of cutting down 350 acres of trees." by saying, I do think there's some merit to fully experiencing what our troops experienced in 1863."(53) However the *Hanover Sun* took another point of view in an editorial, "The '1863' argument has been put forth ad nauseam by the National Park Service, and frankly it's an insult to the public's intelligence."(54) But one of its readers replied that, while initially opposed, "After learning more about the plan I accepted it."(55) Still another wrote, "People of the area must remember that Gettysburg is not a recreational park. It is not a nature park. It is an historical park and every effort must be made to preserve and accurately interpret it."(56)

In another controversy related to battlefield restoration 77 year old Dion Neutra, son of Richard Neutra, architect of the Cyclorama building, continued his efforts to prevent bulldozers from leveling the building. "I do intend to chain myself there." he declared adding, "The National Park Service makes it look like 1863 after you take our building out? What about all the other crap on the battlefield?"(57)

As restoration efforts continued the appearance of the battlefield slowly began to change. Long missing historic fences were being returned to their original sites, cattle were removed from areas where visitor/cattle confrontations could occur, once cultivated fields were no longer the scene of large modern farm machinery planting and harvesting crops. Under the federal Conservation Reserve Enhancement Program (CREP) farmers, who had before utilized the fields for crops, were now paid to plant grasses and then leave the fields alone. This created a rather ragged look on some portions of the battlefield, especially in front of the North Carolina monument, which led to complaints about its appearance. Supt. Latschar admitted that there was "a nice field of weeds" growing there since that area had not yet been planted in grass. This was scheduled to be done in the fall as part of the 361 acres of the battlefield that qualified under the CREP program. Latschar also noted that in 1863 the Pickett's charge area was primarily "subsistence farming" with small fields and small herds of animals. "when we get the historic fences up and we have nine fields instead of one, people will understand."(58)

Along with restoration of the Pickett's charge fields the park began to replant 160 acres of historic orchards which had been lost over time. The Friends donated $6000 toward the purchase of fruit tree seedlings which would create 12½ acres of new orchards while the eventual cost of restoring the entire 160 acres was estimated at $94,000. Tree varieties were not selected for their productivity – the park had no intention of going into the fruit business – but for their hardiness and disease resistance.

In addition to providing tree seedlings the Friends purchased the 9.3 acre Kump property near the Slyder farm several hundred yards to the east of the Emmitsburg Road. The land was the scene of fierce fighting on July 2, 1863 and the property was the last remaining private in-holding in that part of the park. A modular home and several outbuildings were removed and the property turned over to the park in 2005.

In the fall of that year it was decided to remove all of the trees in the famous Peach Orchard and rehabilitate the orchard completely. Over half of the 25 year old trees had died and the remainder were dying due to a virus spread to the trees by microscopic worms in the soil. Therefore the entire orchard was bulldozed, the diseased trees removed, and the ground left in grass for two years to allow the worms to die off naturally rather than use pesticides to kill them. At the end of the two year period the orchard will be replanted and the Friends, who are financing the entire project, will be able to look forward to "pick-your-own" days, an event that annually raised about $20,000 for the organization.

Unnoticed by anyone except those directly involved, was the return to the battlefield of an animal species last seen there 20 years ago. The Nature Conservancy, using a Legacy grant from the Department of Defense, and in cooperation with park officials, reintroduced the regal fritillary butterfly to the park in September 2005. They were brought to the park from the only remaining population in the U.S. at Fort Indiantown Gap near Annville, Pa. Although missing from the park for over two decades this rare butterfly existed on the battlefield in 1863 and it was hoped that the newly established grasslands in the park would provide suitable habitat for this butterfly species that had been observed in the Wheatfield as recently as 1980.

There were groups other than the Friends who also were deeply committed to battlefield preservation, among them the members of the Gettysburg Equestrian Historical Society. During his time in Gettysburg President Eisenhower had an extensive horse trail marked through the park and increasingly this trail was being used not only by individual riders but for commercially guided horseback tours of the battlefield. This constant use had created severe erosion on some sections of the trail while steep descents on other sections became a matter of concern after the fall of several horses and riders. So it was with particular interest that Society members heard of plans to rehabilitate the horse trail by closing some sections where erosion and dangerous descents were the most prominent, and relocating the trail to utilize historic lanes present in 1863. In June 2003 the park embarked on a three phase plan which would also provide loop trails, including a new trail in the Devil's Den area, all using a weather resistant and highly durable surface that would eliminate closing the horse trail during periods of prolonged wet weather. In the past Society members had built bridges over park streams for the horse trail, removed downed trees and brush from the trail, and in general assisted the park with trail maintenance. Now, pleased that rumors of permanently closing the horse trail were unfounded, the Society added $10,000 to the $70,000 the park allotted for trail construction allowing for the purchase of some much needed heavy equipment.

Two years after the effort to restore all 413 cannon carriages had begun, work on the 100th carriage was completed. After having been on the field for over 100 years the cast iron carriages, which had replaced the original wooden ones, were showing major deterioration. Some had developed serious cracks and most had as many as 30 coats of lead paint on them. At a cost of 120 man hours and $4850 each, the repaired and restored carriages were returned to their exact positions on the battlefield. Funded by the Friends, it was hoped that the entire project would be completed in five years, but it was a hope that would not be realized.

In a report in 2001 that was cause for alarm the financial analysis of park finances showed that 90% of the park's budget was being consumed by labor costs. Federal pay raises mandated by Congress, without sufficient funding to cover the entire cost, meant that the difference had to be made up from the park's operating budget. The park Business Plan stated, "... this trend has reached the point where the park cannot afford to remain fully staffed. ... As a result the park must either rely upon its' partners to fund some of its basic operations, or forego some operations entirely."(59) As time went on the situation did not change so that by 2004 of all the problems the park faced none was greater than continuing budget shortfalls. The park no longer had money to buy property within its boundary from willing sellers, properties which could be developed for any purpose including commercialization. "The bottom line is we're broke." said Supt. Latschar(60) Lack of funding was also affecting the repair and restoration of the deteriorating cannon carriages as qualified personnel left for positions elsewhere and could not be replaced. Rather than restoring 60 carriages per year as had been originally anticipated staffing losses had reduced that number to fewer than 30 per year and the backlog continued to grow at the rate of one per month. Carriages which had been sand blasted to remove the layers of lead paint had to be stored in an open shed where they were slowly rusting from lack of new paint. "It's almost useless." said Dave Drier, chief of maintenance in discouragement.(61) Cuts in park staff, which administrators in Washington, D.C. decreed should be referred to as "service level adjustments" hit Gettysburg hard.(62)

Service wide all parks were suffering, yet in 2003 another Congressionally mandated pay raise of 4.1% for all federal employees had, as before, not been covered by appropriated funds. At Gettysburg 66% of the raise had to come from the park operating budget. In 2004 it was more of the same but worse when 75% of the pay raise was not funded. That meant a $475,000 loss in operating money which in turn translated into the loss of 12 full time employees, including security personnel, and 10 seasonal rangers who formerly worked during the period of greatest visitation. Positions on the park staff left open by retirement, or personnel leaving for other reasons, were not filled. To meet its needs just to stay even with essential upkeep Gettysburg needed an additional $3.6 million. Although the park and its Visitor Center remained open, "What I cannot guarantee is the quality of your visit." said Supt. Latschar.(63)

The only bright spot in an otherwise grim financial picture was an announcement by the Museum Foundation that it had raised $64 million of the $95 million needed for the construction of the new museum/visitor center and complete rehabilitation of the Zeigler's Grove battle line. However the Foundation also declared that construction on the building would not begin until $74 million in funding was assured.

For years it had been assumed that the spot where Lincoln stood when giving his Gettysburg Address was near the Soldiers National Monument in the National Cemetery although some had argued for a location closer to where the New York monument now stands. However in 2001, after carefully examining pictures taken during the ceremony, park chief historian Kathy Harrison determined that the actual site was east of the generally accepted location, on land that is today part of Evergreen Cemetery. Initially identification of the new site was met with skepticism but when noted photographer and historian William Frassanito supported Harrison's research most of the controversy ended. Now a marker in the National Cemetery indicates to visitors that the 1863 speakers platform was "in the Evergreen Cemetery to your left". But there are no plans to otherwise mark the site in part to protect Evergreen Cemetery graves from hosts of visitors wanting to stand on the actual spot where Lincoln stood. Harrison was in complete agreement with the decision saying, "... it's not the site that matters, it's the speech that matters."(64)

A growing number of organizations had joined the efforts to provide endowment funds for the upkeep of park monuments and in May 2002 the Irish Cultural Society had presented the park with a check for $3500 for the perpetual care of the statue of Father William Corby. Irish soldiers in the Union army played an essential part in the battle and Irish organizations next sought funds for the preservation of the Col. Patrick O"Rorke, 140th New York Infantry Brigade, monument. Successful in both these endeavors, efforts were then begun to provide endowment funds for the upkeep of the two Pennsylvania Irish monuments, the 69th Pennsylvania Infantry and the 116th Pennsylvania Infantry.

In early January 2004 work was begun to restore the 4th Ohio Volunteer monument which had been dedicated in 1887. The 32 foot high monument had been made of white bronze, a weak type of metal and as a result the monument began to tilt from the weight of the column and the figure at the top. In the interest of public safety the column and the soldier's statue had been removed and placed in storage leaving only the base on Cemetery Ridge. To repair the entire monument so that it might be replaced on the battlefield the Ohio Sons of Union Veterans raised nearly $25,000 to pay for its restoration.

Although not monuments as such the U.S. War Department, which at the time managed the battlefield, had placed a series of ten informational tablets on West Confederate Avenue in 1895. Another nine tablets were located on Cemetery Hill along the Baltimore Pike. The tablets, which outlined the scenes of fighting in the two areas, were removed in the 1970's along with their stone bases because of traffic concerns. They, along with the many monuments on the battlefield, were considered part of the commemorative features of the battlefield and for this reason the decision was made to return them to their positions. However traffic remained a major concern so the tablets on West Confederate Avenue were moved about 100 yards south of their original positions near the Fairfield Road. Those on the Baltimore Pike were reset facing away from that road so that visitors would have to park and walk to the tablets to read them rather than stop along that very busy highway.

Safety was also the driving force behind a park decision to place traffic lights at the intersection of U.S. 30 and Reynolds Avenue west of town. In addition the speed limit was lowered from 40 mph to 25 mph. This was met with resentment by some local residents, one of whom wrote, "It seems that tourists (occasional visitors) garner all the respect and consideration when decisions are made about traffic. The local citizen (full time resident) appears to be taken for granted and relegated to a second class citizen. Local residents shouldn't be punished daily to accommodate the tourists."(65)

But far more vehement protests arose when the park administration announced in April 2005 that it was considering changing the closing hours of the battlefield from 10 p.m. to sunset – a practice followed by a number of other national parks. The proposal was brought about by concerns over vandalism, visitor safety, and cuts in the budget which necessitated a reduction in the number of law enforcement rangers available for patrol duty. The proposal was open for public comment for a 30 day period and brought about a storm of objections. Some ghost hunters predicted that the park would lose 100,000 visitors during the first year alone. On the other hand Mark Nesbitt, owner of "Ghosts of Gettysburg" said, "... This is not going to affect ghost stories. Of the 600 stories, 45% occur during the day. ... As far as paranormal investigations, there are plenty of places in the town of Gettysburg. Most people don't realize the town itself was a battlefield."(66)

Ghosts not withstanding there were many other voices raised in protest. "We moved to Gettysburg primarily to enjoy the battlefield's facilities and I think the Park Service is doing us and others who enjoy the battlefield a great disservice by the imposition of restrictive hours."(67) wrote one local resident. Another declared, "Once again it seems the Gettysburg National Park Service, under the dictatorial rule of Dr. John Latschar is planning yet another in your face move to the people who live in Adams county. ... To be honest I believe them wanting to change the park hours is just 'lazy' law enforcement.

I myself plan to spend more time on the battlefield after dark, and I invite many others to do the same."(68) Others threatened to cease coming to Gettysburg if the park hours were changed, "...lest we sit bored in a motel room once the park closes."(69) Another opponent wrote, "It is unfair to assume that changing the park hours will preserve the park when the people who cause the problems would continue to go there after dark anyway."(70) Over 200 letters were received from the public and after considering their input the park administration announced a compromise: from November 1 through March 31 the park would close 3 hours early, with hours from 6 a.m. to 7 p.m.; from April 1 through October 31 the familiar 6 a.m. to 10 p.m. hours would be continued.

Fund raising for the new museum/visitor center received a major boost when, in April 2005, Philadelphia philanthropist H.F. Lenfest offered a $4.5 million challenge grant requiring the Foundation to match his funds with another $4.5 million in new gifts. If this all-or-nothing challenge was met the Foundation would realize an additional $9 million in funding. In May the Foundation announced a $3 million gift from the Ford Motor Company and because of this, coupled with other donations, the Foundation announced in July that the conditions of the Lenfest challenge had been met and thus the Foundation would receive his $4.5 million gift.

Five years after its' demolition the Ottenstein tower still remained a center of controversy. A three judge panel of the Third District Court of Appeals threw out the $6.6 million judgement awarded the tower owners and owners of the land on which it had been built. According to the panel the value of the tower and land might have been overstated by as much as $2.7 million. For this reason the court returned the issue to the lower court for further analysis. Hans Enggren, owner of the land expressed his disappointment with both the ruling and the length of time it took the court to reach it. "All of this is amazing" he said, "They shouldn't be able to treat people like this."(71)

Volunteers are an essential part of park operations, providing services that a short handed staff have no time to perform. Therefore, as part of the battlefield rehabilitation program the Friends took on the task of replacing the historic fences in the Pickett's charge section of the battlefield. "We wanted to get across that it wasn't one big pasture ... that there were a lot of fields and it was difficult for the Confederates to cross. The goal is to allow the public to see how the soldiers saw it in 1863." said Katie Lawhon.(72) A mile of fencing was restored by volunteers from the Friends participating in one of their periodic work days on the battlefield.

On May 22, 2005 another group of volunteers from the Greater Pittsburgh Civil War Roundtable spent the day trimming grass, cutting brush and pulling weeds around the 155th Pennsylvania Volunteers monument on Little Round Top. Afterward they recalled some of their experiences as visitors observed their activities. "One woman asked me if I was stealing trees." said one member, while another recalled talking with two older women who were covering the park on foot. "They weren't really interested in the Civil War but said the battlefield was a great place to find mushrooms."(73) Another volunteer, not a part of the Pittsburgh group described working in the Visitor Center parking lot and approaching a car parked in the roadway. When asked if he needed help the rather bewildered driver replied, "Yes. We're looking for West Virginia."

That same year 30 acres of non-historic woods were being cleared from the Devil's Den area. Supt. Latschar termed it, "the most interesting" tree clearing project of the entire 576 acres slated for removal. He noted that Pickett's charge is easily understood because the land has remained open. Now the same will be true of the Confederate advance under Gen. John Bell Hood on July 2, 1863. The difficulty of the terrain had lain hidden beneath a more than 60 year old covering of brush and trees. Rocks, gullies, and stone walls which had split the advancing Confederate line and disrupted the push toward Devil's Den, were now being revealed. Once the area was cleared "Visitors can stand on South Confederate Avenue and see what Hood's boys saw when they stepped out.... . It's going to be a whole new perspective." said Latschar, adding that people complained about taking shade trees out. "But shade trees at Devil's Den are about as appropriate as shade trees on Normandy beaches."(74)

As was to be expected some local residents were less than enthusiastic about the tree removal. "Once the battlefield trees are hacked, think of how unspectacular our barren, hallowed ground will look. Our soon-to-be timberless acreage of rolling ridges and captivating views will appear ghastly sickening and morbidly abnormal." wrote one.(75) Another complained, "In regards to the Gettysburg National Parks plan to mutilate 500 more acres of trees from the public land I would first like to say this is public land not John Latschar's private domain. ... This administration of the Gettysburg National Park should be charged and prosecuted with mutilation of public property and endangering wildlife. This project, like others, adds to the maintenance dollars that are stolen from the pockets of taxpayers."(76) And again the frequently heard complaint was raised by a local resident, "The truth about the battlefield will not be verified until the monuments are removed. Every single one of them."(77) To these and other complaints one local citizen replied, "The park is not an arboretum, it is not a bird and wildlife sanctuary, and it certainly is not intended ... to have a role in sustaining the property values of its neighbors. ...Some people in town seem to think that the purpose of the battlefield is to provide local residents with a manicured country park for hiking and biking ... . It is not the property of a handful of local landowners with private and personal agendas for it."(78)

But such reasoning fell on deaf ears when it became known that 27 acres of non-historic woods on West Confederate Avenue would be removed. Some residents of the development bordering the park just to the west of those woods complained that removal of the woods would take away their privacy and reduce their property values. One resident declared, "If they take out the trees there will be standing water which will be a breeding habitat for mosquitoes and the West Nile virus."(79) Another resident of the development said "I find it most interesting that the people who make the decisions weren't born here, grew up here, or live here."(80) He added that he remembered playing on the battlefield as a child but because of the changes could now barely bring himself to visit it. "You're ripping out a part of my childhood. It doesn't look like it did when I was a kid."(81)

Finally the long awaited day for the Museum Foundation arrived when the ground breaking ceremony for the new museum/visitor center took place on June 2, 2005. Among the speakers was U.S. Senator Rick Santorum (R Pa) who had been a steadfast supporter of both the new facility and of efforts to restore the battlefield as much as possible to its 1863 appearance. "This was the most important battle, in the most important war, in the most important country in the world." he told his listeners. "It deserves something special."(82) It was anticipated that the Foundation would operate the facility for 20 years after which both the land and the building would be donated, debt free, to the National Park Service. Barring unforeseen circumstances the building was due to open in 2008.

However not everyone shared Santorum's enthusiasm. Eric Uberman continued his longtime opposition. "The infrastructure that was set up to serve the tourists is not being considered in the move." he complained. "The visitor will not have the option to walk from downtown to that site. It's land locked. They've set up a virtual monopoly."(83)

As the year drew to a close work on the museum/visitor center continued. Guinn Run, a small creek through that section of the battlefield, had been dammed to create two ponds for paddle boats when the Fantasyland amusement park was in operation on the site. Now, in the first phase of work, the dams had been removed, the creek restored to its original course, and 1? acres of wetlands created to compensate for wetlands lost to parking areas and access roads during construction.

2006 opened on a familiar theme as the battle over tree removal continued without letup. Residents long used to seeing trees along Oak Ridge and behind the Peace Light monument were appalled when those non-historic trees were removed. Referring to the exit lane from the Peace Light one wrote, "That drive used to be a beautiful tree lined lane. Now it is completely barren. I drive past it every day and can hardly bear to look at it."(84) Another resident complained, "I am horrified and sickened by the removal of the trees along the ridge near the Peace Light ... . Let the trees alone and use your limited resources to take care of what you already have. For heaven's sake, enough is enough."(85) But in reply another resident wrote, "Under federal law money allocated for one purpose – in this case – landscape rehabilitation – cannot be used for any other purpose. ...any such allocated funds not used must be returned to the federal treasury." The writer then went on to say, "There can be little doubt that where trees have been removed the battlefield lacks some of the beauty it previously acquired through benign neglect but ...on July 1, 2, 3, 1863 the field had no beauty whatsoever. Nor was the land later preserved to be beautiful but to honor those who experienced its' stark horror... , and if in its' bareness it reminds us of just how horrible war is so much the better."(86)

Animals are frequently abandoned on the battlefield by heartless owners but on January 4, in what the rangers called "an unconscionable act of cruelty" seven puppies, only a week old, were left in a milk crate on East Cavalry field to die of cold and starvation. Found by a local resident who heard them whimpering and turned them over to the park, all the rangers could do was place them with the local SPCA and hope for the best. In this case at least, the story had a happy ending when Candy and Steve Gebhart of New Oxford, Pa. adopted the entire litter of three female and four male puppies.

The park too was the beneficiary of a true act of conscience when, on February 17, it received a package from Canada containing a bolt which, according to the anonymous sender, had been removed from a cannon in 1968. An unsigned e-mail to the park explained that "The reason for taking it is long and inexcusable." and it was the sender's desire that it be returned to the park.(87) The value of the bolt was estimated to be $20 but the value of the act was priceless.

On the night of February 15 occurred one of the worst acts of vandalism in the history of the park. Three monuments, the 114th Pennsylvania Volunteers, the 11th Massachusetts Volunteers, and the 4th New York (Smith's) artillery battery were heavily damaged by vandals who pulled the monuments over, and in the case of Smith's Battery, pulled the toppled monument down the road. The 114th Pennsylvania monument, topped by the figure of a Zouave infantryman, stood in front of the Sherfy house on the Emmitsburg Road. The monument was pulled over and the 500 pound statue fell onto an historic decorative wrought iron fence in front of the house. The 11th Massachusetts monument, on the Emmitsburg Road at Sickles Avenue, which had a sculptured arm and hand holding a sword at the top, was pulled over, the arm destroyed and the hand and sword stolen. But the worst damage was done to the 4th New York Battery on Houck's Ridge above Devil's Den. Here the vandals not only pulled down the bronze statue of a Union artilleryman but dragged it 162 feet, in the process breaking off the head, which was stolen.

State Representative Harry Readshaw, who had long been active in securing funds for the upkeep of Pennsylvania monuments called the vandalism, "A planned, heinous act. If they are willing to do something as repulsive as this, what else are they capable of doing next?"(88) He challenged Civil War preservationists in the three states affected to raise funds for the repair of the statues as the park had no such money available. The cost of repairs to the monuments were estimated to be: the 114th Pennsylvania - $8000; the 11th Massachusetts - $20,000; and the 4th New York Battery - $35,000 to $50,000. The damaged monuments were erected between 1885 and 1888 when Union veterans returned for their dedications and before Gettysburg had been declared a national park.

Vandalized monument 4th New York Artillery   *photo courtesy of GNMP*

The Friends joined with the Museum Foundation, Adams County Crime Stoppers, the Gettysburg Civil War Roundtable, and the Licensed Battlefield Guides to offer a $31,000 reward for the arrest of the vandals. These groups were joined by local residents David and Jennifer LeVan who added $5000 to the reward money and also offered the Friends $25,000 to be put toward the repair of the monuments.

On a more positive note Federal Judge Christopher Conner granted the Park Service access to the building adjoining the Wills house, access which was essential to repairing a common wall between the two buildings. Prior to his verdict John and Antionette Koscinski, owners of the building in question, had refused to grant the NPS entry to their property forcing the Park Service to seek relief in court. Conner described the Wills house condition in his memorandum: "The chimney is collapsing under its own weight, the roof is sagging, bricks are missing from the common wall in the attic, and beams and rafters are rotting. In the basement the common wall is crumbling into piles of dust. The electrical wiring is antiquated and substandard, water pipes are suspended from the ceiling by duct tape, and the property lacks a firewall to afford protection to the adjoining properties." Conner then declared, "The time to begin preservation of this significant landmark is upon us."(89) Park Service officials estimated that the renovations would provide $130,000 in benefits to the Koscinski property.

In another court action the U.S. Middle District Court in Harrisburg, Pa. finally put an end to the Ottenstein tower controversy when a judgement was handed down awarding $3.932 million to the tower and land owners combined. It was left to those two parties to decide how the money would be allocated between them. Thus after five contentious years the situation was resolved and the park could turn its full attention to other matters.

The coming months and years are certain to hold more controversies, certainly over battlefield rehabilitation, and possibly others as yet unforeseen. On the other hand construction of the long awaited, and badly needed, new museum/visitor center was under way with 2008 the hoped for completion date. As the 1863 scene continues to emerge with the removal of the existing Visitor Center and Cyclorama buildings along with other non-historic buildings and woodlands the battlefield will, when work is completed, have been returned to a landscape familiar to the men in blue and those in gray who sacrificed so much on this holy ground.

Chapter 10

"steadfast leadership and persistent dedication"

As spring 2006 arrived significant changes were evident on the battlefield. The Ford garage on the Biglerville Road passed into history and open grassland restored that portion of the battlefield to its' 1863 appearance. Meanwhile non-historic tree removal continued on various sections of the battlefield much to the consternation of some opponents of the project. It was obvious that the "battle of the trees" would continue into the foreseeable future although one resident, in defending the tree removal quoted President Dwight D. Eisenhower who said, "I think it is a pity this one piece of terrain is not kept so that youngsters can see it nearly like it was in 1863." (1)

Federal budget cuts continued to have a negative impact on park maintenance as projects were postponed, employee positions eliminated and the purchasing of needed supplies curtailed even further while the backlog of essential work grew to over $13 million. The park had already lost 13 permanent employees and 23 seasonal ones in the preceding five years with further cuts anticipated. "This is the reason that volunteers are absolutely critical.", said Superintendent Latschar. "We used to say that they were our margin of excellence. Now we say that they are our margin of survival." (2)

Meanwhile a new partnership emerged as the Friends of the National Parks at Gettysburg and the Gettysburg National Battlefield Museum Foundation merged to form what is now called simply the Gettysburg Foundation. It was for each a step forward, increasing the operational efficiency and fund raising capabilities of both groups.

Although groundbreaking for the new visitor center/museum had taken place in June, 2005 actual construction had to await a series of state and local permits. The result was that work on the new building did not begin until the spring of 2006.

As construction got underway on the new visitor center, efforts continued to repair the three monuments badly damaged by vandals in February. Pennsylvania state representative Harry Readshaw was successful in raising $7,325 to repair the 114th Pennsylvania Volunteers monument. The excess funds beyond the $5,800 needed to repair this monument were allocated to help repair the badly damaged 4th New York Battery and the 11th Massachusetts monuments. Beginning in 1997 Readshaw had continued to raise funds for the repair and upkeep of the more than 140 Pennsylvania monuments on the battlefield. Unfortunately the culprits who inflicted the 2008 damage have yet to be caught.

On very rare occasions an event takes place on the battlefield that is neither welcome nor approved by the National Park Service but for which, under the U.S. Constitution, a permit cannot be denied. Such was the case in July, 2006 when the Ku Klux Klan scheduled a protest demonstration for September 2. Exercising their constitutional right to free speech, as they had earlier at the Antietam National Battlefield, the Klan secured a permit to gather on federal land. In opposition to the Klan local community organizations held "unity rallies" while counter demonstrations by the Sons of Confederate veterans, Daughters of the Confederacy, and the 37th Texas Cavalry reenactors took place a short distance from the Klan activities. U.S. Park Police from Washington, D.C., Pennsylvania State Police, and local law enforcement officers supplemented the park security force to ensure visitor safety and prevent violence. When the day arrived the event went off without any major incident and both local citizens and government officials breathed a sign of relief when the 30 white robed visitors left.

In July tree cutting resumed on the battlefield, this time along West Confederate Avenue. Here the intent was to open up the view the Confederates had of the Union positions across the valley on Cemetery Ridge in 1863. Due to the unrestricted growth of non-historic trees the Confederate artillery appeared to be shooting into dense woods rather than across an open valley. But historical accuracy did not quell the anger of local citizens opposed to tree removal as part of the battlefield restoration program. One citizen wrote, "Does the Park Service really want to contribute to this devastation and consequent loss of birds, plants and mammals? And finally the aesthetics –need I say more? I believe the time has come to maintain what we currently have in the park and stop the impossible task of trying to restore its' appearance to that of 1863." (3)

However another writer declared, "…it is a marvelous transformation… . Now the open land lies as it should have been… . What was confused is now revealed. I agree with what Superintendent Latschar, the National Park Service, and the hundreds of volunteers have done to give us a fully restored battlefield. It is in the interests of all." (4)

While construction of the new visitor center/museum got under way restoration of the Cyclorama painting continued. A staff of 20 workers, including several conservation experts from Poland, spent long hours under the direction of chief conservator David Olin repairing the huge painting. "Now it's hung like a shower curtain.", said Olin (5), noting also that the 14 original panels of the painting had been cut into 27 pieces. He added that when completely restored the painting would hang in a parabolic shape as was originally intended, with a diorama at its' base to create a three dimensional effect. Not only had the painting been improperly hung but lack of a controlled environment had caused severe damage to both the painted surface and the fabric of the painting. But Olin's team painstakingly cleaned the painting inch by inch, repairing ripped sections and replacing the backing no longer able to bear the 1.5 ton weight of the 365 foot long, 42 foot high painting. As they progressed features, long hidden by dirt and grime, were revealed and the 125 year old painting was slowly brought back to its' original glory.

In a major departure from the usual construction practices the new visitor center/museum is, for the most part, heated and cooled using a geothermal system of 168 wells drilled 550 feet deep connected by closed pipes containing glycol which circulates through the pipes and transfers the constant 55° temperature of the earth into the cooling and heating systems. Covered by the parking lots the pipes are not visible to the public. The building is also serviced by a conventional heating system in order to provide sufficient warmth in the colder months of the year. The expectation was that the building would receive a "Silver" rating from the U.S. Green Building Council for adhering to voluntary sustainable building standards.

Furthermore, in November, Alcoa awarded the Gettysburg Foundation $100,000 to be used to enhance environmentally sustainable practices within and around the new building. "… we are truly pleased to be involved in this unique and functional, self-sustaining preservation and restoration project.", (6) said Meg McDonald, president of the Alcoa Foundation.

On a less pleasant environmental note Gettysburg resident Daniel Bowers was accused of dumping two drums of used motor oil along Confederate Avenue in the East Cavalry section of the battlefield. Investigators estimated that between 20 and 40 gallons had been dumped. Bowers was eventually cleared of criminal charges but was required to pay clean-up costs.

Following a consistently discouraging pattern a $100.4 million reduction in the National Park Service budget for the upcoming fiscal year caused fear that the appropriation again would not cover federally mandated pay raises. Should that happen Gettysburg, along with national parks across the country, would be forced to allocate part of their operational budget to cover the shortfall. This would, in turn, require them to reduce programs, delay repairs, and eliminate ranger positions, all with a negative impact on visitors. "I worry about money because we have less and less every year.", said Superintendent Latschar, adding "It's not about stretching money because we can't stretch what we don't have. Instead we're doing less with less and we're making choices. Some of those choices are with visitor services." (7)

In February 2006, a federal judge had ruled on a lawsuit brought by the National Park Service against the owners of the building next to the Wills house. The owners of the adjacent building had refused access to a common wall between the two buildings which was badly in need of repairs. The ruling opened the way for work to begin on the historic structure although the delay had cost the Park Service $360,000. It was hoped that the building, where President Lincoln spent the night before his historic speech, could be opened to the public by the spring of 2008 but unforeseen problems caused by greater than expected deterioration of the building set back that widely anticipated event.

Although removal of the Cyclorama building had, from the beginning, been a part of the new General Management Plan to restore the core area of the battlefield to its' 1863 appearance, a Virginia group, the Recent Past Preservation Network, joined by architect Richard Neutra's son Dion, brought suit to prevent the building's demolition. They proposed moving the huge building to a new location. "We have brought suit because the Park Service, in our opinion, did not adequately address the historic significance of this structure... ." (8) said Christine M. French, president of the network. The suit was brought despite the fact that in 1999 the Federal Advisory Council on Historic Preservation had declared that, "with rare exceptions the millions of people who have visited the Gettysburg National Military Park since 1962 have come to see the battlefield not Neutra's architecture." The report went on to say that, "There are other Neutra buildings, there is only one battlefield...", and added that because of the historic nature of the site, "The building must yield." (9) Despite the Advisory Council's conclusion another supporter of retaining the building wrote, "The Cyclorama's demolition is tantamount to rewriting history... . The National Park Service stewardship of our nation's history should be in preserving it, not destroying it." (10) But a proponent of removing the building stated, "The Cyclorama doesn't fit in with the surroundings. When sighting across the killing fields of the Civil War, the Cyclorama certainly stands out but so would a giant concrete mixing bowl... . The Gettysburg battlefield is supposed to be a monument to the men who fought here, not a monument to the fight to save avant-garde architecture." (11) Still others noted that the building stood on ground where nearly 900 men fell during Pickett's charge on July 3, 1863.

One restoration effort to which no one had raised an objection was the removal of the entire Sherfy peach orchard. The Gettysburg Foundation volunteered to cover the cost of the project and in April, 2008 tests showed that the worms' responsible for the disease fatal to the trees, were no longer present in the soil and therefore the famous peach orchard could safely be replanted. In a few years the young seedlings would grow into mature trees and the orchard would have the same appearance as it did in the bloody days of 1863.

While the Sherfy orchard site lay fallow a $17,972 bequest from the estate of Francis L. Wolf of Harrisburg, PA made it possible for the park to replant other historic orchards no longer in existence. Unlike the Sherfy peach orchard the restored orchards were planted in hardy apple trees, selected not for their fruit bearing qualities but for their disease resistance and longevity. The intent is to help visitors understand how the soldiers used cover provided by the orchards for protection. "We want to bring back the feature in a general way so people can see it the way the soldiers did." (12) said park spokeswoman Katie Lawhon. She noted however that the park did not intend to go into the fruit production business.

In March, 2007 the Gettysburg Foundation released a new estimate of the cost of the new visitor center/museum based on, among other factors, the decision to install a geothermal heating/cooling system, and a doubling of the cost of the exhibits due to the use of advanced interactive technology which was not available when the exhibits were first planned. Because of this it was anticipated that the total cost of the new facility would exceed $100 million. The announcement raised a storm of criticism from longtime project opponent Eric Uberman. With the release of the new estimate Uberman turned his attention from the building itself to the report of Foundation expenses. "(For the project cost) to go from $40 million to well over $125 million with minimal explanation is something that shouldn't be tolerated by anyone." (13) he declared.

Occasionally a discovery is made either on the battlefield or in some collection of historic artifacts that offers a poignant reminder of the terrible cost of the battle. Such was the case in 2007 when Karen Bohleke was doing research on 19th century clothing at the Adams County Historical Society. In a box she found a small pouch containing an even smaller wad of yellow paper. Carefully wrapped inside the paper was a tooth which an enclosed note said was taken from a skull found in the Rose woods a year after the battle. The skull was located at the head of a grave marked Lt. W.L. Daniel, Co I, 2nd S.C.V. The note was signed by Lt. W. T. King, company G, 209th Pennsylvania Infantry. Through extensive research Wayne Motts, director of the Historical Society discovered that William Daniel, and his brother James, fought with the Confederate troops at Gettysburg and fell, mortally wounded, within 100 yards of each other. James was buried in an unmarked grave in Richmond, Virginia, but William's grave had never been found, as happened to many Confederate soldiers who fell at Gettysburg. After locating John O. Clark of Johnston, South Carolina, whose great, great grandmother was William Daniel's sister, arrangements were made to bury the tooth in South Carolina in a box made of wood from that part of the battlefield where

William Daniel was fatally wounded. This tiny fragment of the young Confederate soldier was buried near some other members of his family in a proper military fashion.

Despite the offer of $36,000 in reward money for the arrest and conviction of those involved in the greatest vandalism the park had ever experienced the culprits in the 2006 incident remained at large. Although the 14th New York Artillery monument was heavily damaged a statue in New Hampshire, created by the same artist, provided an exact copy of the artilleryman on the 14th New York monument making it possible to replace the stolen head and ammunition rammer of the park monument. Sadly that was not the case with the 11th Massachusetts Volunteer Infantry monument. That monument was "so badly damaged, so much of it stolen, that we will probably just have to have a new one carved out of stone."(14) according to supervisory exhibits specialist Vic Gavin.

Meanwhile senseless vandalism continues to plague the park. In April, 2007 a visitor found the 155th Pennsylvania Volunteer monument on Little Round Top damaged. A musket tip had been broken off and placed on another monument nearby. It was the second time in two years that particular monument had been damaged.

But while some seek to destroy parts of the battlefield others spend time, effort and money to preserve the historic fields. 82 year old Ken Bridgen of Sewickley, Pennsylvania was one of those individuals. He periodically spent more than 40 hours making hundreds of bags of dog treats which he then sold, for a $3 donation, outside of hardware and grocery stores. The money thus gained was turned over to the Gettysburg Foundation to help further the work of battlefield preservation. Although he admitted that some questioned his sanity Bridgen said simply, "It's the kind of guy I am. I love to be involved." (15), and each year he would come to Gettysburg for the Friends annual fund raising march.

With so many historic structures to be preserved fire is a constant concern at the park but sprinkler systems installed in several park structures in 2002, helped save the 1850's Biggs farmhouse on Taneytown Road. Although the cause of the fire was found to be accidental the roof and attic of the house were heavily damaged. Fortunately the resident, a park employee, and his family escaped injury but the damage was so extensive that alternative housing was needed while repairs were being done.

Progress on the new visitor center/museum continued on schedule and at a meeting of the Adams County Historical Society Superintendent Latschar listed four objectives it was hoped the new building would fulfill: 1)provide a permanent home for the Cyclorama painting; 2)provide visitors with a basic

Old Visitor Center on Cemetery Hill

understanding of the battle at Gettysburg and its' place in the overall scheme of the Civil War; 3)create a permanent, environmentally sound home for the park's extensive artifact collection; 4)help restore the battlefield to its' 1863 appearance. Referring to that final objective, "That's the one that is near and dear to my heart." said Dr. Latschar, adding, "Approximately 971 Union soldiers died or were wounded on ground that is currently covered with blacktop." (16)

And it was this very restoration that caused a seemingly unending controversy. One writer called the vegetation which had grown up on the battlefield an example of, "...nature's healing power. ...that loveliness can grow where terror once reigned. To destroy that wonder of nature is to destroy that message"... .(17) Still another complained, "I am sick and tired of the things they are doing to make it look like it did in 1863. First they got rid of a beautiful auction house, then an educational tower, then all the deer, then the trees and now the power lines. Maybe the next thing they will think of is to use live ammunition when they play those "war games" on the Fourth of July. Then there would be bodies of men and horses strewn over the battlefield and it would really look like it did in 1863."(18) The writer apparently did not realize that the "war games" she referred to were annual re-enactments held on private property and are in no way affiliated with Gettysburg National Military Park. But another citizen expressed a different opinion, "The battlefield is preserved for one purpose; to help visitors understand what happened here. The rehabilitation program is a very positive step in support of that mission."(19)

As construction of the visitor center/museum continued concerns about the fate of the well known electric map began to surface. It had become federal property in 1971 when it was included in the $2,350,000 sale of the old visitor center to the National Park Service. Still some local citizens protested vehemently at the prospect that it would be destroyed when the old building was razed. Efforts to find a non-profit or government group to take the map had proven futile as the difficulty of removing it from the building and the expense involved had discouraged any would be takers. Again John Latschar was the target of a letter writer's wrath. "I am concerned and dismayed at the decision of the Gettysburg National Military Park Service to demolish the electric map. ...I am concerned that this is a unilateral decision made by a Park Superintendent who is determined to eliminate as much as possible of the old Gettysburg traditions." (20)

However, rather than demolish the electric map the park and the Gettysburg Foundation decided to place it in storage with a final decision on the fate of the map to be left for the future. Although the Gettysburg Foundation would provide the funds to remove and store the map the Park Service would retain ownership.

In July tree removal began again in the park and as usual so did the chorus of protests against the action. Park personnel continued to meet with local citizens and others to explain the rationale for the tree cutting. Park historian Kathy Harrison pointed out that in some areas of the battlefield the two armies appeared to be engaged in "jungle warfare." Areas where cannon appeared to be shooting into dense woods were, in 1863, actually open ground and the very openness affected the movements of both armies. Once the non-historic trees are removed she explained, visitors will gain a greater understanding of what happened and why.

But these explanations fell on the deaf ears of critics who called the tree removal "hellacious" and ridiculous. (21) And again Superintendent Latschar was at the center of the firestorm. One writer attacked him as "...a dictator...who sees the park as his personal backyard and playground, making his own rules and disregarding advice and public requests." (22) The writer then went on to demand that he be replaced.

Again other citizens came to the defense of Dr. Latschar and the park. "...this is a MILITARY PARK, for people to interpret what went on 144 years ago. The soldiers literally saved our nation by their sacrifice here at Gettysburg. To meaningfully ponder and reflect on that is to look upon these fields and see them as the soldiers and residents saw them back then. Please do not belittle what those soldiers did for all of us, by wishing the battlefield is something it is not." (23)

But still the verbal battle raged on. One Ohio resident wrote, "...the National Park "Service" has already cut down acres of trees at Gettysburg National Military Park. The sick, twisted logic behind this meaningless eradication is that the trees weren't there when the original battle of Gettysburg took place. How could such an absurd idea even be considered...? What visitor would expect a place to be unchanged anyway?" The writer then went on to call the tree cutting "...selfish, shortsighted manipulation of our irreplaceable wilderness..." (24)

But another citizen felt differently as he wrote, "The fields of Gettysburg are not about woodlands, or quiet strolls, or the beauty of nature.... Our vistas are of war, gunfire, death and battle at its' fiercest. ...I want my grandchildren to see the field as noble Armisted did as he made the long walk to the Angle and death.... I want them, in the solitude of Culp's Hill, to remember a boy from Gettysburg who came home with the invaders to die on his family farm. I want them to begin to comprehend the terrible cost of war.... Trees can be replanted, woodlands cultivated, secluded walks installed. But the fields of Gettysburg and others like them, can never be duplicated. Rather they must remain forever frozen in time, a living memorial for those who died and an inspiration for present and future Americans to harden their resolve for the tasks that lie ahead." (25)

In a similar vein another citizen wrote, "I send my congratulations to Superintendent Latschar for his vision and his tenacity in getting this important work done in spite of the hue and cry from so many locals who seem to think that the battlefield exists to provide them with a pleasantly landscaped nature park. It exists to preserve the heritage of the Battle of Gettysburg, and Superintendent Latschar has accomplished a great deal in pursuit of that mission. Rather than be vilified, he ought to be congratulated. ...I believe that Latschar will go down in history as perhaps the greatest superintendent the battlefield has ever had." (26)

In October, 2007 an act, not of vandalism but of nature, wreaked havoc on the 6th New York Cavalry monument on Buford Avenue not far from the Peace Light. During a severe thunderstorm lightning struck it causing $100,000 in damage to the 118 year old granite monument. Pieces of the monument were tossed 10 feet away, mortar joints were blown open, and the stones comprising the upper section were moved sideways several inches. According to monument supervisor Vic Gavin, "the damage may be even worse inside the structure where lighting superheated the moisture that is naturally present in the stone and mortar." (27) Eventually all but the bottom five feet of the monument had to be removed in order to repair it. Prior to this event the last recorded lightning strike on a battlefield monument occurred in

1930. Again a New York monument, the 58th New York Infantry near Barlow's Knoll, was damaged.

Since 2002 one of the most moving sights on the battlefield takes place in the Soldiers National Cemetery during the evening of November 17, a day known in Gettysburg as Remembrance Day. This day was set aside to honor all those who sacrificed their lives in the great battle. The Friends of the National Parks at Gettysburg began the project that year when volunteers placed more than 3500 luminaria on the graves of the Civil War dead. The lighted candles create a haunting scene for the hundred of local residents and visitors who solemnly walk through the cemetery in the evening twilight.

Despite the fact that the Cyclorama has been owned by the American people for nearly a century critics of the new visitor center/museum continued to complain bitterly about funding to restore it. The original estimate had been somewhat over $1 million but as closer inspection revealed far more damage to the painting than had originally been thought the price to restore it rose to $15 million. Despite statements from both the park and the Foundation that no requests for additional funding had been made congressional earmarks, primarily sponsored by U.S. Representative John Murtha of Pennsylvania elicited a strong response and criticism from those who had opposed the entire project from the very beginning. Officials of both the park and the Gettysburg Foundation were accused of intrigue and illicit actions when, in December, 2007 Congress appropriated $3.8 million to complete the restoration project.

6th New York Cavslry monument on Buford Ave. struck by lightning October 2007.

Another group complaining about park actions had planned to bring at least 540 people to Gettysburg to conduct paranormal (ghost) investigations on the battlefield. However as park spokeswoman Katie Lawhon pointed out, "Our mission is to preserve and protect the resources associated with the Battle of Gettysburg and the Soldiers National Cemetery".... . (28) Ghost hunting is not considered consistent with that mission and therefore no permit was granted. Since local residents and businesses were reluctant to grant access to their properties the event was cancelled.

Finally, on April 14, 2008 the new visitor center/museum was opened to the public which gave an overwhelmingly positive response to the new building. This event was considered a "soft" opening. The "Grand" opening was scheduled for September when, after nearly three years of restoration work, the great Cyclorama painting would again be on view to the public.

In defining the difference between the old park museum and the new facility, Superintendent Latschar explained that the old museum was a "collections" museum with hundreds of artifacts on display but no central theme. "We've got rows and rows of rifles and pistols and cases full of battle debris, and no story. What we're creating is a story line museum, where you use artifacts to illustrate the story line. So we have no need for 40 varieties of muskets. We're trying to provide our visitors with a basic understanding of the Battle of Gettysburg in the context of the war and in the context of America, so when they get out on the battlefield they know not only who shot what, but what they were shooting about." (29)

Upon its opening the building while, as expected, was not universally accepted was effusively praised by most visitors and the media. An article in the *Washington Post* stated, "...there's little doubt that the new building is the right one for Gettysburg. ...the success of the building isn't architectural.... . What makes it work is its' basic seriousness." (30) The local *Gettysburg Times* headlined, "Magnificent facility." (31) And one resident after visiting the new building declared, "That's magnificent back there—that museum is the best thing that ever hit Gettysburg." (32)

Borough councilman Ted Streeter, referring to the strong initial resistance of many townspeople to the construction of a new visitor center/museum, observed, "We certainly started off with some differences, and it was a long a protracted struggle. But they produced a wonderful facility that will benefit the borough, the park, the park visitors and the entire Civil War community." (33) George Gelles, a Gettysburg resident said the difference between the old and new museums was "from a tent to a palace."(34) And borough council president Dick Peterson declared, "The museum is laid out beautifully. It's got something for everybody." (35) Bob Kummerich, another borough council member said, "It exceeds my expectations. The facility is the crown jewel of all American Civil War visitor centers and museums." (36)

In an article describing the new visitor center/museum the *York Sunday News* praised Robert Kinsley with these words: "One of the people who played a leading role in the development of the new center is Robert Kinsley. The York based builder is chairman of the foundation and his company designed and built the center. At cost. The company did not make a profit. It was a labor of love for Mr. Kinsley, a student of Civil War history... . The Kinsley Foundation also purchased and donated to the (Gettysburg) Foundation the original 50 acres on which the building was constructed." (37) Further afield the *Boston Globe* described the facility as "a handsome, high-tech portal for exploring and understanding the impact of what happened here all those years ago." (38)

As is the case with any project of this magnitude, there were some naysayers. One local resident complained bitterly that there were fewer artifacts on display than in the old building. "Are there other reasons the Park Service is showing so few artifacts? To save maintaining the exhibits? Are they taking care of the artifacts or hiding problems?... Did the Park Service build offices for themselves as lavish as the rest of the building?" (39) She later complained, "If you want to see a Civil War collection about the Battle of Gettysburg the visitor center is a bust... . Most of the wonderful items from the old museum are nowhere to be seen. How much of this Taj Mahal was socked to the taxpayers?" (40)

But complaints such as these were countered by other citizens, one of whom wrote, "I've been going to Civil War museums for more than 50 years and I've never seen the equal of this one. If the old visitor center was a bit of a flea market display of artifacts, the new one is an equivalent of the Louvre in comparison... . The layout is great, the graphics and story line understandable and logical, and the displays absolutely superb. ...I've never seen anything that does a better job." (41)

As work continued on restoration of the Cyclorama painting members of the press were given several opportunities to follow the work in progress and report to the public. Malcolm Jones of *Newsweek* magazine wrote in the April 14th, 2008 issue, "Much work remains to be done. But even partially restored the painting seethes with life—and death. This in no mindless celebration of war but a balancing act of horror and heroism. Phillippoteaux stared straight into the face of battle, and he didn't flinch." (42)

It had been 10 years since the new park General Management Plan, encompassing a new visitor center/museum had been proposed. In the interim

although many harsh words had been spoken in opposition, many bitter letters written, John Latschar never wavered in his determination to see the project through to completion.   Upon the opening of the new building Dick
Peterson, borough council president, initially one of the most severe critics of
Dr. Latschar and Gettysburg National Military Park was quoted by the local
newspaper.   In a striking, very welcome reversal of opinion he said to the
superintendent, "John, the visitor center is absolutely breath taking. It is first
class in every way and even better than I expected. ...It was only 10 years ago
that I, and most of my compatriots on Steinwehr Avenue, condemned the idea
of a new museum/visitor center. We feared that the new facility would draw
customers away from our shops and attractions. Subsequently we formed a
coalition to oppose the new center and argued our points at every Park Advisory Board meeting.   Regrettably during that period harsh words were
exchanged. As a result bitter feelings prevailed. So what happened to change
my mind and the minds of countless others? The answer can be summed up
in two words...working together. ...the very people who rarely communi-
cated a decade ago—some of them adversaries—are now on many of the
boards who are working to improve this community. And they are serving
together. ....The town changed because people changed. Former adversaries
are friends. Even old guys like me are capable of that."(43)

One of the projects dear to the hearts of the borough council was the
opening of a restored Wills house on the square downtown. But the grand re-
opening, originally planned for November 17, 2008, had to be delayed. The
lawsuit against the owners of the building next door, the deteriorated condition of the building itself—far more serious than originally thought, and difficulty in locating historically accurate materials needed for proper restoration,
all were major set backs for completion of the work. For these reasons the Park
Service was unable to open the building until February 12, 2009. However it
was well worth the wait. Careful preservation of as much of the structure as
could be saved, and meticulous re-creation of those elements too far gone to
be useable, created a superb restoration of one of the town's most historic
buildings. Largely through the generosity of the descendents of David Wills
furniture, including the bed upon which Lincoln slept the night before his historic speech, bring history to life as visitors are now able to see a piece of American history that hitherto they could only read about.

Meanwhile as visitors continued to flock to the new visitor
center/museum there were, as expected, continuing differences of opinion.
Some scoffed at the idea of a "storyline" museum, others complained that
there were not enough artifacts, especially weapons, on display. The bookstore
and the presence of a refreshment area were also criticized. But the vast major-

ity of writers viewed the new facility in a far more favorable light. One article stated, "For museum visitors, the Gettysburg Museum of the Civil War is visibly the personification of a modern museum. The weapons, uniforms and buttons that are exhibited are given a context and a meaning. When you leave the museum you begin to feel and understand what it was like to be alive and directly involved in this turbulent era." (44) Further defense of the new approach came in another article. "The NPS and it's private partner the Gettysburg Battlefield Foundation, who together have receive considerable public condemnation from those favoring the traditional "guts and glory" view of the war, should be commended for NOT sticking to their guns. Moreover the lofty, yet basic box-store interior space of the new museum and center is a staging ground of infinite possibilities. Indeed its' flexibility is one of its' planners wisest bequests. There is ample room for new interpretations, for another age. Have all the brouhaha surrounding the new center and chunks of taxpayers money expended on it been worth it? Absolutely. The details, and much of the whole, bespeak a genius of enlightened intelligence."(45)

In August, with activity at the new visitor center/museum in full swing, nature dealt another blow to the park when a strong wind and thunderstorm caused severe damage to a honey locust tree in the Soldiers National Cemetery. Known as a "witness tree" it is one of a number of trees within the park that were present as saplings in 1863 and survived the ravages of shot, shell and charging soldiers. Now grown to a large, imposing size a number of these trees have been identified in areas where the park has conducted surveys, with doubtless others in sections of the battlefield not yet studied. These "witness trees" are identified using a method developed by the International Society of Arboriculture. Such trees were marked and carefully protected when found in areas where non-historic vegetation was scheduled to be removed. In the case of the honey locust, "The tree was not entirely destroyed.", said Superintendent Latschar. "Some of the main trunk and several living branches were unharmed. According to Randy Kritchen, a certified arborist on the park staff, the honey locust is a resilient tree and we have high hopes that it will live." (46) The wood from the damaged tree was donated to the Gettysburg Foundation which will use it in appropriate ways to raise money for the Foundation.

Despite the overwhelming pleasure expressed by visitors to the new visitor center/museum by August it had become apparent that revenues from the venues in the building were not meeting projected levels and steps needed to be taken to eliminate the shortfall. "We've tried just about everything." said Dr. Latschar adding, "We're just not meeting our goals and hitting our numbers."(47) This despite salary and personnel cuts. Originally it had been announced that the museum would be free but in examining the fee structure it became evident that including the museum in the new fee scale was necessary. So an entire restructuring of fees, to include admission to the museum, was decided upon. There would be single fee of $7.50 for adults with lesser amounts for children, senior citizens, and members of the military. Entrance to the building and bookstore would still be free.

There were howls of protest, primarily from the local public, when the proposal was announced although the $7.50 admission charge for all three venues was significantly lower than the $12 fee originally planned for the movie plus Cyclorama alone. One writer called the new fee "a disgrace." (48) Another said, "It's a visitor center. It should be free." (49) And still another said he would not return because of the fee change. But others were not so harsh. One visitor wrote, "I think you can understand why they can't have it free. I personally think that's absurd." (50) And the *York Daily Record* stated, "…$7.50 seems a reasonable price for all the museum has to offer." (51)

Although the new visitor center/museum was certainly the major object of attention and controversy in the park the Gettysburg Foundation was quietly assisting in battlefield protection when it purchased the 80 acre Spangler farm on the eastern edge of the battlefield. Long a top priority for

George Spangler farm barn. The farm was purchased by the Gettysburg Foundation in 2008

park acquisition it appeared destined to fall to an outside developer since the park itself had no land acquisition funds. However thanks to a lead gift from the Williams Family Foundation of Georgia, the Gettysburg Foundation was able to secure funding for the purchase. The farm was the location of artillery which aided Union forces in holding their positions on July 2 and 3, 1863. But perhaps it is best known as the Union hospital site where Confederate general Lewis Armistead died after being mortally wounded leading his men during Pickett's charge on July 3. The Foundation plans to use it for educational purposes but the farm is in need of significant repairs and will not be opened to the public until these are completed. "The farm is literally untouched from the time of the battle.", according to park historian John Heiser. "This is the last true surviving corps hospital site on the battlefield that has stood virtually untouched. It's almost immaculate." (52)

In the fall another, quite stunning announcement made headlines when it was announced that Superintendent Latschar would retire from the National Park Service after having been selected by the Gettysburg Foundation board of directors to succeed Robert Wilburn as president of the Foundation. Wilburn had announced earlier that he would be leaving the Foundation in the spring of 2009 and Dr. Latschar was the unanimous selection of the board to assume that position.

Comments from members of the Gettysburg borough council revealed the respect and admiration with which local officials had come to regard the superintendent over the years. Said Main Street Gettysburg director Bill Kough, "One word describes Dr. Latschar when I think of his attributes, "Brilliant. His priorities are family, country, history and community." (53) "We started at arms length the first time we had any reaction with him. But honestly, we gained a lot of respect for each other over the years." (54), was councilman Ted Streeter's reaction; while borough council vice-president Holly Giles stated, "Whatever project John Latschar takes on, especially with the Borough of Gettysburg, it is very apparent that he uses all of his expertise and knowledge for all to benefit." (55) And borough council president Dick Peterson, one of Superintendent Latschar's most severe critics when the park decided to relocate the visitor center from its' site adjacent to Steinwehr Avenue, praised the man he had grown to consider a friend. "He's taken a lot of criticism over the years and he's survived. He's changed and we've changed. Twenty years from now we won't even remember all of the controversy. We'll remember John Latschar for his vision and what was accomplished here." (56)

But despite the heartfelt accolades there were a few who had bitterly opposed Dr. Latschar from the very beginning and had continued to oppose his every action for over 14 years. They again swung into action claiming a conflict of interest and demanding a review of the appointment. In January, 2009, despite the fact that the National Park Service had approved of Dr. Latschar's change of office the Department of the Interior provided new guidance that placed such severe restrictions on any action he might take as president of the Foundation that it was apparent he would be unable to function effectively in his new job and therefore his acceptance of the offer was withdrawn. The Foundation reluctantly accepted his decision and so John Latschar remained as superintendent of Gettysburg National Military Park.

Because assurances had been given that no taxpayer money would be used in the construction of the new visitor center/museum critics were quick to point out that much of the cost of restoring the Cyclorama painting was being paid for with funds allocated by Congress i.e. taxpayer money. Others, delighted to see the painting restored, argued that the painting belonged to the American people and therefore it was quite proper for Congress to appropriate the money to restore it.

Public viewing of the restored Cyclorama painting also marked the "Grand Opening" of the visitor center/museum which had been informally opened to the public in April. Reaction to the painting was overwhelmingly positive. Robert Hancock of Chambersburg, Pa. said the difference in the appearance of the painting before and after the restoration was like "…night and day. Before it was good, but since the restoration it's incredible." (57) Grace Fernandes of Costa Rica said, "You can't help but feel something deep down inside." (58), and her brother Dale Fernandes of Fayetteville, Pa. added, "It makes you feel like you're really there." (59) Dwayne Beggs called the results, "Incredible. Anything they spent to do that was well worth it." (60)

As the restored painting was opened to the public the lawsuit to retain the old Cyclorama building was making it's snail-like way through federal court. At this time both Eric Uberman and Robert Monahan offered to take the building although Uberman admitted he probably would not have room on his property for the entire building "But we could at least take the cylindrical part." (61) he said. However neither Monahan nor Uberman indicated a willingness to pay the cost of moving the building which court documents showed could reach over $5 million. As to who would pay these costs the president of the group seeking to preserve the building stated, "We haven't gotten to that point yet.", (62) while Monahan admitted that the logistics of moving such a large structure had not been discussed.

Amid all the attacks and criticisms by those who had been opposed to Superintendent Latschar from the time he arrived in Gettysburg the National Parks Conservation Association, the country's largest Park Service support

Cyclorama building in Zeigler's Grove

group, hailed him as a model for the Park Service when it presented to him the Steven T. Mather Award as the nation's most outstanding park superintendent. "John not only works to protect our parks, he leads us in rethinking where, how, and why these resources impact our environment, our communities, and our national identity.", said Joy Oaks, NPCA mid-Atlantic Regional director. The award recognized Dr. Latschar "for his steadfast leadership and persistent dedication." (63) to our national parks.

Despite such praise from the NPCA and from local officials the drumbeat of criticism of John Latschar not only continued but seemed to increase following his decision to remain in the Park Service. Vitriolic letters to the editor continued to appear, especially in the local paper. One writer called him "arrogant" stating, "He rules his park with a reign of terror... . There is likely merit in many charges that have been made against him and they should be investigated." (64) Accusations were made that the visitor center/museum was approved and constructed under a veil of secrecy between the Park Service and the Gettysburg Foundation. In addition the old refrain that Foundation CEO Robert Kinsley had made money on the project was raised again although records show that he donated $8.4 million to the Gettysburg Foundation through the Kinsley Family Foundation, Kinsley owned partnerships, construction management done "at cost", and donations of personal funds. In reaction to the continued stream of negative comments about Superintendent Latschar and the Gettysburg Foundation the *Hanover Evening Sun,* in a March 1, 2009 article called Gettysburg, "...a town where criticizing the National Park Service is practically a spectator sport." (65)

Amid all the negative actions tragedy struck the park not once but twice in January, 2009. On the 5th Deputy Superintendent John McKenna died unexpectedly in his sleep. Known for his kind and gentle nature McKenna had come to the park in 1995 and had served as John Latschar's second in command throughout his tenure at the park. Losing John McKenna was, "like losing a brother.", (66) said John Latschar. Three weeks later Ranger Greg Coco lost his battle with cancer. The loss of both men was deeply felt not only among park administrative staff but among rangers, guides, volunteers and local officials who had known and worked with both men.

One bright spot amid the storm of park bashing was provided by Gary Gallagher, one of the country's most noted historians who, after visiting the new visitor center/museum and observing the landscape rehabilitation efforts wrote, "There has never been a better time to visit Gettysburg. ...I make this claim on the basis of more than a hundred visits to the battlefield. My first visit...came in 1965, my most recent, with middle and high school teachers just a few weeks ago. ...Resolute leadership by Superintendent John Latschar over the past dozen years has yielded spectacular results. ...I believe the critics care deeply about Gettysburg but miss several key points. ...Most of the 1.5 million yearly visitors are neither experts on the battle nor well informed about the Civil War... . But if they gain some knowledge about the battle's tactics, why the armies were in Adams County, and how the site became the site of reconciliation I would judge their visit a success. Because of exemplary work at the park over the past few years, the chances of success are much greater than before." (67)

Restoration of the battlefield took a major step forward in February, 2009 when a contract was awarded to Interior Specialists of Maryland for the demolition of the old visitor center on the Taneytown Road. "This work represents step one of the larger rehabilitation projects that will return the Ziegler's Grove area of the battlefield as closely as possible to its 1863 appearance." (68) said Gettysburg Foundation spokeswoman Dru Neil. Although not included in the initial phase, the completed project included the removal of the entire old visitor center parking lot and all but a small portion of the Cyclorama building parking lot which was retained to accommodate visitors to the Soldiers National Cemetery. The land itself was restored to the meadow it was in 1863 when over 900 men became casualties on Cemetery Ridge. Demolition of the Cyclorama building awaited the federal court decision.

On April 30, 1864 Pennsylvania governor Andrew Curtin signed legislation establishing the Gettysburg Battle-field Memorial Association. Section 2 of that act states, *"That the object of said Association shall be To hold and preserve the battlegrounds of Gettysburg... with the natural and artificial defenses as they were at the time of said battle."* (69)

Over time that mandate, inherited by the National Park Service in 1933, had fallen into neglect until 1995. It was then that John Latschar, a new superintendent of an old and somewhat neglected park, determined to fulfill the mandate of 1864. Bitterly opposed by forces both within the town and beyond, he never wavered and today the battlefield speaks to visitors as it has not since those early post-war years. As a result Gettysburg serves as a model "for preservation, partnership, and management practices for the entire national park system." (70)

No other superintendent in the history of Gettysburg National Military Park has had such a positive impact on the park and the community in which it is located. Despite continual efforts, by critics, to derail his programs and besmirch his reputation, John Latschar has persevered, often at great personal cost. From the very beginning of his tenure he firmly believed that this battlefield, this park, is truly a sacred place and that those men who fought here, whether clad in blue or clad in gray, deserve a memorial worthy of the sacrifices they made on this holy ground. He has succeeded.

Dr, John Latschar

BIBLIOGRAPHY

All of the material in this volume is drawn from the archives of the Gettysburg National Military Park, Gettysburg, Pa. The greater number of sources are newspaper articles from the various periods in the park's history. Some of these newspapers are no longer in existence or have undergone name changes through the years. Specific volumes of material utilized are also in the park archives and some of the more recent ones are available from Gettysburg National Military Park upon request. All are listed below.

An Act of the General Assembly of Pennsylvania to Incorporate the Gettysburg Battlefield Memorial Association – April 30, 1864

The Battle Veterans Interpret the Battlefield – Gettysburg Memorial Landscape – author and date unknown

Annual Reports to the Secretary of War from the Gettysburg Battlefield Commission – 1899, 1919, 1920

General Management Plan for Gettysburg National Military Park and Gettysburg National Cemetery – Mid-Atlantic Regional Office, National Park Service, U.S. Department of the Interior – December 1982

Boundary Study – Gettysburg National Military Park, National Park Service, U.S. Department of the Interior – August 1988

Administrative History – Gettysburg National Military Park and National Cemetery, U.S. Department of the Interior – July 1991

"Land Exchange Between National Park Service/Gettysburg National Military Park and Gettysburg College" – Hearing before the Environment, Energy and National Resources sub-committee of the Committee on Government Operations, U.S. House of Representatives – May 4, 1994

The Changing Faces of Gettysburg, The National Park Service at Gettysburg – Karlton O. Smith, Fourth Annual Gettysburg Seminar – March 4, 1995

Request for Proposals – Visitor Center and Museum Facilities – Gettysburg National Military Park, National Park Service, U.S. Department of the Interior – December 11, 1996

Hearing of the U.S. Senate sub-committee on National Parks, Historic Preservation and Recreation; "Oversight hearing on the issues relating to the visitor center and museum facilities at Gettysburg National Military Park" February 24, 1998

Report from a Panel of Historians Peer Review of the Process Developed by Gettysburg National Military Park Planning Staff and Historians to Determine Significant 1863 Landscape Features, Their Relationship to the Outcome of the Battle and Extent of Their Change Over the Past 135 Years. Commissioned by the Executive Committee of the Gettysburg National Military Park Advisory Commission. Published March 1998

Final General Management Plan and Environmental Impact Statement, Volumes 1 and 2, Gettysburg National Military Park, Department of the Interior – June 1999

Summary Groundwater Resources of Adams County Pennsylvania - by Larry E.Taylor and Denise W. Royer, Commonwealth of Pennsylvania – Bureau of Topographic and Geologic Survey 1981

National Railroad Historic Society Bulletin – First Quarter, 1945

Newspapers and Magazines:

Gettysburg Compiler	
Philadelphia Public Ledger and Daily Transcript	(Pa)
Gettysburg Star and Sentinel	
Gettysburg Times	
Columbus Dispatch	(Ohio)
Rochester Democrat and Chronicle	(NY)
Washington Star	(DC)
Cleveland Plain Dealer	(Ohio)
Washington Post	(DC)
Hanover Evening Sun	(Pa)
Civil War News	
Philadelphia Inquirer	(Pa)
Harrisburg Patriot News	(Pa)

York Sunday News   (Pa)
USA Today
York Dispatch   (Pa)
Lancaster News   (Pa)
Civil War Times Illustrated
Adams County Independent   (Pa)
National Railroad Historical Society Bulletin

News Releases
The Boston Globe   (MA)
Newsweek Magazine
Crossties   (Rutgers University, NJ)
Inside NPS
National Parks Conservation Association

ENDNOTES

Chapter 1

1.	Gettysburg National Military Park Administrative History	pp 5	July 1991
2.	Personal letter – McConaughey to Curtin		7-25-1863
3.	Gettysburg National Military Park Administrative History	pp 4	July 1991
4.	ibid		
5.	Gettysburg National Military Park Administrative History	pp 6	July 1991
6.	Gettysburg National Military Park Administrative History	pp 10	July 1991
7.	Personal letter – Wills to Curtin		3-21-1864
8.	Establishing Act for Battlefield Memorial Association by Pa. Legislature		4-30-1864
9.	Gettysburg National Military Park General Management Plan	pp xxiii	June 1999
10.	Gettysburg National Military Park Administrative History	pp 49	July 1991
11.	Gettysburg National Military Park Administrative History	pp 53	July 1991
12.	"The Battle Veterans Interpret the Battlefield" author unknown		circa 1992
13.	ibid		
14.	ibid		
15.	ibid		
16.	ibid		
17.	The North American		2-20-02
18.	Preliminary Survey of the Springs Hotel Road Development - J.M.Sheads	1939	
19.	Ibid		
20.	Gettysburg Compiler		10-16-1868
21.	Gettysburg Compiler		11-20-1868
22.	ibid		
23.	Philadelphia Public Ledger and Daily Transcript		6-17-1893
24.	The Press		7-9-1893
25.	Philadelphia Public Ledger and Daily Transcript		6-2-1893
26.	Evening Star		5-27-1893
27.	Star and Sentinel (Gettysburg)		1-22-1895
28.	Gettysburg Compiler		2-4-1896

Chapter 2

1.	Gettysburg Star and Sentinel	1-28-1896
2.	Adams County Independent	8-14-1897
3.	ibid	
4.	Gettysburg Compiler	5-14-1895
5.	Gettysburg Compiler	5-21-1895
6.	ibid	
7.	Star and Sentinel (Gettysburg)	3-1-1898
8.	Annual Report of the Gettysburg National Military Park Commission to the Secretary of War	1899
9.	The Press	3-4-1898
10.	Star and Sentinel (Gettysburg)	9-10-1895
11.	ibid	
12.	Star and Sentinel (Gettysburg)	11-20-1894
13.	Star and Sentinel (Gettysburg)	12-18-1901

14.	Gettysburg Compiler		3-6-1900
15.	Gettysburg Compiler		3-5-1901
16.	Star and Sentinel (Gettysburg)		8-29-1899
17.	Gettysburg Compiler		10-28-1908
18.	Gettysburg Compiler		?-?-1908
19.	Public Ledger and Philadelphia Times		1-24-1903
20.	ibid		
21.	ibid		
22.	Gettysburg Times		7-29-1915
23.	Gettysburg Compiler		5-17-1917
24.	Gettysburg National Military Park Administrative History	pp 117	July 1991
25.	Annual Report of the Gettysburg National Military Park Commission		1919
26.	Annual Report of the Gettysburg National Military Park Commission		1920

Chapter 3

1.	Gettysburg National Military Park General Management Plan	pp xxvi	June 1999
2.	Gettysburg National Military Park Boundary Study	pp 13	August 1988
3.	Gettysburg National Military Park Boundary Study	pp 14	August 1988
4.	Gettysburg Times		6-25-1935
5.	Gettysburg Times		9-24-1935
6.	Gettysburg Times		4-?-1934
7.	Gettysburg Times		2-17-1934
8.	Personal letter – Richard H. Little to Sec.of the Interior Harold Ickes		5-1-1937
9.	Gettysburg Compiler		1-30-1937
10.	Gettysburg Times		6-25-1938
11.	Gettysburg Times		6-24-1938
12.	Personal letter J.R. McConaghie to S.B. Cabell		11-28-1938
13.	Memo F. Tilberg to NPS Regional Director		8-14-1940
14.	Gettysburg Times		5-7-1945
15.	Report of Maj. Laurence C. Thomas "Location of the Prisoner of War Camp on the Gettysburg Battlefield During World War II – 1944-1945" 1945		
16.	Gettysburg Times		1-9-1946
17.	Gettysburg National Military Park Administrative History	pp 211	July 1991
18.	Gettysburg National Military Park Administrative History	pp 247	July 1991
19.	ibid		
20.	Gettysburg National Military Park Administrative History	pp 267	July 1991
21.	Wall Street Journal		1-8-1959
22.	Gettysburg Times		3-17-1959
23.	Columbus (Ohio) Dispatch		5-7-1959
24.	Gettysburg Times		4-17-1959
25.	Gettysburg Times		4-13-1959
26.	Public meeting – author's personal recollection		1959
27.	New York Times		6-14-1959
28.	Gettysburg Times		6-6-1959
29.	Gettysburg Times		2-31-1959
30.	Gettysburg Times		9-12-1959

Chapter 4

1.	Rochester (New York) Democrat – Chronicle		April 1959
2.	Gettysburg Times		4-28-1960
3.	Gettysburg Times "Parade" article		2-12-1960
4.	Gettysburg Times		2-4-1960
5.	Gettysburg Times		8-?-1962
6.	Gettysburg Times		3-17-1960
7.	Gettysburg National Military Park Administrative History	pp 273	July 1991
8.	Gettysburg National Military Park Administrative History	pp 258	July 1991
9.	Washington Star		2-11-1962
10.	Gettysburg National Military Park Administrative History	pp 288	July 1991
11.	Gettysburg Times		9-11-1962
12.	Gettysburg Times		2-1-1960
13.	Cleveland (Ohio) Plain Dealer		7-14-1963
14.	Gettysburg Times		7-22-1964
15.	ibid		
16.	Gettysburg National Military Park Administrative History	pp 296	July 1991
17.	ibid		

Chapter 5

1.	Gettysburg Times	9-19-1970
2.	Gettysburg Compiler	8-28-1878
3.	Gettysburg Times	9-19-1970
4.	Gettysburg Times	10-13-1970
5.	Washington Post	12-19-1973
6.	ibid	
7.	ibid	
8.	ibid	
9.	ibid	
10.	ibid	
11.	Gettysburg Times	7-12-1971
12.	Gettysburg Times	7-27-1974
13.	Gettysburg Times	7-24-1974
14.	Gettysburg Times	7-27-1974
15.	Gettysburg Times	10-27-1970
16.	Gettysburg Times	6-22-1971
17.	ibid	
18.	Gettysburg Times	2-15-1972
19.	Gettysburg Times	10-27-1970
20.	Bill of Sale between Angela Rosensteel Eckert and the United States Government – Gift of Personal Property	12-21-1971
21.	Gettysburg Times	10-4-1972
22.	Gettysburg Times	5-26-1973
23.	Gettysburg Times	5-19-1975
24.	Gettysburg Times	5-3-1972
25.	Philadelphia Inquirer	1-27-1972

Chapter 5 (cont)

26.	Evening News – Harrisburg, Pa.	7-10-1973
27.	Gettysburg Times	2-15-1973
28.	Gettysburg Times	11-22-1974
29.	Sunday Patriot News (Harrisburg, Pa.)	2-17-1974
30.	Sunday Patriot News (Harrisburg, Pa.)	3-17-1974
31.	Gettysburg Times	4-8-1974
32.	Gettysburg Times	11-15-1974
33.	Gettysburg Times	12-24-1974
34.	Gettysburg Times	12-27-1974
35.	Gettysburg Times	12-24-1974
36.	Gettysburg Times	1-6-1975
37.	Gettysburg Times	1-24-1975
38.	Gettysburg Times	2-1-1975
39.	Evening Sun (Hanover, Pa.)	1-22-1975
40.	ibid	
41.	Gettysburg Times	7-27-1977
42.	Gettysburg Times	7-11-1977
43.	Gettysburg Times	7-23-1976
44.	Gettysburg Times	7-22-1977
45.	Gettysburg Times	3-28-1979
46.	Patriot News (Harrisburg Pa.)	2-4-1979
47.	ibid	
48.	Gettysburg Times	1-9-99

Chapter 6

1.	Gettysburg Times	3-8-1980
2.	Gettysburg Times	3-12-1980
3.	ibid	
4.	ibid	
5.	York (Pa.) Sunday News	2-14-1982
6.	Gettysburg Times	8-28-1980
7.	Gettysburg Times	3-18-1980
8.	Gettysburg Times	4-10-1981
9.	Gettysburg Times	3-27-1980
10.	ibid	
11.	Gettysburg Times	3-19-1980
12.	Gettysburg Times	4-13-1980
13.	Gettysburg Times	3-10-1980
14.	Gettysburg Times	4-16-1980
15.	Gettysburg Times	3-17-1980
16.	Sunday Patriot News (Harrisburg, Pa.)	4-28-1980
17.	Gettysburg Times	9-20-1981
18.	Sunday Patriot News (Harrisburg, Pa.)	5-10-1981
19.	Gettysburg Times	6-11-1982
20.	Gettysburg Times	9-3-1982
21	Sunday Patriot News (Harrisburg, PA)	10-3-1992
22.	Gettysburg Times	6-18-1988
23.	York (Pa.) Dispatch	10-25-1988
24.	Gettysburg Times	3-24-1987

25.	Gettysburg Times	11-3-1988
26.	Sunday Patriot News (Harrisburg, Pa.)	8-2-1987
27.	York (Pa.) Sunday News	3-26-1989
28.	ibid	
29.	ibid	
30.	Gettysburg Times	6-28-1988
31.	Philadelphia Inquirer	6-17-1986
32.	Gettysburg Times	7-17-1986
33.	Sunday Patriot News (Harrisburg, Pa.)	6-22-1986
34.	Hanover (Pa.) Sun	7-10-1987
35.	Gettysburg Times	8-27-1987
36.	York (Pa.) Sunday News	9-3-1989
37.	Lancaster (Pa.) News	1-29-1989
38.	ibid	
39.	York (Pa.) Sunday News	1-8-1989
40.	ibid	
41.	York (Pa.) Dispatch	

Chapter 7

1.	York (Pa.) Sunday News	3-18-1990
2.	York (Pa.) Sunday News	1-7-1990
3.	Gettysburg Times	7-13-1991
4.	Civil War News	May 1990
5.	Philadelphia Inquirer	9-6-1990
6.	ibid	
7.	York (Pa.) Sunday News	8-4-1991
8.	ibid	
9.	York (Pa.) Sunday News	6-10-1990
10.	Gettysburg Times	2-25-1991
11.	Hanover (Pa.) Evening Sun	3-7-1991
12.	Hanover (Pa.) Evening Sun	11-17-1991
13.	Gettysburg Times	2-14-1992
14.	Gettysburg Times	3-9-1992
15.	Gettysburg Times	4-6-1992
16.	Gettysburg Times	3-19-1992
17.	Hanover (Pa.) Evening Sun	3-28-1992
18.	Gettysburg Times	4-6-1992
19.	Gettysburg Times	12-30-1991
20.	Gettysburg Times	7-10-1991
21.	Gettysburg Times	2-4-1991
22.	Hearing of the U.S. House of Representatives sub-committee on the Environment, Energy, and Natural Resources pp 6	5-9-1994
23.	Gettysburg Times	1-11-1991
24.	Gettysburg Times	1-24-1991
25.	Gettysburg Times	1-23-1991
26.	Gettysburg Times	2-12-1991
27.	Gettysburg Times	2-1-1991
28.	Gettysburg Times	2-2-1991
29.	Gettysburg Times	1-25-1991
30.	Gettysburg Times	2-4-1991

31.	Hanover (Pa.) Evening Sun		1-17-1991
32.	Hanover (Pa.) Evening Sun		5-5-1991
33.	York (Pa.) Sunday News		3-24-1991
34.	ibid		
35.	Hanover (Pa.) Evening Sun		7-22-1991
36.	ibid		
37.	York (Pa.) Sunday News		3-24-1991
38.	Hanover (Pa.) Evening Sun		9-7-1991
39.	ibid		
40.	York (Pa.) Sunday News		12-8-1991
41.	Civil War Times Illustrated		March / April 1992
42.	ibid		
43.	ibid		
44.	ibid		
45.	ibid		
46.	ibid		
47.	ibid		
48.	ibid		
49.	ibid		
50.	Gettysburg Times		2-4-1991
51.	Hanover (Pa.) Evening Sun		7-23-1992
52.	Gettysburg Times		8-23-1993
53.	Hanover (Pa.) Evening Sun		12-30-1993
54.	Gettysburg Times		9-4-1993
55.	Hanover (Pa.) Evening Sun		12-30-1993
56.	Hanover (Pa.) Evening Sun		4-10-1993
57.	York (Pa.) Sunday News		3-14-1993
58.	ibid		
59.	York (Pa.) Sunday News		5-30-1993
60.	York (Pa.) Sunday News		8-8-1993
61.	Hanover (Pa.) Evening Sun		6-25-1993
62.	ibid		
63.	Harrisburg (Pa.) Patriot News		7-31-1992
64.	Hanover (Pa.) Evening Sun		8-5-1992
65.	Gettysburg Times		2-5-1994
66.	Gettysburg Times		7-22-1994
67.	Civil War News		July 1994
68.	Hanover (Pa.) Evening Sun		12-?-1994
69.	Gettysburg Times		9-2-1994
70.	Civil War News		January 1994
71.	ibid		
72.	Hearing of the U.S.House of Representatives sub-committee on the Environment, Energy and Natural Resources	pp 109	5-9-1994
73.	ibid	pp 115	
74.	ibid	pp 161-162	
75	ibid	pp 163	
76.	York (Pa.) Sunday News		5-15-1994
77.	Harrisburg (Pa.) Patriot News		5-10-1994
78.	Harrisburg (Pa.) Patriot News		5-10-1944
79.	Hanover (Pa.) Evening Sun		5-15-1994
80.	Harrisburg (Pa.) Patriot News		5-10-1994

Chapter 8

1.	Hanover (Pa.) Evening Sun		7-25-1995
2.	Gettysburg Times		1-20-1995
3.	Gettysburg Times		12-23-1994
4.	Gettysburg Times		5-5-1995
5.	Gettysburg Times		5-5-1995
6.	Civil War News		September 1995
7.	Philadelphia Inquirer		2-9-1995
8.	ibid		
9.	Gettysburg Times		4-7-1995
10.	Gettysburg Times		4-12-1995
11.	Civil War News		June 1995
12.	ibid		
13.	Gettysburg National Military Park Advisory Commission minutes		4-20-1995
14.	ibid		
15.	Gettysburg National Military Park Request for Proposals	pp 2	12-11-1996
16.	ibid	pp 3	
17.	ibid	pp 8	
18.	ibid	pp 26	
19.	ibid	pp 32	
20.	Gettysburg Times		4-19-1996
21.	ibid		
22.	ibid		
23.	Harrisburg (Pa.) Patriot News		5-6-1996
24.	Civil War News		June 1996
25.	Hanover (Pa.) Evening Sun		10-16-1997
26.	Hanover (Pa.) Evening Sun		10-17-1997
27.	Washington Post		10-28-1997
28.	Gettysburg Times		11-13-1997
29.	ibid		
30.	Personal correspondence Rep. Goodling to author		7-28-1998
31.	Report to Gettysburg National Military Park Advisory Commission by Historians Peer Group Panel – Nelson, Gallagher		March 1998
32.	ibid		
33.	Hanover (Pa.) Evening Sun		10-15-1997
34.	Gettysburg Times		11-21-1997
35.	Harrisburg (Pa.) Patriot News		9-27-1998
36.	Washington Post		6-11-1998
37.	Gettysburg Times		2-24-1998
38.	Gettysburg Times		2-3-1998
39.	Gettysburg Times		2-16-1998
40.	Gettysburg Times		10-1-1998
41.	Gettysburg Times		2-11-1998
42.	U.S. Senate sub-committee on National Parks, Historic Preservation and Recreation – hearing:Powell statement		2-24-1998
43.	ibid Senator Bumpers statement		
44.	ibid Senator Santorum statement		
45.	Gettysburg Times		3-3-1998
46.	Gettysburg Times		6-19-1998
47.	Gettysburg Times		3-3-1998

48.	ibid		
49.	York (Pa.) Sunday News		5-3-1998
50.	Gettysburg Times		2-25-1999
51.	Gettysburg Times		4-20-1999
52.	Washington Post		4-6-1999
53.	Gettysburg Times		4-20-1999
54.	Gettysburg Times		6-7-1999
55.	National Park Service hearing (General Management Plan) pp 738-739		10-1-1998
56.	ibid	pp 744	
57.	ibid	pp 745-748	
58.	ibid	pp 757	
59.	ibid	pp 778-779	
60.	ibid	pp 790	
61.	ibid	pp 806	
62.	Civil War News		August 1999
63.	Civil War News		May 1999
64.	Determination of Eligibility – Keeper of the National Register		September 1998
65.	Report of the Advisory Council on Historic Preservation		May 10, 1999
66.	E-mail message received by Gettysburg National Military Park		2-15-2000
67.	Gettysburg National Military Park Advisory Commission minutes		4-15-1998
68.	Personal correspondence to Superintendent Latschar – unsigned		9-15-1998
69.	Washington Post		4-23-1999
70.	Gettysburg Times		4-23-1999
71.	"A Bill" released to press		October 1999
72.	"Plain Talk" – Representative William Goodling newsletter		10-20-1999
73.	Gettysburg Times		6-21-2000
74.	Washington Post		7-4-2000
75.	USA Today		7-3-2000
76.	Harrisburg (Pa.) Patriot News	Longanecker comment	7-4-2000
77.	ibid	Baker comment	
78.	Washington Post	Szczytko comment	7-4-2000
79.	ibid	Ray Butara comment	
80.	ibid	Bob Butara comment	
81.	Harrisburg (Pa.) Patriot News	Finfrock comment	7-4-2000
82.	Gettysburg Times		6-26-2000
83.	Gettysburg Times		6-26-2000
84.	Gettysburg Times		6-27-2000
85.	Gettysburg Times		7-4-2000
86.	Personal conversation – Superintendent Latschar and visitor		6-30-2000
87.	Personal comment – Gerald Bennett		7-3-2000

Chapter 9

1.	Evening Sun (Hanover, Pa.)	July 13, 2000
2.	Gettysburg Times	July 25, 2000
3.	Gettysburg Times	July 27, 2000
4.	Gettysburg Times	Aug. 1, 2000
5.	Evening Sun (Hanover, Pa.)	July 26, 2000
6.	Memorial Association Charter	Apr. 30, 1864
7.	Gettysburg Compiler	Feb. 4, 1896
8.	Gettysburg Times	Oct. 9, 2000
9.	Gettysburg Times	Oct. 16, 2000
10.	Gettysburg Times	Sept. 14, 2000
11.	Evening Sun (Hanover, Pa.)	Oct. 9, 2000
12.	Gettysburg Times	Oct. 25, 2000
13.	Naugle statement	Feb. 15, 2001
14.	Gettysburg Times	Feb. 16, 2001
15.	Patriot News (Harrisburg, Pa.)	Mar. 8, 2001
16.	Evening Sun (Hanover, Pa.)	Mar. 2, 2001
17.	Evening Sun (Hanover, Pa.)	Sept. 2, 2001
18.	Evening Sun (Hanover, Pa.)	May 27, 2001
19.	Gettysburg Times	Dec. 7, 2001
20.	Civil War News	Oct. 2001
21.	Evening Sun (Hanover, Pa.)	Aug. 17, 2001
22.	Civil War News	Nov. 2004
23.	Gettysburg Times	July 30, 2001
24.	Gettysburg Times	July 3, 2001
25.	Preservation Online	Mar. 4, 2004
26.	Gettysburg Times	June 2, 2005
27.	Evening Sun (Hanover, Pa.)	June 30, 2003
28.	Patriot News (Harrisburg, Pa.)	Nov. 25, 2003
29.	Gettysburg Times	Nov. 25, 2003
30.	Pittsburgh Post Gazette (Pittsburgh, Pa.)	Feb. 29, 2004
31.	York Sunday News (York, Pa.)	Sept. 4, 2005
32.	Gettysburg Times	June 30, 2002
33.	Gettysburg Times	Sept. 6, 2003
34.	Gettysburg Times	Apr. 2, 2004
35.	Evening Sun (Hanover, Pa.)	June 13, 2003
36.	Civil War News	Sept. 2001
37.	York Sunday News (York, Pa.)	Jan. 13, 2002
38.	York Sunday News (York, Pa.)	Jan. 20, 2002
39.	Civil War News	Feb./Mar. 2002
40.	Evening Sun (Hanover, Pa.)	Mar. 7, 2002
41.	Evening Sun (Hanover, Pa.)	Mar. 17, 2002
42.	Sub-committee briefing paper	Mar. 21, 2002
43.	Paul Hoffman statement before sub-committee	Mar. 21, 2002
44.	Bob Wilburn statement before sub-committee	Mar. 21, 2002
45.	Todd Platts statement before sub-committee	Mar. 21, 2002
46.	Gettysburg Times	Mar. 22, 2002
47.	Evening Sun (Hanover, Pa.)	Mar. 22, 2002
48.	Civil War News	Apr. 2002
49.	Evening Sun (Hanover, Pa.)	Mar. 24, 2002
50.	Gettysburg Times	Apr. 5, 2002
51.	Gettysburg Times	Apr. 17, 2002

52.	Gettysburg Times	Oct. 29, 2002
53.	Gettysburg Times	Feb. 8, 2002
54.	Evening Sun (Hanover, Pa.)	Feb. 10, 2003
55.	Evening Sun (Hanover, Pa.)	Feb. 14, 2002
56.	Evening Sun (Hanover, Pa.)	Feb. 16, 2002
57.	Evening Sun (Hanover, Pa.)	Sept. 27, 2004
58.	Civil War News	Oct. 2004
59.	GNMP Business Plan	2001
60.	Evening Sun (Hanover, Pa.)	Nov. 6, 2004
61.	Cleveland Plain Dealer (Cleveland, Ohio)	Oct. 16, 2004
62.	Patriot News (Harrisburg, Pa.)	May 31, 2004
63.	Newhouse News Service	June 24, 2004
64.	York Sunday News (York, Pa.)	Nov. 11, 2001
65.	Gettysburg Times	Feb. 9, 2005
66.	Evening Sun (Hanover, Pa.)	Apr. 10, 2005
67.	Gettysburg Times	Apr. 12, 2005
68.	Gettysburg Times	May 5, 2005
69.	Gettysburg Times	May 23, 2005
70.	Evening Sun (Hanover, Pa.)	July 7, 2005
71.	Evening Sun (Hanover, Pa.)	May 3, 2005
72.	York Sunday News (York, Pa.)	Apr. 20, 2003
73.	Pittsburgh Post Gazette (Pittsburgh, Pa.)	May 30, 2005
74.	Preservation News	Dec. 2005
75.	Gettysburg Times	June 18, 2005
76.	Evening Sun (Hanover, Pa.)	Oct. 13, 2005
77.	Gettysburg Times	Oct. 19, 2005
78.	Gettysburg Times	Oct. 26, 2005
79.	Evening Sun (Hanover, Pa.)	Oct. 12, 2005
80.	Evening Sun (Hanover, Pa.)	Oct. 7, 2005
81.	Gettysburg Times	Oct. 7, 2005
82.	Gettysburg Times	June 3, 2005
83.	Evening Sun (Hanover, Pa.)	June 3, 2005
84.	Gettysburg Times	Feb. 1, 2006
85.	Gettysburg Times	Feb. 1, 2006
86.	Gettysburg Times	Feb. 21, 2006
87.	GNMP Report	Feb. 28, 2006
88.	York Sunday News (York, Pa.)	Feb. 19, 2006
89.	Gettysburg Times	Feb. 16, 2006

Chapter 10

1.	Gettysburg Times	Feb. 21, 2006
2.	Gettysburg Times	Apr. 10, 2006
3.	Gettysburg Times	Aug. 29, 2006
4.	Harrisburg (Pa.) News	Nov. 10, 2006
5.	Gettysburg Times	Sept. 9, 2006
6.	Gettysburg Times	Nov. 17, 2006
7.	Gettysburg Times	Oct. 9, 2006
8.	York (Pa.) Sunday News	Dec. 10, 2006
9.	ibid	

10.	Hanover (Pa.) Evening Sun	Dec. 28, 2006
11.	Hanover (Pa.) Evening Sun	Dec. 1, 2006
12.	Hanover (Pa.) Evening Sun	Dec. 8, 2006
13.	Hanover (Pa.) Evening Sun	Mar. 16, 2007
14.	York (Pa.) Sunday News	Apr. 15, 2007
15.	Hanover (Pa.) Evening Sun	Apr. 16, 2007
16.	Gettysburg Times	May 2, 2007
17.	Gettysburg Times	June 7, 2007
18.	Gettysburg Times	July 4, 2007
19.	Gettysburg Times	June 12, 2007
20.	Hanover (Pa.) Evening Sun	July 6, 2007
21.	Hanover (Pa.) Evening Sun	Aug. 10, 2007
22.	Hanover (Pa.) Evening Sun	October, 2007
23.	Gettysburg Times	Oct. 4, 2007
24.	Gettysburg Times	Oct. 5, 2007
25.	Gettysburg Times	Oct. 16, 2007
26.	Gettysburg Times	Nov. 1, 2007
27.	ibid	
28.	Hanover (Pa.) Evening Sun	Mar. 5, 2008
29.	Civil War News	April, 2008
30.	Washington Post	Apr. 14, 2008
31.	Gettysburg Times	Apr. 11, 2008
32.	ibid	
33.	ibid	
34.	Hanover (Pa.) Evening Sun	Apr. 11, 2008
35.	ibid	
36.	Gettysburg Times	Apr. 15, 2008
37.	York (Pa.) Sunday News	Apr. 13, 2008
38.	Boston Globe	Apr. 13, 2008
39.	Gettysburg Times	Apr. 22, 2008
40.	Gettysburg Times	Apr. 23, 2008
41.	Gettysburg Times	Apr. 24, 2008
42.	Newsweek	Apr. 14, 2008
43.	Gettysburg Times	Apr. 18, 2008
44.	Civil War News	Apr. 18, 2008
45.	Cross Ties - Rutgers University, N.J.	Summer, 2008
46.	Inside NPS	Aug. 19, 2008
47.	Gettysburg Times	Aug. 29, 2008
48.	Gettysburg Times	Sept. 17, 2008
49.	York (Pa.) Sunday News	Aug. 31, 2008
50.	ibid	
51.	York (Pa.) Daily Record	Sept. 4, 2008
52.	Civil War News	June, 2008
53.	Gettysburg Times	Nov. 8, 2008
54.	ibid	
55.	ibid	
56.	ibid	
57.	Hanover (Pa.) Evening Sun	Sept. 27, 2008
58.	ibid	
59.	ibid	
60.	ibid	
61.	Gettyburg Times	Oct. 29, 2008

62.	Hanover (Pa.) Evening Sun	Oct. 30, 2008
63.	National Parks Conservation Association press release	Dec. 16, 2008
64.	Gettysburg Times	Feb. 25, 2009
65.	Hanover (Pa.) Evening Sun	Mar. 1, 2009
66.	Gettysburg Times	Jan. 7, 2009
67.	Civil War Times	February, 2009
68.	Gettysburg Times	Feb. 27, 2009
69.	Establishing Act for Battlefield Memorial Association by Pa. Legislature	Apr. 30, 1864
70.	National Parks Conservation Association press release	Dec. 16, 2008

INDEX

G

H

I